Writing for Comics
& Graphic Novels
With Peter David

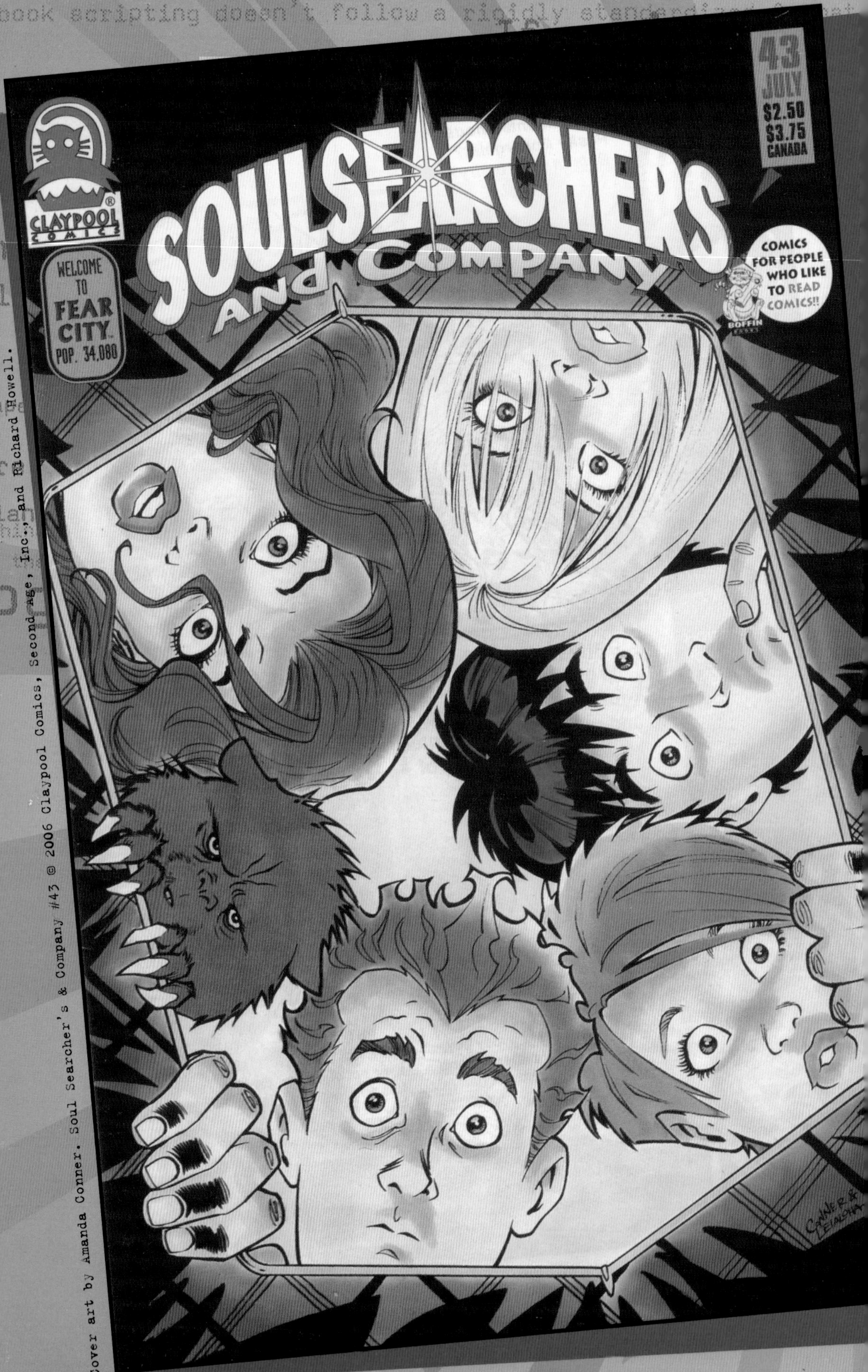
CLAYPOOL COMICS
43
JULY
$2.50
$3.75
CANADA
SOULSEARCHERS
AND COMPANY
WELCOME TO FEAR CITY POP. 34,080
COMICS FOR PEOPLE WHO LIKE TO READ COMICS!!
BOFFIN

Cover art by Amanda Conner. Soul Searcher's & Company #43 © 2006 Claypool Comics, Second Age, Inc., and Richard Howell.

FOREWORD BY
GEORGE PÉREZ

WRITING FOR COMICS & GRAPHIC NOVELS

WITH PETER DAVID

REVISED EDITION

IMPACT
CINCINNATI, OHIO
www.impact-books.com

book scripting doesn't follow a rigidly standardized format
If you're writi
writin

ACKNOWLEDGMENTS

Writing for Comics and Graphic Novels with Peter David.
Copyright © 2009 by Peter David. Manufactured in China.
All rights reserved. No part of this book may be reproduced in
any form or by any electronic or mechanical means including
information storage and retrieval systems without permission in
writing from the publisher, except by a reviewer who may quote
brief passages in a review. Published by IMPACT Books, an
imprint of F+W Media, Inc., 4700 East Galbraith Road, Cincinnati,
Ohio, 45236. (800) 289-0963. Second Edition.

Other fine IMPACT Books are available from your
local bookstore, art supply store or direct from the
publisher at fwmedia.com.

13 12 11 10 09   5 4 3 2 1

DISTRIBUTED IN CANADA BY FRASER DIRECT
100 Armstrong Avenue
Georgetown, ON, Canada L7G 5S4
Tel: (905) 877-4411

DISTRIBUTED IN THE U.K. AND EUROPE BY DAVID &
CHARLES
Brunel House, Newton Abbot, Devon, TQ12 4PU, England
Tel: (+44) 1626 323200, Fax: (+44) 1626 323319
Email: postmaster@davidandcharles.co.uk

DISTRIBUTED IN AUSTRALIA BY CAPRICORN LINK
P.O. Box 704, S. Windsor NSW, 2756 Australia
Tel: (02) 4577-3555

Library of Congress Cataloging in Publication Data
David, Peter (Peter Allen)
  Writing for comics and graphic novels / with Peter David.
-- 2nd ed.
     p. cm.
  Includes index.
  Second ed. edited by Sarah Laichas ; page layout by Clare
Finney.
  ISBN 978-1-60061-687-7 (pbk. : alk. paper)
  1. Comic books, strips, etc.--Authorship. I. Title.
  PN6710.D383 2009
  808'.066741--dc22

                              2009004397

First edition edited by Mona Michael
Second edition edited by Sarah Laichas
Designed by Wendy Dunning
Second edition page layout by Clare Finney
Production art by Kathy Bergstrom
Production coordinated by Matt Wagner

A number of people have put in work above and beyond the call in order to make this book happen. These include:

Mona Michael, my long-suffering editor, who developed the remarkable skill of saying, "You need another month? No problem," several times in our association and then waiting until she was off the phone before she started screaming.

Brent Frankenhoff, who deftly filled in the copious gaps in my art resources by providing needed visuals.

Glenn Hauman, for putting together the plotting charts and word balloon samples.

The fine folks at Marvel, Dark Horse, Warp Graphics, Claypool Comics and IDW for making the approval process for their material smooth and painless. Also thanks to Jay Kogan and Paul Levitz.

My beloved wife, Kathleen, for being helpful and supportive, and keeping me sane during the editing process.

Maggie Thompson, who actually didn't have all that much to do with the production of the book, but if she and Don hadn't offered me the regular slot that became "But I Digress" in *Comics Buyer's Guide*, this book would likely never have existed.

My guest writers—Marv Wolfman, Wendy and Richard Pini, and Andy Schmidt— for taking time out of their busy schedules to contribute to the proceedings.

The fans. You know who you are.

Peter David is a prolific author whose career, and continued popularity, spans over two decades. He has worked in every conceivable media: television, film, books (fiction, nonfiction and audio), short stories and comic books, and has acquired followings in all of them.

Peter has had over seventy novels published, including *Tigerheart, Darkness of the Light, Sir Apropos of Nothing, Knight Life, Howling Mad* and the *Psi-Man* series, garnering numerous appearances on the *New York Times* Best Seller List. He is the co-creator and author of the best-selling *Star Trek: New Frontier* series for Pocket Books, and has also written such Trek novels as *Q-Squared, The Siege, Q-in-Law, Vendetta, I, Q* (with John de Lancie), *A Rock and a Hard Place* and *Imzadi*. He produced the *Babylon 5: Centauri Prime* trilogy novels, and has also had his short fiction published in such collections as *Shock Rock, Shock Rock II,* and *Otherwere,* as well as *Asimov's Science Fiction* magazine and *The Magazine of Fantasy & Science Fiction.*

Peter's comic book résumé includes an award-winning twelve-year run on *The Incredible Hulk,* as well as such varied and popular titles as *X-Factor, She-Hulk, Fallen Angel, Friendly Neighborhood Spider-Man, Supergirl, SpyBoy, Young Justice, Soulsearchers and Company, Aquaman, Spider-Man 2099,*

Photo by Maggie Thompson

Captain Marvel, Wolverine, The Phantom, Sachs & Violens and many others. Peter also scripted the comics of Stephen King's *The Dark Tower* series and has written comic-book-related novels, such as *The Incredible Hulk: What Savage Beast.* Furthermore, his opinion column, "But I Digress," has been running in the industry trade newspaper *Comics Buyer's Guide* since 1990, and in that time has been the paper's consistently most popular feature and was also collected into a trade paperback edition.

Peter's awards and citations include the Julie Award, 2007; the Haxtur Award (Spain), Best Comic Script, 1996; OzCon Award (Australia), Favorite International Writer, 1995; *Comics Buyer's Guide* Fan Awards, Favorite Writer, 1995; Wizard Fan Award Winner, 1993; Golden Duck Award for Young Adult Series (*Starfleet Academy*), 1994; UK Comic Art Award, 1993; and Will Eisner Comic Industry Award, Best Writer-Artist Team, 1992.

Peter lives in New York with his wife, Kathleen, and his four children, Shana, Gwen, Ariel and Caroline. Visit his website, www.peterdavid.net.

DEDICATION

To my wife, Kathleen, and my daughters, Shana, Gwen, Ariel and Caroline.
All of whom have had to learn the meaning of the words: "Daddy's on deadline."

Stan Lee and Steve Ditko   "Final Dr

Page 9 from SpyBoy™ #2 ©1999 Dark Horse Comics, Inc.

Cover Illustration for Fallen Angel #1, Art by J.K. Woodward. Published by I.D.W Publishing, Peter David and J.K. Woodward.

Tracer from Friendly Neighborhood Spider-Man: ©2005 Marvel Characters, Inc. Used with permission.

EXERCISES

cond is called "full script."

what the writer wants on the p

Stan Lee and Steve Ditko   "Final Dr

writing

the pag
al Draft

"PAN
gapes at Bru

more words

Alan Moore

logue

WOW. TALK ABOUT INTIMIDATING.
I'VE BEEN ASKED TO WRITE THE FOREWORD TO A BOOK BY PETER DAVID ABOUT WRITING COMICS. A COMIC BOOK ARTIST—EMPHASIS ON THE WORD ARTIST—HAS BEEN ASKED TO WRITE AN INTRODUCTION TO A BOOK BY AN AWARD-WINNING WRITER ABOUT WRITING. YEAH, THERE IS SOMETHING INCREDIBLY INTIMIDATING ABOUT THAT.

But then again, I've always felt just a wee bit intimidated by Peter David. After all, it was my dear wife Carol who, having been impressed by Peter's work on one of his *Star Trek: The Next Generation* novels, suggested that I should try and work with him on some comic book project. My wife is a voracious reader, especially of books dealing with science fiction, fantasy and the supernatural, so impressing her is no mean feat. While I had met Peter several times at comic book conventions and other similar settings, I honestly didn't know if he really wanted to work with me—or, to be more specific, if we would gel as a team. Nevertheless, I called Peter to pass on my wife's compliments and tell him that I would like to work with him some day in the future.

Well, that future was less than five seconds away—and part of the title of our first project together: *The Incredible Hulk: Future Imperfect*. This particular project had been in development for some time and had two other artists attached to it at one time or another. For whatever reasons, both artists had to bow out and the project lay dormant without an artist until that fateful return phone call to Peter.

This allowed me the unique opportunity to read a plot that wasn't specifically written with me in mind—but you'd never know that from reading it. Peter has a natural gift that firmly places him in the top tier of the comic writers' hierarchy. The man knows how to write visually. He understands the language of comics, how a story should be paced, how a scene should be constructed, how much information should be related by the art and how much by the word. While all this may seem rather fundamental, it is amazing how many writers have great difficulty in achieving this happy balance. When I read Peter's plot, I knew how I was going to draw it. He created images in my head—and all I needed to do was bring them to life in pencil and ink.

But, as much as I was impressed with Peter's plotting, I was also bowled over by his actual script, the finished dialogue written after the artwork is completed. Peter's dialogue has become quite noted for its wonderful mixture of humanity, drama, intelligence, tension and a unique sardonic wit (traits that are evidenced in his conversation and commentary as well, in person or through his opinion column, "But I Digress"—the guy knows how to work an audience) and all that was sprawled out in front of me in the final script that both enhanced and respected my visuals. We were storytelling partners, each trying to challenge the other without stealing the spotlight from each other. That's the kind of partnership a comic book artist relishes—and one that you wish to repeat.

Photo by Maggie Thompson

Alas, due to our hectic respective schedules, Peter and I would only work on one more project together, the wild and kinky urban adventure *Sachs & Violens*, but that second visit into the crazy mind of Peter David was yet another high point for me and allowed me to stretch my storytelling muscles in directions I'm seldom called upon to explore.

I've become a better artist working with Peter David. I've become a better storyteller. I've even been asked to write this foreword.

And, hopefully, I'm better at that now than I was a few paragraphs ago. Read on—you, too, may be the better for it.

—**GEORGE PÉREZ**

PREFACE

WELCOME TO THE SECOND EDITION OF MY BOOK ON WRIT-ING FOR COMICS.

WE'VE ADDED "GRAPHIC NOVELS" TO THE TITLE, BUT I'LL BE TOTALLY HONEST WITH YOU, BECAUSE I REALLY CAN'T TALK ABOUT WRITING IN ANY MANNER OTHER THAN WITH TOTAL HONESTY: WE HAVEN'T REALLY MADE ADJUSTMENTS TO THE BOOK TO ADDRESS GRAPHIC NOVELS SEPARATELY. THE FOLKS IN MARKETING SIMPLY FEEL THAT ADDING THE TERM "GRAPH-IC NOVELS" TO THE TITLE WILL PROVE ATTRACTIVE TO A WIDER AUDIENCE. THE ONLY ONE WHO DETERMINES THE ACCURACY OF THAT SUPPOSITION IS YOU. IF YOU PICKED UP THIS BOOK BECAUSE "GRAPHIC NOVELS" LEAPED OUT AT YOU FROM THE SHELVES, THEN MISSION ACCOMPLISHED.

Everything in the world seems to be renamed anyway. "Shellshock" became "post-traumatic stress disorder." A "used car" is now "previously owned," perhaps suggesting that whoever had the car before simply kept it in the driveway to look at and never actually drove it. It may well be that the very term "comic books" has been outdated for decades. It made sense when comics were, y'know...funny. But most comics nowadays, with the exception of certain manga and such stalwarts as Archie Andrews and com-pany, are very serious affairs. Heroes battle for their lives, lose their lives (although invariably wind up being resurrected) and everything from truth and justice to the American way are at stake. So the term "graphic storytell-ing" and a collection of such—graphic novels—may well be more accu-rate. Of course, even "graphic" can have shadings of meaning. Do action sequences or sex scenes in graphic novels qualify as graphic violence or graphic sex? I'm not sure; I'm still trying to determine why, if an adult home is opened in your neighborhood, that's okay, but if an adult bookstore opens up, people freak out. Go figure.

Just as much of the advice I give you herein is applicable to everything from novels to screenplays, so too is it applicable to graphic novels. Graphic novels are simply comic books presented in a different format. There's no secret trick to them, no special code, nothing you need to know in writing a graphic novel that differs appreciably from writing the typical twenty-two page comic, any more than writing a novel requires a different skill set than writing a novella. Indeed, that's one of the questions aspiring writers ask: How do you transform a short story into a novel? The answer is that you don't. Stories find their own length. (Which is why, for instance, "Flowers for Algernon" is such a brilliant short story and such a failure, in my opinion, as an expanded novel.) The more you write, the longer your stories tend to become as you see the inherent possibilities and the various possibilities your premise suggests that can be explored. You also develop both the patience and the technique to do justice to your concepts. Typically these are not talents you develop overnight.

Think of your imagination as a muscle, no different than any other muscle in your body. You build it up over time through constant use. The more you work it, the longer and more involved the stories you craft can become. And if that muscle cramps up, we call it Writer's Block. The way you deal with Writer's Block is the same as with any cramped muscle: Work it through and keep massaging it until it loosens up.

A single issue of a graphic story is a sprint. A graphic novel is a marathon. Do enough of the former and you'll be ready to undertake the latter.

Speaking of questions (which I was several paragraphs ago), I decided to open up the floor to questions from readers this go-around. I issued an invitation on my website to anyone who had read the first edition to ask about anything they felt I had left unaddressed, so I could rectify the omission this time around. The result was a bevy of thoughtful and even provocative queries that have been included herein.

And those are just a sample of the

Fallen Angel #1 cover by J.K. Woodward © 2006 by Peter David.

IDW
ISSUE #1
$3.99

FALLEN ANGEL

"Having been selected as Spokesperson for virtually everyone in the known world, I am pleased to advise that we all greet the return of Peter David's excellent *FALLEN ANGEL* with unalloyed rejoicing. Anyone dissenting is simply uncool."

HARLAN ELLISON
—Spokesperson for Everyone (virtually)

c book scripting doesn't follow a rigidly standardized format
If you're writi
writing
od
the page
nal Draft"

many questions I have received, and continue to receive, in the time since I wrote the first edition. I have done a number of seminars throughout the country (typically at Wizard conventions, although elsewhere as well), not to mention IMPACT University, which has become a staple at the San Diego Comic-Con. Would-be writers are always keeping me thinking with their questions of how to handle this, that and the other thing. I try to pretend that I have all the answers, but I don't really. No one does. There's any number of professions where it's possible to learn pretty much all you can about it and be good to go for the rest of your career. Writing is not one of those professions.

Your growth as a writer is constantly shifting due to both changes in the world around you

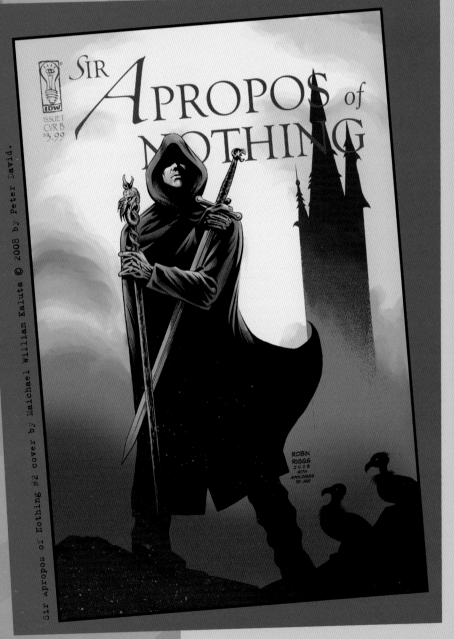

Sir Apropos of Nothing #2 cover by Michael William Kaluta © 2008 by Peter David.

and changes in you yourself. As an example: When I was hired to script Stephen King's *The Dark Tower* series, it prompted me to sit down and read all seven books in the series in one shot. Okay, actually I didn't sit down the whole time; I got up and walked around every so often. The point is, the series was written over several decades of King's life, and it is a fascinating series of snapshots of a writer's development. His writer's voice changes over the years, affected by everything from simply finding the right narrative tone to the calamitous accident he suffered when he was struck and nearly killed by a van. The final volume becomes more than a story; it's a dissertation on art affecting life and life affecting art to the point where it's impossible to distinguish the two. The real world intrudes on your writing whether you realize it or not. And it will affect how your readers view your work as well.

Andy Schmidt was also gracious enough to take the time to update his remarkably useful essay on breaking into comics. Things have changed in the market and will continue to change, and hopefully if we do another edition of his book in a few years we'll be updating it again.

Producing this book's predecessor and this newest volume, not to mention the classes I've taught, is all part of the ongoing learning experience that writing represents. I wish you the best of luck on your continued journey.

—**Peter David**

writing

od

the pag

nal Draft

s

"PAN

i gapes at Bru

more words

Alan Moore

rything

are the

logue

INTRODUCTION

JUST AS MANY DO NOT COMPREHEND THE JOB OF AN INKER, THINKING HIM A MERE TRACER OF SOMEONE ELSE'S LINES AND NOT REALIZING THAT A GREAT INKER CAN ELEVATE A PENCILER WHILE A LOUSY INKER CAN DESTROY THOSE SAME PENCILS (I, WHO CAN BARELY DRAW CRUDE FIGURES, COULD LOOK LIKE DA VINCI IF TOM PALMER WERE DOING THE INKS), MANY DO NOT UNDERSTAND THE WRITER'S JOB IN COMICS.

Indeed, any number of times, I've encountered "civilians" (usually fellow travelers on airplanes, for some reason) who, upon learning that I'm a writer, press to know what I've written. I always mention comics last, because as often as not, I will get blank or surprised looks as they say, "You mean you draw comics?"

"No, I write them."

"Comics have writers?"

The answer is, yes, comics have writers. They are part of the team. I know this because in 1992 I won an Eisner Award along with Dale Keown for "Best Writer-Artist Team," a category that was done away with shortly thereafter, so draw your own conclusions.

THE BALLOON TYPIST

If you think Rodney Dangerfield got no respect, no respect at all...then allow me to tell you what you can expect as a comic book writer, especially insofar as the "outside world" is concerned.

There is no single writer more universally recognized, beloved or renowned than Stan "The Man" Lee. The father of the Marvel Universe, creator of the Fantastic Four, Spider-Man, et al. Naturally, since Stan is not an artist, these concepts did not spring to life on the comics page all by their lonesome. Stan had help from co-creators and legends in their own right, such as Steve Ditko and, most notably, Jack "The King" Kirby.

Some years ago, there was a heated dispute over who contributed what to the genesis of these characters and concepts, most of it stemming from a contretemps involving the return of Kirby's art by Marvel Comics. Now, anyone who has ever been involved in any sort of co-creative endeavor can

> "The **WRITER** is the only one who must pull his contribution out of the ether, drag it *kicking and screaming* from the recesses of his mind and put it down on paper."

tell you that it's nearly impossible to recall—even mere days after the creation, much less decades—who exactly was responsible for what. This did not deter various commentators, none of whom were present during the creative process and many of whom were not even born, from taking sides and trying to place the lion's share of credit to one side or the other. And since it was Marvel vs. Kirby, and Stan was part of Marvel, many sided with Kirby to Stan's detriment.

The most notable was no less an authority than *The Village Voice*. One of the most famed anti-establishment newspapers in America referred to Stan Lee as—get this—"a typist of word balloons." That was it. That was all. Stan's contribution, according to the *Voice*, was balloon typist.

HOW SIGNIFICANT ARE WRITERS TO COMICS?

Consider this simple fact: Writers are the only part of the creative team of a comic that begin with absolutely nothing. The penciler has the script with which to work, the inker has the pencils, the letterer has the dialogue, the colorist has the finished art, and the editor oversees it all. But the writer is the only one who must pull his contribution out of the ether, drag it kicking and screaming from the recesses of his mind and put it down on paper (or a computer screen) so that everyone else can do his job. The writer can't be bypassed. You can produce a comic that's been shot from pencils only, or in black and white, or utterly silent and still have a good comic. You can produce a story without art: It's called a novel. But produce a comic book without a story, and all you've got is a pinup book. Which is fine as far as it goes, but if you really want a pinup book, I'd suggest bypassing comics and going straight to the *Sports Illustrated* Swimsuit Edition. For starters, they're real women.

ARE COMIC BOOK WRITERS UNIVERSALLY DISSED?

Not at all. Mention the names Marv Wolfman or Len Wein, Gardner Fox or Otto Binder, Neil Gaiman or Alan Moore, and you'll see nods and smiles of recognition or even reverence. These writers and many others—including the *Voice*-maligned Stan Lee—are the backbone for a world of illustrated literature that is truly the current equivalent of myth building. What else are Superman and the Justice League if they're not the modern-era version of King Arthur and his Knights of the Round Table? What else is Batman if not a combination of Sherlock Holmes and Zorro? What else is Spider-Man if not a creation in the spirit of classic tricksters ranging from Coyote to Br'er Rabbit, outwitting opponents with sass and smart-alecky quick-thinking?

Len Wein, creator of Swamp Thing, the new X-Men and, oh yes... Wolverine. A god among men.

Marv Wolfman, creator of Teen Titans, Blade and author of *Crisis on Infinite Earths*. A man among gods.

writing

od

the page

al Draft"

"PANEL

gapes at Bruce

more words in

Alan Moore

rything

are the

logue

And like such myths, writers come in and build upon the foundations of that which has gone before. New elements are introduced from varied sources and are adopted into canon as if they've always been there. Lancelot had no place in Arthurian legend until the French decided that what the tales of Camelot really needed was a French knight who could kick everyone else's butt and cuckold the king (big shock there). By the same token, kryptonite—now such an accepted part of the Superman legend—didn't originate in the comics at all, but rather sprang from the minds of the writers of the Superman radio program.

So, as with all things, to become a comic book writer is to grip firmly a double-edged sword. On the one hand, you are joining a grand tradition of aiding in an epic narrative, should you happen to tell stories set in preexisting universes. For that matter, you can produce tales, characters and universes of your own devising, and as varied as Mike Baron's *Nexus* (with Steve Rude), and Joss Whedon's *Fray* (an offshoot of *Buffy the Vampire Slayer*).

On the other hand, if you're not a writer/artist, be prepared to encounter a lot of people who don't have the faintest idea of just what the heck it is you actually do. Personally, there are days I wonder much the same thing. Nevertheless, I'm going to try and impart to you my understanding and theories of just what it is we *do* do. These are, of course, just my opinions and, as William Goldman has often said about show business, "Nobody knows anything." But of all the nothing I know, I'll do my best to share it with you.

Since I've worked in pretty much every medium there is, I'm often asked which form of storytelling I like the most. I've given this a good deal of thought and have come to the conclusion that the honest answer is: novels. That might seem a heck of a thing to say in a book about writing comics, but here's the thing. Short of sitting in a chair and telling a story aloud to an enraptured audience, the novel is the purest form of storytelling there is. It's you and your audience. As long as you have a typesetter who doesn't fill the book with typographical errors (and believe me, these days

Neil Gaiman, the writer's writer. Veddy British, and the creator of the critically acclaimed *Sandman*. Also a close personal friend who remembers my name two times out of every five.

Stan "The Man" Lee, creator of Spider-Man, the Fantastic Four, the Hulk—Mr. Presents himself.

that's not exactly a given), there's nothing between you and your readership. It's the literary equivalent of working without a net: If the story's successful, it's all to your credit. If it's lousy, there's no one else upon whom you can pin the blame.

Furthermore, novels give you latitude since you don't have to worry about making the story especially visual. You can have characters in one room yak for pages on end, and as long as the dialogue is interesting, the reader will remain engaged. You can't really get away with that in comics, or if you do, you'd best have a phenomenal artist penciling it.

Comics, however, are a close second to novels. I was writing and drawing my very own comic books back when I was twelve years old. It didn't take long for me to become convinced that I had neither the patience nor the talent to become an artist. The love of writing, though, never diminished.

The advantage that comic books offer is that you can produce, in conjunction with an artist, a story that is better than either of you could have, or would have, produced on your own. Granted, a lousy artist can kill a well-written story. A gifted artist, though, can elevate a mediocre story (not that you should aspire to mediocrity) and knock a great story out of the park. Pictures may or may not be worth a thousand words, depending on your point of view. But they pack an inarguable punch all their own. And when powerful pictures are combined with powerful words, the result can be more than just a great story. If the blending of the two is seamless, you can have magic.

To that end, I'll be covering ways to tell the best stories you can. I will show you the sorts of scripts I write, and how I write them, in order to convey the story to both the editor and the artist. Comics are not movies, but there are strong similarities in that one must think visually when producing a comic book script. So, you'll be delving into the type of storytelling arcs and techniques that are applicable to both movies and comic books.

To be honest, this book is not the easiest of endeavors for me. A lot of what I do is very instinctive. When you're flying by the seat of your pants, it's tricky to tell people to sit in your lap (and, under certain circumstances, will probably get you strange looks). Nevertheless, I'll do the best I humanly can to break down for you the hows, whys and wherefores. I will make the inexplicable explicable and the ephemeral...uh...phemeral.

to tell
the second is ca

mo

A: Rick Jo
Banner inc

styles of pre

that's going
director. Eac

Not so with co

ond is called "Full script."

what the writer wants on the p

Stan Lee and Steve Ditko   "Final Dra

WHERE DO THEY
THOSE

IT'S THE SINGLE MOST-ASKED QUESTION THAT A WRITER—ANY WRITER—WILL HEAR: "WHERE DO YOU GET YOUR IDEAS?"

This question stems from the simple lack of understanding of what a writer is and what a writer does. Any number of times people have said to me (upon learning that I'm a novelist), "Y'know, I've always wanted to write a book. I've jus never had the time." The implication is that, if they could only engage in some proper time management, they'd be able to do what writers do. Artists don't get that attitude. If people lack the ability to draw, they generally know it. They don't believe they've never drawn a comic or painted a masterpiece simply because they haven't gotten around to it. But they figure they know how to write a sentence (subject-verb-object). A paragraph is just a bunch of sentences, and a book is just a bunch of paragraphs, so really, anyone should be able to write a book, right? If only they had more hours in a day, and by the way, they could also use some of those pesky ideas. Where do you get those, anyway?

It's difficult to explain that one doesn't decide to become a writer and then go scavenging for ideas. One becomes a writer because the ideas keep coming to you, whether you want them or not. It's just how your mind is wired. And it's not only that: Once particular ideas take up residence in your skull, they won't leave. They just sit there, occupying gray matter and shouting at you to attend to them *now*, like Veruca Salt demanding an Oompa-Loompa.

You don't become a writer because you want to. You become a writer because you have to. Because—and I court double-negatives here—you cannot not become a writer. It's the only way to quell, however temporarily, the voices in your head that demand you become their vessel.

How do you explain this? You can't. Not really.

Now, you might be asking yourself at this point (because I'm not in the room with you, so you can't really be asking me), "Is Peter saying that if I have a desire to write, but no immediate ideas bouncing around, then there's no hope for me?"

Heck no. Because my assumption is that you're reading this book for one of two reasons: Either you're simply a fan of mine and interested in what goes through that which is laughingly referred to as my mind when I'm writing comics; or you have a driving ambition to become a writer.

If it's the former, Hi. Sit back, get comfortable. Try the veal, and be sure to tip the waitress.

If it's the latter, you're displaying the first, most important trait that a writer has to have: a determination to learn as much about his craft as possible. (Okay, I lied. That's the second most important trait. The first most important

18

trait is a desire to write in the first place. But we'll go on the assumption that the first is implicit in pursuing the second.)

If you don't have ideas percolating yet, don't worry. With any luck, they will come. And if they never come... you may have a promising career as a movie executive, where you can read scripts and make cogent notes like "Too on-the-nose" or "Needs more beats."

Kidding. I'm kidding. I kid because I care.

Yes, there are some people who are spewing forth ideas like Old Faithful before they've learned to shave. But for the vast majority of us, it is a learned skill. Speaking for myself (because no one else will let me speak for them), I didn't start out writing novels. I wrote short stories, and then short novels, and then long novels. And somewhere during all that, I started writing comic books.

I will say that my prose experience has been tremendously useful. Because I've written both short and long form, I can write comic book stories that are eleven pages long or comic book arcs that consume up to four years. So even before you write comics, you might want to consider writing short stories to prepare you for crafting twenty-two-page comic books. Use these to work out the kinks in matters such as dialogue, pacing and other aspects of storytelling that we'll be discussing farther along.

Also keep this in mind: To a writer, ideas often aren't as important as the execution of those ideas. Consider, for instance, *Battlestar Galactica*. The 1978 original TV series, involving the remnants of the twelve colonies of man flee-ing from the robotic Cylons, had more cheese than Wisconsin. The actors did the best they could with what they were given, and John Colicos was a bril-liant villain as always. But the series was schlocky on its best day, and many science-fiction fans didn't take it seriously.

Now flash forward to the 2003 incarnation. Same names. Same characters, although genders have been switched around. Same terminology. Same con-cept. Same idea. But the new series is riveting television, admired and extolled by even the most hard-core SF fans. Completely different execution of ideas and story lines that were less than compelling the first time around.

This isn't to say that you can sigh in relief and say, "Ah! So if I have no ideas, I can just fake it!" Well, no. That's like saying that if you have no foundation, you can fake building a house. The ideas are the foundation upon which you will exe-cute your story, so ideally there should be something at home before you start.

Let's figure out from where you can pull them.

WRITE TO SCHENECTADY

Noted writer Harlan Ellison came up with another explanation. People asking Ellison where he gets his ideas would receive the following response (or a variation thereof, depending on his mood):

"Schenectady. That's where I get my ideas. That's where all writers get their ideas. There's this little guy who lives in Schenectady, and you send him thirty dollars, and every month he sends you three ideas."

Invariably people will nod or look surprised and then say, "I knew it was something like that!" and demand to know where they can find the guy's address.

So if you're reading this, live in Schenectady, and want to earn some money, you may be in a position to hose a few suckers. As for the rest of you...if you've already got your muse and are simply looking for a little guidance, I'll steer you as best I can.

As I said earlier, if you've taken the time to buy this book, obviously you're determined to learn about writing and improve yourself as a writer. For what it's worth, I still buy and read books on writing, and I've had over fifty novels and hundreds of comics published. You never stop learning. In fact, the day you've decided that you've learned everything one needs to know on how to write is the day you know way more than I do.

Actually—and I'm going a little off point here, but it's still early in the book, so what the heck—to be a writer, you have to possess an odd combination of humility and towering ego. The humility is what you need to admit to yourself that the more you think you know, the less you really do know. Writing is a devastatingly humbling profession. A plumber isn't going to wake up one day and suddenly discover he's powerless to fix a leaky pipe. But there are days where a writer is going to stare at his computer screen (or, yes, the paper in his typewriter) and come to the terrible realization that he's got nothin'. The words aren't coming. The ideas aren't flowing. A grocery list would be too challenging to scribe.

To that end, it helps to remain humble. To know that no one is above the occasional mental log

jam, and the important thing is to push through it. If what you're working on isn't coming to you, work on something else. Anything else. Another story. A diary entry. A poem. A dirty limerick. A letter to the editor. A book on how to write comics. Anything. Because writer's block is not the problem. It is the fear of writer's block that is the problem. It is the belief that what you're going to write isn't going to be good enough. You know what? It might not be. And, yeah, that can be a problem for a writer. If the average paper pusher has an off day at the office and does the best he can but it's inadequate, so what? It'll have no long-lasting impact. If I have an off day at the office, it may well see print six months later and fans are going to say, "Not Peter David's best work by a long shot." And there it sits in a box, stinking up the place. Well, you know what? In the words of Super Chicken, I knew the job was dangerous when I took it. But it's worth it if you do it right.

At the same time, writers must have huge egos. Massive egos. Consider the fundamental conceit of being a writer: You think you have something to say that is so important, so brilliant, so clever, that it should be distributed to as many people as possible, with your name on it (and preferably in as large letters as possible). Your ego can and will be your best friend when it comes to dealing with everything from hostile fans to acerbic editors, shielding you from crumbling under the pressure.

One of my earliest fantasy novel manuscripts was sent to one of the top editors in the field. She read it and sent the following short note back to my agent: "I could barely wretch my way through the first hundred pages. I couldn't imagine vomiting my way through the entire book. I'd be very interested to know who would buy something like this." My agent sent me the note, worrying I would be devastated. Instead I simply shrugged and said, "Okay. Who do we send it to next?"

And for the record, the manuscript was called *Knight Life*, it was purchased by Ace Books, and the sequels, *One Knight Only* and *Fall of Knight,* came out a few years ago. My ego is intact and the editor is long gone.

Anyway...

When it comes to ideas, one should always remember the basics.

All stories—all stories—can be boiled down to three fundamental conflicts:

* Man vs. Man (*The Lord of the Rings*)

* Man vs. Himself (*The Strange Case of Dr. Jekyll and Mr. Hyde*)

* Man vs. Nature (everything from *Moby-Dick* to *Armageddon*)

Everything else—everything else—is simply a variation or some combination of those three.

It's not simply the story you're telling but how you tell it. When you're first composing a story, there may be a temptation to produce a litany of "events." You know: This happens, then this happens, then this happens. But you're going to quickly discover that the story is just sort of sitting there, with nothing really compelling to recommend it. It may help to ask yourself which of these three conflicts represents the core of your story.

Furthermore, you need to have a solid grasp of your theme. If ideas and conflict are the skeleton of your story, the theme is your spine. I define theme as that aspect of the human condition upon which your story offers commentary. Ideally everything that transpires in your story should somehow connect to your theme. It sounds simplistic, I know, but you must have a clear idea of your theme, and whence the conflict stems, before you embark upon telling your story. Without that, your story will be unfocused and vague.

You begin to see that the public fascination with "ideas" and from where writers get them barely scratches the surface of the true writing challenge. And yet, since it is the preoccupation of many would-be writers ("I want to write, but I don't have any ideas!"), let us investigate them further.

Photo by Maggie Thompson.

HARLAN ELLISON
Raconteur, bon vivant and man-about-town, whose works in realms ranging from nonfiction to speculative fiction, horror to mystery, have won so many awards that they're going to have to come up with new ones just for him.

Photo by Richard Phillips.

MONTHLY
IDEAS FOR SALE IN SCHENECTADY
Granted, the sign should read, "Home of the Idea Guy." But then, everyone would know.

SEE THE WORLD NOT AS IT IS, BUT AS IT COULD BE

When I was about ten, my parents and I went on a family trip to Switzerland. My father noticed me gazing with fascination at the Swiss Alps. This particular section had long steel cables leading to the top via which cable cars could carry tourists who wanted a gorgeous view.

"You're thinking about how beautiful the mountains are, right?" he asked proudly.

"Actually," I replied, "I was wondering if Batman and Robin would be able to climb up the cables to get to the Joker who was hiding on the top of the mountain..."

This did not sit well with my dad.

I once was on a promotional tour for *The Incredible Hulk*. With artist Dale Keown and I doing a sweep across the Midwest, we were on a low-flying airplane taking us from one destination to the next. The plane's course took us over the Colorado Rocky Mountains. I stared down at one of the mountain ranges and thought, "Y'know...if I wanted to hide a super-secret organization, I'd probably do it right inside one of these mountains."

Thus was born the Pantheon and their headquarters, the Mount.

That's the joy of writing fantasy. It allows the imagination to run completely wild. You can range far afield of reality yet not lose your readers' suspension of disbelief if you ground it in the realm of that which they see every day. The notion is to get them to see the possibilities that you see. Every time you say, "What if?" you're challenging the reader to say, "Why not?"

For Don Quixote to see windmills and believe they were giants was, of course, madness. But to look at them and say, "They might be giants" is the

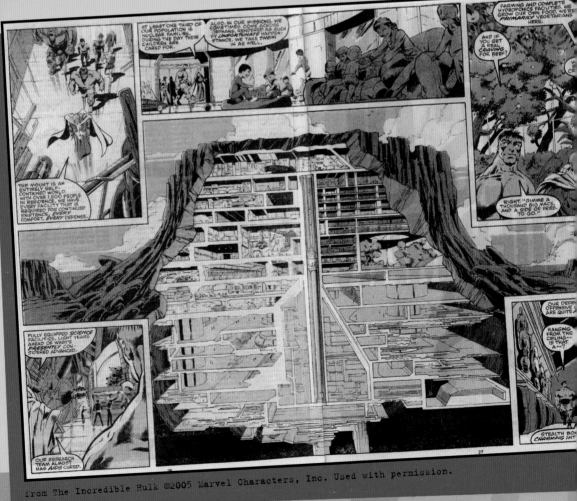

from The Incredible Hulk ©2005 Marvel Characters, Inc. Used with permission.

core of all human imagination and supposition. "What if" is not merely a title for a Marvel comic but the two most important words in a writer's vocabulary. Look at the world around you and see the possibilities inherent in it.

Ever since the Marvel Age ushered in actual cities as venues for superhero action (as opposed to the fictional "Metropolis" or "Gotham"), comic writers have been unleashing their imaginations into the real world and running wild with the possibilities.

> "**WHAT IF** is not merely a title for a Marvel comic but the two MOST IMPORTANT WORDS in a writer's vocabulary."

Mount Rushmore wound up serving as a façade for a super-secret organization, A.P.E.S., in the DC series *Young Justice*.

◀ I was flying over the Rocky Mountains when I came up with the idea for the Mount, the secret headquarters for the super-secret Pantheon in *The Incredible Hulk*.

WHAT IF?

Sit in a public place, such as a park or the middle of a mall. Watch the people go by and come up with entire stories for them based on what you observe. Transform the world into your laboratory for conceiving ideas.

- An elderly man is just standing there, staring at a pocket watch. Perhaps it's a watch he stole when he was seven years old and he is now preparing to return it to the granddaughter of the person he stole it from. Perhaps his wife gave it to him and it stopped running the day she died.

- A young couple is walking by in close, intense discussion. Perhaps she is pregnant and he doesn't know how to react. Perhaps he's just had a psychic flash that a gang shoot-out is going to break out at the movie they were planning to see, and he's trying to figure out how to convince her not to go without sounding insane.

- A well-built woman with a large bag strides past. An actress heading to an audition? A hit woman on her way to assassinate a local crime kingpin? If the former, does she get the job? If the latter, does she make the hit? What if she's both and discovers her target is a director who has just called her agent to say he wants her for the lead in his next movie?

Anything is possible.

Unfortunately, sometimes real life can overtake the imagination. I thought it was the height of cleverness to have an invisible structure suspended between the Twin Towers serve as the HQ for yet another super-secret organization, S.H.I.R.T.S., (yes, their opponent was S.K.I.N.S.) in the pages of Dark Horse's *SpyBoy*.

Page 5, SpyBoy #4 | SpyBoy™ #4 ©2000 Lark Horse Comics, Inc.

A REAL WRITER HAS REAL ISSUES

"Write what you know." That's one of the simplest axioms that any writer is taught. If you've ever taken any sort of creative writing course, that's what they say.

Unfortunately, many young writers respond, "But I don't know anything." Ah, how little you know of what you truly know.

For the purpose of this discussion, I'm going to assume that most of you out there are interested in the realm of superheroes, fantasy beings with powers above and beyond those of mortal men. Some of you may think it's simple to write a story involving such beings: A villain breaks out of confinement, beats the hero, but the hero then figures out a way to overcome the villain, end of story, send it to the artist, collect a paycheck.

Does that sound boring to you? I hope so, because it sounds dull as dishwater to me. As a string of incidents, it qualifies as a story in the broadest sense. And you may well see published stories that are little more than what I've just described. But if you want to break into comics, you can't simply aspire to be "as good as" what's already out there. You need to be at least five to ten times better just to get noticed.

EVERY STORY NEEDS AN ANCHOR

Furthermore, there's a danger when writing fantasy to produce tales so far removed from real-world concerns that there's no anchor to reality. That's a fatal mistake, because your prospective reader likely doesn't live in a fantasy world. He lives in a real world filled with everything from broken romances to paying bills to fear of terrorist attacks.

READERS WANT STORIES THEY CAN RELATE TO

Some readers claim they read comics merely for escapism, so they don't have to think about reality. But they're just saying that. The ultimate in escapist fantasy would be cosmic-level tales featuring such heroes as the Silver Surfer or the New Gods. If the escapist philosophy of readership held true, they would be among the most successful characters out there. Instead, their solo books inevitably

crash and burn due to low sales, irrespective of the quality of the individual work.

What readers really want is stories and characters to which they can relate, stories that have some resonance to their lives. Without that— without the readers being able to make some manner of personal investment in the events you're depicting—they simply won't care about your story or what happens in it.

BLEND FANTASY AND REALITY

Possibly one of the all-time best blendings of fantasy and reality was Joss Whedon's *Buffy the Vampire Slayer*. Here you had a preposterous assortment of vampires, werewolves and demons (most of whom knew kung fu for some reason) converging on one hapless town in California, with its main protector a blonde slip of an erstwhile cheerleader with superstrength and martial arts skills, aided by an only occasionally effective posse of nonsuperstrong friends.

Except *BtVS* wasn't really about vampires and such. Instead, particularly in its first three years, it was about teenage angst. Anyone who ever believed high school was hell would readily buy into the concept that Sunnydale High literally was hell, or at least built on an entranceway to it. *BtVS* ran the entire gamut of adolescent nightmares, from peer pressure to teen suicide to the boyfriend who seemed so nice until his girlfriend slept with him, at which point he underwent a personality change and treated her badly. True, the fantasy element heightened the situation and the stakes. But even that heightening made contextual sense. How often have teenagers, when wrestling with problems of acceptance and rejection, felt as if their entire world hung in the balance? Making the stakes in *BtVS* the literal life and death of the world wasn't outrageous at all, but a simple extension of what already existed.

WHAT'S AT STAKE

Fantasy settings enable you to take aspects of your life and explore them in bigger-than-life situations—to tell tales that are metaphors for what's going on inside you and outside you. By making the *stakes*

> "Here's a news flash: I wrote **THE INCREDIBLE HULK** for twelve years, and I have never been hit with *gamma radiation* and have never been transformed into a *thousand pounds of unfettered green rage.*"

of your story something you yourself can relate to, you've gone a long way toward making your story accessible to your readers.

So when writers are advised to "write what you know," no one is saying you should stick only to those things you have directly experienced. Here's a news flash: I wrote *The Incredible Hulk* for twelve years, and I have never been hit with gamma radiation and have never been transformed into a thousand pounds of unfettered green rage.

YOU REALIZE, OF COURSE, THIS MAKES NO SENSE: STUNTS

It is incumbent upon the writer to not only spot all the potential plot holes, but to cover them as well. You want to anticipate the reader noticing holes and answer them either before the reader can think of it, or right when the reader is noticing it. Sometimes it almost doesn't matter what the explanation is, as long as it's there and makes at least a modicum of sense.

THE MONOLOGUE SOLUTION

That's why you'll see scenes where the hero is trapped by the villain, and the villain explains his fiendish plot, and the hero then asks a series of questions as to why the villain did A, B and C when he could have done D, E and F. Now the real reason the villain didn't do D, E and F is because he'd have accomplished his aims midway through Act 2 and utterly defeated the hero. But the writer obviously doesn't want to admit this. So instead, for no real reason except a made-up one ("Must figure out some way to stall for time... until I can loosen these ropes!"), the hero becomes the villain's biographer and wants to make sure he gets it all straight. Actually, what he's doing is serving as the reader's proxy to anticipate the reader's questions. And the villain explains his scheme point by point, also for no real reason

("I want you to know everything before you die!") when he's really the writer's mouthpiece to try and cover all the questionable choices in the story.

THE "TOO RIDICULOUS TO WORK" SOLUTION

Every so often, though, you'll run up against a fundamental aspect that is so completely ridiculous, it makes no sense. Or perhaps it's a bald-faced rip-off of another story. Five White House press secretaries putting their heads together couldn't come up with a positive spin. In a situation such as that, here's what you do:

You have the characters themselves acknowledge that the whole thing is stupid, or a rip-off, and then move on.

No less a talent than Alan Moore did exactly that in *Watchmen*. At several points in the story, characters comment on the utter absurdity of the main plotter's ultimate scheme. His response is essentially, "Yeah, well, that's what you think." Yes, that's what they think, and that's what I think, and that may well be what Moore thinks. Plus, in this instance, the main plan is uncomfortably close to an old *Outer Limits* episode. So what happens? A character is shown watching the exact episode

Yet one doesn't have to experience those aspects of the Hulk to still write what one knows. Dealing with inner rage, knowing so much frustration over difficulties that you'd just like to smash to bits whatever's bothering you, feeling conflicted as different aspects of your personality drive you in different directions...these are all things that people know about and relate to. The stakes for maintaining control are high in everyday life. If the Hulk goes berserk, he gets the army on his tail. If the average reader flips out and starts doing massive amounts of damage, he'll get in trouble either with his parents or the police, or both. In all cases, it's authority figures attempting to exact punishment for antisocial behavior.

"Write what you know" means that you write about stakes that are personal to you. That mean something to you. That have the element of truth to you. That will serve to make the writing honest, and your readers will then be able to connect with you. If the stakes have personal resonance with you and your readers (a desperate endeavor to win back the love of one who has deserted you; a deep moral quandary over whether or not to rat out a friend whose dangerous actions are putting him at risk; a fear of abandonment that threatens to become real), even if your story trips into the most outrageous of scenarios, it will still have enough "reality" to it that the readers will connect and your story will be successful.

AND SHORTCUTS WHEN NOTHING ELSE WORKS

that's being ripped off. By underscoring it in the text, you're acknowledging in essence, "Okay, yes, I know this is a weak point in the script, but let's all agree to ignore it and keep going."

I once completely wrote myself into a corner in plotting an issue of *The Incredible Hulk* involving Bruce, Betty, Rick Jones and a Skrull saucer. I got to the second to last page of the story, with the saucer going up in a ball of flame, and I suddenly realized to my horror that I'd forgotten to get Rick off the saucer. I was on a tight deadline, the story was already barely squeezing into the allotted pages, so I had neither the time nor the space to try and revise the story.

So what happens? Bruce and Betty begin to mourn the loss of their old friend, and suddenly Rick comes floating safely to earth via parachute. He informs Bruce that he always carries a miniparachute with him in the off-chance he should have to escape from an exploding Skrull saucer. When Bruce expresses the same incredulity that the reader might well feel, saying that such a development is ridiculous, Rick sanguinely replies, "Why? I needed to, didn't I?" To which Bruce has no reasonable comeback.

That's an example of knowing just how far

one can push a gag. The same bit would have NEVER worked with Betty, or Bruce, or even Doc Samson. But Rick's been around so much, in so many places, that the running conceit of his character is that it's impossible to take him off guard. He's seen it all. He's the ultimate Boy Scout in that he's always prepared. So claiming that he carries a parachute with him for just such an occasion, while a stretch, is not beyond the realm of possibility for him.

This isn't limited to comic books. In *Raiders of the Lost Ark*, Indy tells Sallah that he's going to be going after the truck in which the Nazis are transporting the ark. Sallah reasonably asks, "How?" To which Indy responds, "I don't know, I'm making this up as I go." Next thing you know, Indiana Jones is on horseback. Where'd he get the horse? Doesn't matter. The writer has tacitly admitted through Indy's voice that he's got no reasonable explanation. So we might as well just throw Indy on the horse and keep on moving.

It's a shortcut. It's sloppy writing. But that doesn't mean that, if your back is against the wall, you shouldn't do it if you have to. Just don't push it. There's a fine line between a sly wink and a disbelieving blink.

TELL SMALL STORIES AGAINST A WORLD FRAME

Ideas for stories are all around you. You just have to realize they're there.

The approach that has always worked for me is to tell small stories set against a much larger framework.

Consider, for example, World War II. The Holocaust. A vast, sweeping attempt at genocide that took the lives of six million Jews. Yet if asked to name one Holocaust victim off the top of their head, many people would doubtless say Anne Frank, the German Jewish girl who wrote her famed diary while her family was hiding from the Nazis during their occupation of the Netherlands. The evil of the Holocaust is almost too vast to contemplate. But the story of a single girl and her family has captured the minds and imaginations of readers for decades. Granted, her story is a true one. That is not the point. The point is that stories are at their best when they center on a few people rather than a cast of thousands. It is easier and more effective for readers to become involved in the lives of a few people than thousands or millions. Such a story not only touches the heart, but it translates well into other media...in the case of Anne Frank, into stage dramatizations and even an opera.

(Curiously, when it comes to Holocaust deniers, even the story of Anne Frank is too much for them to accept, as they maintain that Anne Frank is a fictional character and her diary a pack of lies. Just goes to show how far people will take their disbelief, especially when it involves something so evil that they figure it just can't have happened.)

That's one of the reasons why a vast, star-spanning comic book cosmic epic makes a problematic read: The stakes are too far away from everyday concerns and the participants can number over a hundred. It's simply too distancing. Try to frame situations, no matter how global or complicated, in smaller, human terms.

For instance, the *Young Justice* story "Liberty Throughout the Land" was inspired by newspaper stories detailing how people of Muslim extraction were being harassed and even brutalized after the events of 9/11. Imagine the notion of being totally innocent of any wrongdoing, loving the country you're in, and suddenly being treated as if you're the enemy by people who have decided you're a threat to them.

Well, in *Young Justice*, the Red Tornado's adopted daughter Traya is a native of the fictional country Bialya, the DC equivalent of a rogue nation, created so that DC writers can tell stories of terrorist activities without ascribing them to real-life countries. The thing is, any story needs a *catalyst* in order to trigger it. A catalyst is some event that occurs to set the tale into motion so you have a reason for it happening "now" rather than at some other time. In this case, I had terrorism strike home for one of the girls in Traya's private school when her parents—volunteer workers in Bialya—are killed by a suicide bomber. The girls turn around and take out their collective anger and grief on Traya. Aided by the magnificent art of Todd Nauck and Lary Stucker, the story practically wrote itself.

In this case, obviously, the ongoing difficulties entailed by global terrorism was the worldwide framework against which the story was set. I wanted to do a story about the ultimate futility of terrorism and how humans themselves become devalued. Now of course it would be possible to do a story about the origins of terrorism, and government battles against it, and the ongoing scourge it represents.

But the bottom line of terrorism is the terrible human cost: how innocent bystanders suffer, and how it makes people suspicious of their neighbors. These were the aspects addressed in *Young Justice*, showing how innocents were hammered by the effects of terrorism in a manner that shook them to their souls. This is underscored when a young girl named Ellen, whose parents are killed by a car bomb while abroad, confronts Wonder Girl and says, "I read somewhere that you Wonders...you and Wonder Woman...get your power from gods. That right?" When Wonder Girl confirms this, and further confirms that they do indeed see gods from time to time (albeit Greek ones), Ellen says angrily, "Okay, well...well, next time you see some gods, you ask 'em why stuff like this happens. Why they let it happen. Why any god would. Then you come back and tell me what they say."

Wonder Girl responds, "My guess is they'd probably say that they give us the right to make choices, for good or bad, and beyond that it's up to us."

To which Ellen replies, "Yeah, well...tell 'em I think they suck, then. And tell 'em people are killing other people in their names, and that sucks even more."

And Wonder Girl admits, "They'd probably agree."

Keeping it small means keeping it real...even when one of your protagonists hangs out with gods and Amazons.

DAVID · NAUCK · STUCKER

EXERCISE

TURN OFF YOUR TELEVISION

An unfortunate truth is that most people get their news entirely from television, where most items are boiled down to sixty-second nuggets of information. If you're looking for the kind of details that inspire stories, that's not the place for it. Instead you want to read newspapers, newsmagazines such as *Newsweek* or *The Week* (particularly if you're looking for a publication that presents varied viewpoints), books... anything that will help keep you wired in to what is going on in the world around you.

When reading about world events, reporters can be your best friends. Everyone has their own story to tell, and many love telling it to reporters. Reading about floods? Look for tales of human conflict (a young man who could have made it out on his own but decided to brave a hurricane's fury because his ailing mother couldn't be moved) or selfless heroism (a man wrestles an alligator to save a pregnant woman). Reading about war? Fictionalize the stories of terrified citizens whose lives have been turned upside down. Create a fictional character based on, say, the real-life angry mother whose son died in a war and is now stoking the fires of an antiwar movement, and see where the story takes you.

You will find that simply writing a story that presents your point of view amounts to little more than a screed, which equals boring. I mean, sure, it's possible (and indeed often happens) for writers to produce stories that are designed to drive home their personal beliefs. But the reason I think it's better fiction not to go that way is, quite simply, it gives your heroes less to overcome.

BELIEVE IN YOUR CHARACTER
Your heroes should always find themselves in opposition to something. If they need to reach a magical object, there should be powerful forces guarding the way. By the same token, if they have deep-seated beliefs upon which the plot turns, they should be facing people with opposing views that are as near and dear to them as your hero's are.

And those opposing beliefs should be well thought out. It may give you personal satisfaction to present the opposition as boneheads, but what triumph is there for your hero if he overcomes a bunch of lamebrains? How much respect will your reader have for him if the challenges he faced were wafer thin?

You will find it not only a valuable experience for writing, but a valuable experience for life, if you make a habit out of understanding and even embracing (at least for story purposes) viewpoints that are opposites of yours. If you're going to write a story about, say, abortion, and you're in favor of a woman's right to choose, pretend you're fervently against it and write an editorial for an imaginary newspaper explaining your position. Don't just give it lip service; for the purpose of the editorial, believe it. When you're a writer, you're basically role playing. The more you believe in each character, the more you share their opinions while inhabiting their skin, the more credible they will be and the more effective your story.

A variety of news stories about capital punishment prompted me to write the story of "Crazy Eight," which appeared in *The Incredible Hulk* #380 with pencils by guest artist Bill Jaaska. Now I happen to believe firmly that capital punishment

MAKE EVERYBODY MAD
Interestingly, we received angry letters from people representing both sides of the issue in "Crazy Eight," each claiming that the story clearly favored the opposing viewpoint. For instance, those in favor of capital punishment were outraged that Crazy Eight, the executed criminal, was remotely sympathetic. Apparently the notion that criminals are human beings, too, and not mad dogs who must be put down with no thought given to morality, made them much too uncomfortable.

On the other hand, those who were opposed to capital punishment felt I had done Doc Samson a disservice by having him remaining simply a witness to the execution, rather than bursting into the chamber, freeing Crazy Eight and helping her escape. To them, I had tacitly made Samson a supporter of capital punishment. It didn't occur to them that such a development would have turned Doc into a criminal.

We also got letters asserting that showing people being executed in comics was far too depressing. My response to that was simple: If capital punishment is so upsetting to you, go out and do something about people who are really being executed, rather than becoming overwrought about the pretend death of a fictional character.

The cover of *The Incredible Hulk* #380, in which we see Crazy Eight in action, happy to be killing guys she thinks deserve it...and Doc Samson a witness not only to her crimes, but to the eventual penalty she will receive.

Hulk #380: ©2005 Marvel Characters, Inc. Used with permission.

should be outlawed. So I crafted the story to be nothing more than a down-and-dirty, straightforward story in which we put a human face on a supervillain who is slated to be executed via electric chair. We not only showed her brutal life of crime for which she was unrepentant, but also her head being shaved, her being strapped into the chair and her pure panic at facing her life's end. Then we executed her, end of story.

Interestingly, one editor at Marvel told me, after reading the story, that he couldn't believe I'd executed Crazy Eight. He said, "After all the work you put into that character, to just kill her off? I couldn't believe it." But that's the whole point of balance. In order to be convincing that the courts felt she deserved to die, I had to make her crimes brutal and herself totally unrepentant. But I also needed to make her as fully rounded as possible, otherwise the reader would have felt no connection to her. No one is upset when a monster dies in a movie. To make Crazy Eight be something other than a monster—and for her death to have meaning so the opposing view was presented—I had to hammer home her fundamental humanity.

REPRESENT THE OPPOSITION

In my general reading, I stumbled across a book by essayist and journalist Nat Hentoff. Entitled *Free Speech for Me But Not for Thee: How the American Left and Right Relentlessly Censor Each Other*, it detailed the ongoing attempts by people at both ends of the political spectrum to suppress opinions they don't like. What particularly caught my attention was the growing trend in colleges—supposedly liberal colleges—to try and shut down invited speakers who espouse viewpoints with which they disagree. Common sense tells you that if you don't like what someone has to say, don't attend his speech.

Remarkably, colleges and universities, which should be pressure cookers of opposing viewpoints and discussion, are populated by students and faculty members who have not only made up their minds that they don't want to be exposed to opposing viewpoints, but they also want to make sure no one else has the opportunity. So I decided to drop this hot button of a topic into *Supergirl* #23 in a story entitled "Double-Edged Sword," drawn by Leonard Kirk and Robin Riggs.

In that tale (based, as they say, on a true story) an anthropologist, espousing a theory that African Americans are biologically inferior to whites, comes to a local college to lecture and is greeted with massive resistance. And just as teachers and scholars in the real incident advocated steamrolling over the concept of free expression, so did John Henry Irons, a.k.a. Steel, oppose the speaker's presence at the college...bringing him into conflict with Supergirl, who didn't quite

In this issue, entitled "Double-Edged Sword," Supergirl battles with Steel over the limits (or lack thereof) of free speech.

understand all the ramifications but felt she'd rather err on the side of free speech.

It's always important to present all sides equally for dramatic purposes, but it's never more so when a guest hero is espousing a viewpoint that is opposite to that of your central character. To play it absolutely safe, I moved beyond my own attempts to present opposing views. I obtained actual opinion pieces from learned professors who held the views that I wanted Steel to have. Obviously I didn't use their statements word for word, but I patterned Steel's commentary on what they said. Massaged the exact phrasing a bit, but the core, the essence of what they said, was presented intact.

Curiously, in this instance, I heard from virtually no one who shared Steel's views. That's understandable; very rarely do people like to step forward and state that they're in favor of squelching free speech. However, I did hear from many free speech advocates who, interestingly, felt I had done Steel a disservice. How could any reasonable person, they argued, possibly feel the way Steel did? The arguments I'd given him, they felt, were totally unconvincing. I always wondered how the scholarly and learned academic men and women whose sentiments had been the basis for Steel's speeches would have felt knowing that comic book fans had dismissed them as unconvincing.

Putting an assortment of characters—both lead and supporting—into opposition with each other enabled me to explore all aspects of an incendiary issue.

No matter how hard you work at it, you aren't always going to satisfy all the readers all of the time. But you owe it to yourself, the integrity of the characters, the quality of your fiction and the readership in general to do the best you can in terms of balance. You want to write a one-sided position piece? Send a letter to the editor. Don't put it in your fiction.

This is not to say that story concepts can only be derived from what's happening around you. Sometimes all you need is a sense of logic, of "what happens next."

For instance, I was once at an X-book writers' meeting, since I was writing *X-Factor* at the time. We were plotting the course of the next year's worth of stories, and one decision that had been made was to bring back Magneto. What was being conceived and discussed at that moment was having a major slugfest between Wolverine and Magneto.

And I said, thinking out loud, "Y'know, I don't understand why Magneto even bothers with Wolverine. Adamantium's a metal, right? If I were Magneto, I'd just yank his skeleton out of his body and be done with him."

There was dead silence around the table for a moment as everyone looked at each other. "My God, what a fantastic idea," said editor Bob Harras.

"No, it's not," I said with a sense of growing alarm. "It's a terrible idea."

"But what a great visual it would be!" said someone else.

"Yeah, but then Wolverine's dead!" I protested.

"No, he's not." It was like something out of Monty Python.

"How can he not be dead after having his skeleton yanked out of him?" I asked.

"He's got a healing factor."

"A healing factor?!?" I practically shouted. "How can he heal from having no skeleton? He'll be a healed pile of goo! What about his brain? His brain's encased in the adamantium skull, did you think of that?! He'll have no brain! If he heals from having no brain or bones, he's not Wolverine anymore! He's a freakin' god! We can't do this!"

Well, they did it anyway and got years' worth of stories out of it. It was the single greatest impact I ever had on the entire mutant universe, and it came from a throwaway comment.

Sometimes we wonder where we get ideas, and sometimes we wish we could ship them back to Schenectady.

THE "CATCH" TO REAL-WORLD IDEAS

There are, of course, downsides to hinging stories on real-world issues. First and foremost, you can make yourself a target for those who disagree with your politics, or even your perceived politics. Second, you run the risk of real-world events outstripping whatever it is you're writing about. For instance, I was once working on a novel that hinged on a presidential sex scandal. But then the Twin Towers fell, and suddenly the peccadilloes of the Clinton administration seemed even more inane and irrelevant to the world stage than they'd been when they were actually happening. I had to throw out the entire concept of the novel and start from scratch.

Plus sometimes, when playing in the corporate structure of comics, you can run afoul of conservative viewpoints—"conservative" as in "not wanting to make waves." I wrote a story for *X-Factor* that centered on abortion and included lively debates from characters on all sides of the issue. The editor said it was the best script I'd ever written. But it wound up being edited into unrecognizability because abortion was a hot-button issue that the Powers-That-Be didn't want to touch.

An extreme example of what can happen if you just ask yourself what happens next. Wolverine suffered terribly as a result of my offhand comment, "If I were Magneto, I'd just yank his skeleton out of his body and be done with him."

CHARACTERS
HEROES

IT'S IMPOSSIBLE TO INVEST TOO MUCH ENERGY IN EITHER CRAFTING NEW HEROES AND VILLAINS OR CHOOSING UNIQUE WAYS IN WHICH TO INTERPRET OR REINTERPRET ALREADY EXISTING CHARACTERS. YOUR STORIES STAND OR FALL ON YOUR CHARACTERS. IF THE READER DOESN'T CONNECT WITH THE CHARACTERS, THE MOST INGENIOUS PLOT IN THE WORLD WILL MAKE NO DIFFERENCE AT ALL.

Your heroes and villains share a curious bond: Without the villains, the heroes have absolutely nothing to do with their time. The hero is defined by the challenges he must overcome, and the villain presents those challenges. Perversely, the villain almost assumes a "heroic" role since—more often than not—he's the one with the aggressive goal. He's the one who wants to accomplish something. The hero needs the villain far more than the villain needs the hero.

If you ask anyone you know whether they need someone who is going to make their life difficult, you would unquestionably get a resounding "no." No person would say that he measures the success of his day by how soundly he manages to overcome an implacable opponent.

And yet, many of us do have "villains" in our lives. Be they oppressive bosses, obnoxious co-workers, bullies at school. On any given day we may find ourselves in a position where we have to outthink, outwit and outmaneuver those who seem to strive to make our lives difficult.

Sometimes, we may even find ourselves with our backs against the wall and have to slug it out with them. It's moments such as these that we might indeed find ourselves wishing we had superpowers. For that matter, it's those real-life moments that provide inspiration for the characters who are the most memorable. Finding yourself in a situation where some total creep is making you angry beyond belief enables you as a writer to connect with a rage-driven character like the Hulk. How about if a girl you like sees you only as meek and mild and dismisses you out of hand? Don't you wish you could dazzle her with the strength and charisma of your alter ego? Heaven forbid you or a loved one suffers at the hands of a criminal. Would that you could blend with the darkness, track down the perpetrator, punch out the criminal and drag him to justice.

And not only can you relate to that as a writer, but such hero/villain dynamics tap a great wellspring of desire within your readership as well. That's what makes such heroes eternally popular and the villains resolutely hissable.

Thor vs. Hulk: ©2005 Marvel Characters, Inc. Used with permission.

Curiously, we tend to think of the hero as the mover and shaker, the protagonist. Yet the opposite is often true: It is the villain who actually drives the plot. He's the one with the plan, he's the one with the goal—anything from robbing a bank to world domination. There is a variety of possibilities and directions to which the villain's foul schemes can go to satisfy his needs. The hero, on the other hand, exists for one reason only: to thwart the villain. On an average day, the Avengers sit around playing pinochle, waiting for the activities of a villain to spur them to action. On an average night, Batman is either hanging out at the Batcave dodging falling bat guano, or else he's patrolling the city looking to find a villain whose endeavors he can thwart.

THE SYMPATHETIC VILLAIN

As a writer, not only do you need to have a hero with whom your reader can connect, but you also want the reader to understand—and perhaps even sympathize with—the villain's goals. Is such a thing possible? Sure it is. Alfred Hitchcock once pointed out that an audience could be watching a scene in a movie wherein a handsome burglar has concocted an elaborate and clever scheme to gain access to a vault inside a wealthy couple's home. As he is working on opening the safe, unbeknownst to the burglar, the couple is on their way home because they left their theater tickets on the bureau in the room he's burgling. Tension mounts as the burglar continues to crack the safe while the couple draws closer and closer to discovering him. And what, asked Hitchcock, is going through the audience's mind during that time? They're mentally urging the burglar, "Hurry! Hurry! You're going to get caught!" Yes, that's right: They're rooting for a bad guy.

It is the ingeniousness of his plan, after all, that is being asked to seize the audience's imagination.

If the villain's plan is lame, if the villain is someone who fails to engage the reader's attention, then not only will the reader not care about his evil doings, but the hero's eventual triumph over his opponent will seem unimpressive.

WHAT'S HIS MOTIVATION?

In order to make the villain sympathetic, it helps to present his motivations and actions from the point of view of the villain himself or others close to him. Everyone, even the most hardened criminal on death row, has reasons for his or her actions. They may not seem like good reasons, but they are reasons nevertheless. When someone climbs up onto the top of a building and starts firing at people with a high-powered rifle, the question that often comes to mind is, "Why would someone be motivated to do something like that?" As a writer, it's your job to provide answers to that question. If you can provide the answer, you can split the readers' loyalties so that, yes, they'll want the hero to succeed in his endeavors, but they'll also feel some degree of sympathy for the villain. Anyone who has seen *Pirates of the Caribbean* cannot help but feel bad for Barbossa at his fate, particularly the moment when an apple rolls out of his hand. Anyone who hasn't seen it won't know what I'm talking about, so I recommend you check out the film for a textbook demonstration of how to create a sympathetic villain.

IS HE A VILLAIN EVERYWHERE?

You can also shift point of view to how others view the villain. Showing a villain who is also a devoted family man humanizes him. Years ago in the Silver Age of comics, Lex Luthor was a fairly one-dimensional villain. Even the nominal reason for

> "EVERYONE, even the **most hardened** criminal on death row, has REASONS for his or her actions."

his hatred of Superman—Superboy being responsible for Luthor going bald—seemed dubious at best. And then the writers had the brilliant idea of sending Luthor to a far-off world where, due to various circumstances, Luthor was hailed as a hero. Not only that, but when Superman showed up to haul Luthor back to Earth, the planetary residents saw Superman as a villain. One almost hated that Superman had an insufferable moral code requiring him to bring Luthor back to justice, because even as kids we sensed that if Superman simply left Luthor on the world where he was worshipped and happy, the planet Earth would never have to fear Luthor again.

Sometimes it's hard to know what's right and what's wrong. And that moral confusion can make for the best stories.

EXERCISE

DESIGN-A-VILLAIN

A little exercise for developing your own villain:

1 Decide who the hero is going to be that your villain will be in opposition to.

2 Select some aspect or aspects of the hero that your villain can mirror. If your hero believes in the government, the villain advocates no government. If your hero is a brilliant detective, your villain obsesses about pulling off crimes that leave no clues.

3 Develop a back story for your villain that explains why he does what he does. We know why Batman tries to stop criminals. Why shouldn't we know why his opponent is a criminal?

4 Develop powers and a "name" for the villain that are reflective of all of the above. For example, if the villain believes in fostering total chaos, you can either give him a name that reflects that (the Anarchist, for instance) or you can go in the opposite direction and, in Orwellian Newspeak, dub him something that is contrary to his actual persona (the Peacemaker). The powers or techniques that you provide for him should grow organically out of everything you've established so far. Say he clips out the names of everyone who was in the newspaper the previous day, puts them in a hat, pulls out two or three of them each morning and goes off to murder them using a gun called the Colt Peacemaker.

WHAT IS A HERO?

So, are the hero and villain interchangeable? Certainly not. What, then, makes a hero a hero? Well, that definition has changed somewhat over the years.

For instance, once upon a time, the hero—particularly the superhero—was the one who showed restraint. Unlike, say, a James Bond or a Robin Hood, who killed their opponents because their opponents were trying to kill them, superheroes always found a way to render their opponents powerless without crossing certain lines. They staked out the moral high ground. Why, I couldn't say. From a story context, you could argue that since they had so much power at their disposal, they considered it their obligation to display restraint. From a real-world context, it may well be that the publishers of what was considered kiddie fare felt that their characters shouldn't be going around willy-nilly killing the bad guys.

There's been a sea change in that attitude over the years, though. It may well have started in an early issue of the Chris Claremont/John Byrne *X-Men*, when Wolverine killed a couple of guards in the Savage Land as his teammates looked on in horror. As a fan at the time, I was as shocked as the other X-Men over this vicious behavior on the part of a nominal hero...even if he was something of an antihero.

Since then, the lines have irrevocably blurred. The Punisher, who kills with abandon, was introduced as a villain because of his tactics but is now seen by readers as a hero. Wolverine could shred a battalion of baddies with his claws and no one would blink an eye. And recently, over in the DC Universe, Wonder Woman was presented with an ultimatum by the villainous Maxwell Lord, who had taken control of Superman's mind and made the Man of Steel a menace. Essentially, Lord told Wonder Woman that the only way she could stop him from performing his evil deeds was to kill him.

Once upon a time, what would have defined Wonder Woman as a hero was that, faced with two untenable options, she would be clever, wise and heroic enough to find a third way that wouldn't violate her moral code. Not this time. Without hesitation, she broke Lord's neck. Mission accomplished. Either it's brilliant writing to show that even the most heroic of individuals must resort to unheroic means when there's no other choice, or it's sloppy writing because the authors simply weren't clever enough to find a way for Wonder Woman to keep her hands clean. Take your pick.

WHAT MAKES HEROES HEROIC?

So, if the line is becoming more and more blurred in terms of the tactics that heroes are using in fighting the villains...and if the villains are the movers and shakers who have active goals to pursue while the heroes simply live to thwart the villains...what is it about the heroes that makes them heroic at all?

The answer to that is: Who benefits?

Villains' plans almost always center around something that will benefit them personally. They see mankind as something that exists either to be conquered or to benefit them. Heroes, on the other hand, work to benefit the commonweal. They use their powers in the service of others for a number of reasons:

* Their upbringing has instilled a higher moral calling (Superman, Wonder Woman).

* Some personal trauma has set them onto this path and they couldn't turn away even if they wanted to (Batman, Spider-Man).

* They model themselves on an already existing hero (the Silver Age Flash, for instance, was a fan of the Golden Age Flash).

As much as it seems that their main mission is to thwart villains, when you get down to it, that's really their secondary goal. Their first goal is to protect the innocent. Even the Punisher, with his brutal methods, is concerned about making sure that criminals don't prey on the helpless.

HEROIC WEAKNESSES

The best and most compelling heroes are those who must overcome weaknesses in order to accomplish that goal. With the classic literary heroes, those weaknesses come from within: Sherlock Holmes, for instance, and the boredom that led to his drug addiction. Or shift to the modern day where, on television, detective Adrian Monk is a mass of psychoses that both aid and impede his solutions of mysteries.

In the old days of superheroes, the heroes were so much bigger than life, with so few personality foibles, that their weaknesses were manufactured: Superman with kryptonite, Green Lantern with wood or the color yellow, Martian Manhunter with fire. In later years, superheroes became more down-to-earth, subject to more human impediments. The Fantastic Four, for instance, were as likely to be fighting with each other as they were the villains who were their opponents. And Spider-Man...some days you wondered why he even got out of bed in the morning, and he often wondered the same thing.

WHY DID SPIDER-MAN BOTHER GETTING OUT OF BED IN THE MORNING?

Because he was a hero. Because, even though he tried repeatedly, he couldn't find it within himself to stand by and let others be hurt by criminals. And neither could Superman or Batman or Green Lantern or Flash or any of the other heroes who constitute your list of protagonists.

The reasons why they feel that way, and how they react to that responsibility, are not only what makes them unique, but also provide you with endless fodder for exploration into what makes them tick and how they react to different situations.

If the audience doesn't care enough about the hero to share his journey, he might as well stay on the farm (or in the Shire or Krypton or wherever). But you can have two characters sit around and talk in a restaurant for twenty-two pages, and if the talk is interesting and the characters are engaging and there's character development of some kind, you've got a story.

BRINGING THE SUPERHUMAN "DOWN TO EARTH"

In the production of comic books, the greatest challenge presented to any writer is to make the characters as "real" as possible. This is not an easy undertaking. If you're writing a straight-up work of fiction that features Joe and Jane Average, there are fewer challenges involved in establishing the connection between audience and character... the connection that leads to the all-important willing suspension of disbelief. But when writing of superhuman characters, it's much more difficult to make them "down-to-earth" as well so they will engage the readership.

WRITER OR LUNATIC

Fictional characters—to state the obvious—aren't real. If a man walks down the street muttering to himself, "And there's this big green guy, and he's smashing through a wall, and he picks up this car and he's throwing it and people are running and screaming," it's called "lunacy." If I'm engaging in the same process, it's called "plotting" or, if you will, "working." But there's only really two intrinsic differences between the scenarios: I'm actually aware of where I am (theoretically) and you guys are willing to shell out money to find out what happens next (theoretically) as opposed to, say, crossing to the other side of the street.

See, we humans are skeptical creatures. More often than not, when something is presented to us, we tend to view it with skepticism. We doubt the speaker's sincerity and try to discern what's in it for him. We try to perceive reasons that the speaker might be lying or trying to hose us.

Readers always embrace the small touches that serve to make characters, no matter how much bigger-than-life they are, more down-to-earth. The Hulk was given a love of baked beans by one writer years ago, and another gave the Martian Man-hunter a fascination with Oreo cookies. Neither development is especially major in regards to the character overall, but it's years later and fans still remember those little bits of business.

Indeed, the greater a contrast between the character and his foible—the more outlandish the character as opposed to the more mundane the trait you're introducing—the more memorable it will be because of that discrepancy.

CALL ATTENTION TO TRAITS

Embrace the reality of character interaction. If you have a character with a particular trait, don't hesitate to have another character draw attention to it. Reed Richards would regularly express himself in the most elaborate and florid terms imaginable. Every time he did, you can bet Ben Grimm was there to make a snide comment demanding to know why the heck Reed couldn't simply talk the way that normal people did. "Do you have to use them five-buck words?" the Thing would complain at him. That was one technique that helped to make the Fantastic Four so vivid, so much like a family. After all, everyone has family members who display certain traits that drive other family members absolutely nuts.

SPEAKING OF FAMILY

It can also help to give your heroes some sort of family background. When you think of your own life, you think of loved ones, of family, of parents. Too many heroes exist in a vacuum. They have no siblings (unless they're superpowered) and their parents are either dead or never touched upon.

We know nothing of their background or the forces that made them what they are.

It used to be that all heroes had origins that explored their backgrounds all the way back to childhood. Anything you can present to give the reader an idea of the circumstances that form your characters is a good thing.

One of the great television series in history was *Hill Street Blues*. One character, Mick Belker, was depicted as a cross between Serpico and a mad dog. Grizzled and streetwise, he would tackle perps and literally sink his teeth into them. When sitting at his desk and his phone would ring, he'd answer it with an irritated "Belker!" But at least once an episode, his expression and face would soften, and he would say, "Hi, Ma." You'd see a tender side to the character that the criminals he arrested would never believe existed. It fleshed him out, gave him multiple dimensions. One episode they even brought his sister in for a one-shot appearance...and, when a criminal hassled her, she offered to rip out one of his lungs.

REAL CHARACTERS HAVE MANY LAYERS

That's what you should be striving for when crafting a character. Give him as many shadings as possible, either through personal foibles or through how he interacts with other cast members or family. Because the chances are that everyone reading your book either has little personality tics of their own or relationships with family or loved ones, and thus your characters—no matter how fantastical or bigger-than-life they are—will still be accessible to your readership.

USE THE SUPPORTING CAST

Your supporting cast is crucial to accomplishing this. The most successful characters are the ones with a supporting cast almost as memorable as they themselves are. Spider-Man in his lifetime has had Aunt May, Mary Jane, Betty Brant, J. Jonah Jameson, Robbie Robertson, Gwen Stacy and her father, Captain Stacy, Harry Osborn, Flash Thompson...characters who have such staying power

GIVE THEM SOME FRIENDS

Making characters accessible isn't always easy. It's certainly one of the greatest challenges I faced with *Fallen Angel*. Since the protagonist is a woman of mysterious background and ambiguous morals, she was, by design—at least to start out—inaccessible. This changed over time, but the trick was getting fans patient enough to stick around to see what I was doing.

To compensate, I expand upon the backgrounds and experiences of supporting characters, angling to get the readers involved in those characters' fates. I endeavor to make the entire environs of the Fallen Angel "real," rather than individual characters.

I couldn't do much to make the protagonist in *Fallen Angel* seem "common," so I surrounded her with some more "common" characters with whom readers could relate.

that, even though some of them are dead, they continue to have influence on Spidey's life. And that makes sense: All of us have family or friends whom we've lost that we still think about.

Superman has the most celebrated supporting cast in all of comics: Lois Lane, Jimmy Olsen, Perry White, Lana Lang...characters with such a life of their own that some of them even wound up getting their own titles for a time.

CHANGING ROLES

What's interesting is to see how supporting cast members have changed over time, and there's no more apt individual to consider than Lois Lane.

Lois, for the longest time, existed for one main reason: to show how clever Superman was. This was done by painting her in the shal-

lowest of terms. She dismissed Clark Kent out of hand while pining endlessly for Superman. Essentially, she was oblivious to the worth of Clark Kent while blinded by the scintillating wonderfulness of Superman. Since much of what spurred Superman's very creation was teenage wish fulfillment, Lois's view of Clark and Superman played directly to the core of male teenage angst: "If only she knew the guy I was underneath, and knew how wonderful I was, she would love me without reservation."

The fact that it made Lois appear shallow didn't really matter. As long as Superman looked good in comparison, that was the important part.

When Lois began to suspect that Clark and Superman were one and the same, she proceeded to use all her reporter's instincts to prove it. This gave Superman further opportunities to prove how much smarter he was than Lois...and considering the stories were aimed at young boys who thought girls were dumb anyway, it didn't matter that Superman often came across as needlessly cruel in his endeavors. Many was the story in the Silver Age wherein Superman would "teach Lois a lesson" and then heartlessly laugh about it afterward (often with his coconspirator, Batman). Granted, from time to time, Superman got hoist on his own petard...enough so you'd think Lois would want to have nothing to do with the big jerk. But no, she was always back for more the very next issue.

But time passed, and two things happened: first, women's liberation. And second, the age of comic book readers began to skew older. Eventually, Superman no longer needed a punching bag; he needed a female lead to share his life with him. Thus did Lois go from being a cheap joke to being emotionally equal to the Man of Steel and, eventually, his partner in life. All of which reflected well on Superman, giving him more dimensions, layers and new relationships to explore.

Which is what a supporting character (or cast, for that matter) is supposed to do.

CONSISTENT CHARACTER INCONSISTENCIES

The difference between people and characters is that it's accepted that people can act out of character, but not accepted that characters can act like people.

THE PROBLEM

For instance: You can have a pillar of the community. A good, decent man. He's driving along late at night and sees a red light ahead. But there's no one around. He figures, what the heck, no one will know, sails through the red light...and mows down a kid crossing the street. He gets out of the car and finds the kid's brains splattered all over the place. Clearly he's dead.

Anyone who knows the guy will tell you that he will contact the police and stay with the corpse. Instead, he panics. Terrified at what he's done, certain his life is going to be ruined, horrified of what people will think, he leaps back into his car and drives off. In short, he engages in behavior that he would "never" do. Why? Because human beings are fragile creatures, and the fact is that for all we tell ourselves that we're people of conscience or bravery, we don't really know what we would do when our fat's in the fire. Not really.

However, try to do such a story where it's Mary Jane Watson at the wheel of a car, and you've got a tough slog ahead of you. Make it someone like, say, Cyclops, and it becomes even more problematic.

It's a strange dichotomy that one of the things that defines us most as humans—unexpected reactions to unexpected events—runs into the greatest problems when it comes to convincing the audience to follow along for the ride. The knee-jerk reaction from readers when presented when aberrant behavior on the part of a long-standing, established character is: "He would never do that."

"Would never do that."

Fine words, but laughable ones. Ask any girl whose main squeeze has ever dumped her for her own best friend. Ask any husband who suddenly discovers that his wife has cleaned out the bank accounts and hired a divorce lawyer. Ask any loved one of a soldier filmed gleefully abusing prisoners in a foreign land, and they'll tell you, "There's no way. No way. This is a kind, gentle, loving person, and he would never do that to another person."

Real people are simply not defined by the boundaries of the absolute. Given a certain set of circumstances, virtually anyone is capable of acting in ways that would totally stun everyone who has known them their entire lives. That unexpectedness, that unpredictability, is what makes people humans, and what makes humans interesting. But have a fictional character act in a manner that's contrary to his previously established personality, and the fans will howl.

So, is it impossible to have a character act human? That is to say, out of character? No, it's not. The way to finesse your way around this potential pothole is simple, and once I alert you to it, you'll be amazed how often you see writers do it.

THE SOLUTION

Have the character acknowledge and address up front that he's acting out of character—before the reader does. The ideal situation is to have the character justify his behavior to himself (and, by extension, the reader) *as it's happening*. If things are happening too quickly for the character to be properly introspective, you can address it with, "I can't believe I'm doing this." "This is so unlike me." Or an exchange: "Why are you doing this?" "I have no idea, now shut up and let's go." Realistic dialogue this is not, but it will be enough to at least keep the reader along with you, and then—presuming it's necessary—you can come back after the dust has settled as the hero goes into more detail to explain his actions.

If you have some breathing space within the story while the actions are being taken, the character can muse upon his reasons, either through thought balloons, narrative captions or even exchanges with another character. Again, this is not remotely realistic. People don't generally have epiphanies of self-realization while they're in the midst of a situation. That comes later. But keep in mind that you're trying to accomplish something that truly is realistic, namely having someone behave in a manner that is surprising not only to the audience but to themselves. If the only way to make that believable action acceptable to the reader is by having him acknowledge it in an unrealistic manner, that's what you have to do. You're writing a story, you need to keep your reader with you.

WRITE WHAT YOU KNOW: YOURSEL

Your first, best source for characters is your own personality. Your own past, your own life experiences. The more honest you can be building fragments of yourself into your characters, the more chance that they'll strike a chord with the readership and gain the sort of acceptance and popularity you want them to.

Writers invest pieces of themselves into their characters in all manner of ways. Joe Straczynski, when creating the commanders of *Babylon 5*, dubbed them John Sheridan and Jeffrey Sinclair... both of whom happened to share the initials of their creator. My main character in *Sir Apropos of Nothing* shares my impatience for the fantasy tropes of daring knights and breathless maidens waiting to be rescued, and strides through his fictitious medieval world with rampant cynicism and frustration with the world around him.

And I very much doubt that Peter Parker would have rung true to so many readers if Stan Lee weren't, to some degree, drawing on his own personality in crafting the character. It's unlikely that Stan didn't experience some degree of teenage frustration in his formative years, and those frustrations bubble to the surface in Peter Parker's struggle for acceptance.

Another aspect of my own personality that I'm not especially proud of is that I'm very, very impatient with any situation that requires my waiting in line for extended periods. Naturally, being a writer, I made use of this character flaw by giving it to Quicksilver, a Marvel speedster who was usually depicted as being angry at the world for no good reason.

▶By investing someone who always wants to be moving quickly with my own personality flaw of despising being slowed down, Quicksilver explained away three decades worth of annoying behavior so simply that we were deluged with letters from readers saying, "My God, I hated Quicksilver for years, but now I finally understand him! The poor guy!" Of course, it didn't hurt that the art was by future Marvel Editor-in-Chief Joe Quesada.

TIPS TO PUTTING ASPECTS OF YOURSELF INTO YOUR CHARACTERS

- **Don't hold back.** Writers have to be willing to metaphorically drop their pants and invite the world to take its best shot. If there are aspects of yourself that you really don't like, be willing to explore them within a fictional construct. Not only might you create a compelling character, but you might find out interesting things about yourself.

- **Make a list** of positive attributes that you want to explore.

- Now take those same attributes and **explore them as negatives.** For instance:

  – A guy who's a smooth and engaging talker. Write a character study that depicts him as a successful teacher, engaging the students' attention.

  – A guy who's a smooth and engaging talker. Write a character study in which he's a con man who cons the wrong guy and winds up getting the crap kicked out of him.

  – If you're feeling ambitious, you can even write a story in which the two guys are brothers, leading lives that take them in drastically different directions.

Be willing to explore any possible road that can lead you to ideas and directions for stories.

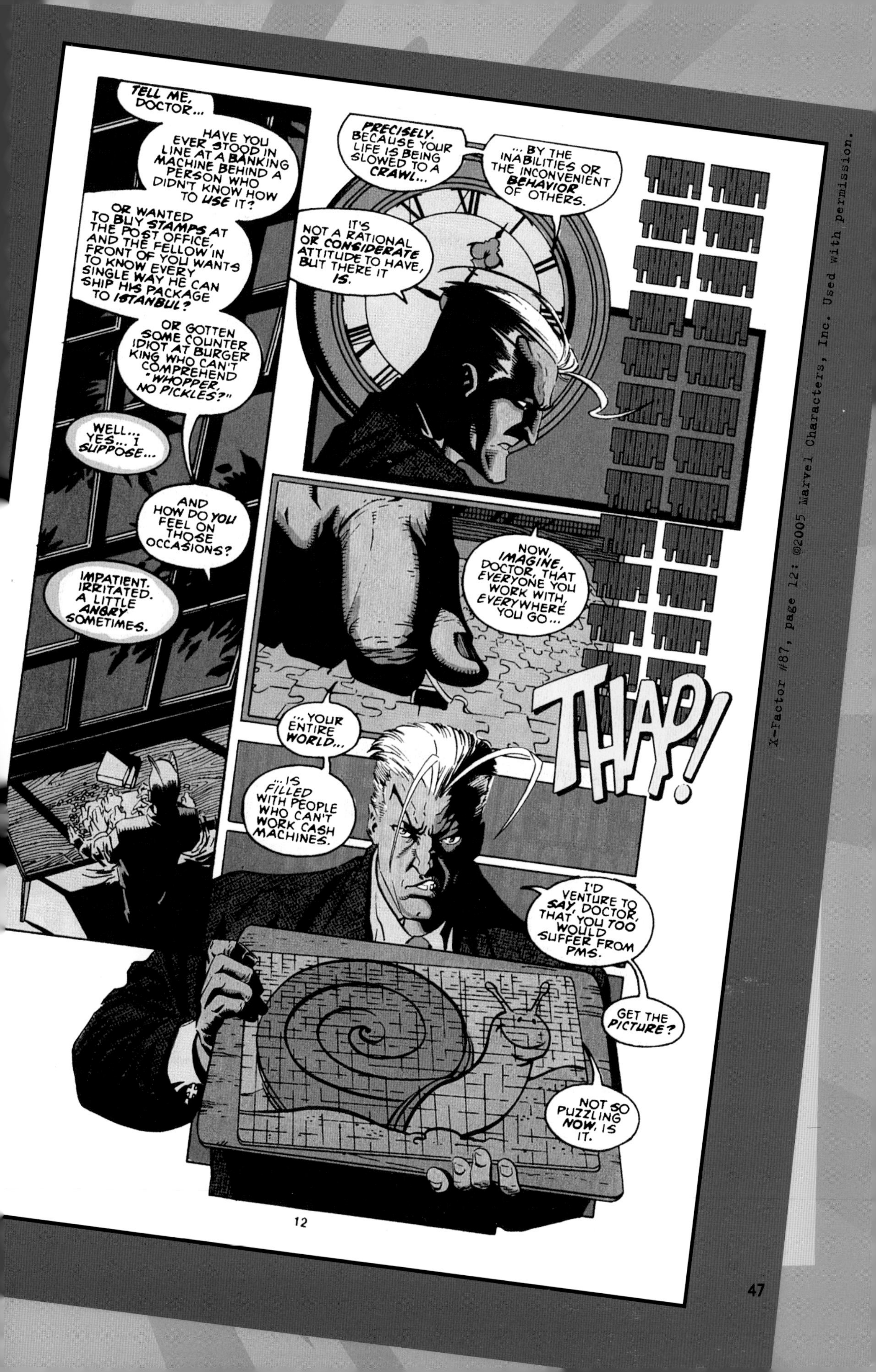

TELL ME, DOCTOR...
HAVE YOU EVER STOOD IN LINE AT A BANKING MACHINE BEHIND A PERSON WHO DIDN'T KNOW HOW TO USE IT?
OR WANTED TO BUY STAMPS AT THE POST OFFICE, AND THE FELLOW IN FRONT OF YOU WANTS TO KNOW EVERY SINGLE WAY HE CAN SHIP HIS PACKAGE TO ISTANBUL?
OR GOTTEN SOME COUNTER IDIOT AT BURGER KING WHO CAN'T COMPREHEND "WHOPPER, NO PICKLES?"
WELL... YES... I SUPPOSE...
AND HOW DO YOU FEEL ON THOSE OCCASIONS?
IMPATIENT. IRRITATED. A LITTLE ANGRY SOMETIMES.
PRECISELY. BECAUSE YOUR LIFE IS BEING SLOWED TO A CRAWL...
... BY THE INABILITIES OR THE INCONVENIENT BEHAVIOR OF OTHERS.
IT'S NOT A RATIONAL OR CONSIDERATE ATTITUDE TO HAVE, BUT THERE IT IS.
THAP! THAP! THAP! THAP! THAP! THAP! THAP! THAP!
NOW, IMAGINE, DOCTOR, THAT EVERYONE YOU WORK WITH, EVERYWHERE YOU GO...
...YOUR ENTIRE WORLD...
...IS FILLED WITH PEOPLE WHO CAN'T WORK CASH MACHINES.
THAP!
I'D VENTURE TO SAY, DOCTOR, THAT YOU TOO WOULD SUFFER FROM PMS.
GET THE PICTURE?
NOT SO PUZZLING NOW, IS IT.
12

DRAWING ON YOUR FRIENDS

Do not hesitate to fictionalize friends, in part or whole, as a basis for characters you want to create. For instance, while working on *Space Cases* in Canada, our story editor was a woman named Valri. A wonderfully funny comic actress and comedy writer of long standing, Valri was also a very much in-your-face individual when it came to her sexual preferences. The first time we met was for lunch and she told me within two minutes that she was a lesbian...and all I'd said was, "Tell me about yourself."

By the end of the lunch, I knew I had to "use" her somewhere, and she wound up being incarnated in the pages of *Supergirl* as an aggressively gay stand-up comedienne named Andy Jones.

Now, I cannot emphasize this enough: For the love of all that's holy, do not, do not, use the actual name of the actual friend. This can lead to all manner of complications that you simply do not want any part of. For that matter, using the names of anyone who is an actual person, friend or not, is something to be avoided. Even flattering portrayals can sometimes land you

in legal hot water. And unflattering ones? Forget it. Writer/artist Todd McFarlane spent years in legal battles stemming from his ill-advised transformation of hockey player Tony Twist into villainous crime lord Tony Twist.

By contrast, in one issue of *Young Justice*, I introduced a sheik named Ali Ben Styn, a verbal and visual parody of pundit and game show host Ben Stein. Before the character saw print, however, I contacted Stein (e-mail is a wonderful thing), told him what I wanted to do, sent him all the dialogue, cleared the use of his likeness and got his written blessing.

And that's just dealing with people you haven't met. When it comes to friends, the stakes can be raised. I know of one writer who

BY THE WAY...

Amusingly, "Andy" generated more hate mail than any other *Supergirl* character, decried by letter writers (none of them gay, mind you) as being unrealistic and insulting to lesbians. A year or so later, however, Andy received vindication of sorts when the Gay & Lesbian Alliance Against Defamation (GLAAD) gave one of their annual awards for positive portrayal of gays and lesbians to *Supergirl*, specifically because of Andy Jones.

thought it would be fun to base a character in his comic series on a female friend of his, and named the character after her. As long as he was writing the book, she was in relatively safe hands. Alas, the writer eventually departed. But since it was work-for-hire, the character remained the property of the company and another writer took over the book. Let's just say that some truly awful and horrific things happened to the comic book incarnation of the young lady. That can't have been fun.

So, when basing characters on friends, you're well-advised simply to stick to general character traits: their peculiar likes and dislikes, their individual ways of expressing themselves, their priorities in life, that sort of thing. Don't lift them whole cloth, name included, into your comic. By the way, this practice is commonly referred to as "Tuckerizing," named after writer Wilson "Bob" Tucker, who was renowned for sticking the names of friends and fans into his work. Why was Tucker able to get away with it and you should avoid it? Because he started the practice in a far less litigious time, and because he's Bob Tucker and you should be so lucky to have your name in his work.

If you are going to use someone's name in your work—if you're bound and determined to—make absolutely certain you've cleared it with them and they're cool with it. Getting permission in writing certainly wouldn't hurt.

For what it's worth, my name has shown up in any number of works of fiction. Curiously, I usually wind up getting killed. I'm not sure what's up with that.

In this issue, the kidnapped and brutalized Andy is forced to relive some difficult aspects of her life, very loosely based on some incidents that Valri, her character model, told me.

EXERCISE

FICTIONALIZING YOUR FRIENDS

1 Write a 100-word first-person narrative in which you have a character based on a friend of yours describing him- or herself.

2 Write another 100-word first-person narrative in which that same character is describing you.

3 Write a third 100-word first-person narrative in which that same character is describing a mutual acquaintance.

4 If you're feeling extraordinarily brave, show the three essays to the friend upon whom you've based it. More often than not, people won't recognize characters based on themselves. If your friend does happen to recognize the portrayal and doesn't consider it flattering, go to step 5.

5 Find new friends.

What do readers want from new heroes and villains? What could constitute the new Superman? Guys, let's be honest...if I knew that, I wouldn't be writing a book about how to create him. I'd be creating him myself and making billions.

But let's figure out instead what constitutes the old Superman. What is it about him that gives the character such resonance that he's been the gold standard of superheroes for seventy years?

WISH FULFILLMENT

Superman, first and foremost, is driven by one of those most primal teenage urges: wish fulfillment. Teens Jerry Siegel and Joe Shuster crafted a character who was, on the outside, everything they likely were—shy, nerdy, nebbishy. But within Clark Kent beat the heart of the greatest hero on earth: stronger and faster than anyone around. In the late 1930s, when young men were worried about being sent off to war, Superman was capable of kidnapping warring leaders with impunity, bringing them face-to-face and telling them to settle their differences man to man and stop sending youngsters to die in battle.

TWISTED ICONS

Batman is arguably the second most popular hero ever created. Bereft of parents (as was Superman, and eventually Robin, Spider-Man and many others), he wasn't exactly original. He was a combination of Zorro, Sherlock Holmes, the protagonist of Mary Robert Rinehart's *The Bat*, and even possessed the master-of-disguise aspects of Baroness Orczy's Scarlet Pimpernel. He was completely different... but, again, familiar.

DRAWN FROM ICONS

Not only was Superman rooted deeply in the most manifest desires of teens, but his lineage was easily traceable. Superman was an amalgam of the protagonist from Philip Wylie's novel, *Gladiator* (Knopf, 1930), and Doc Savage, the Man of Bronze (as opposed to the Man of Steel, who took his first name of "Clark" from Clark Savage Jr., not to mention eventually the concept of his Arctic Fortress of Solitude), and his origin was vaguely Biblical to boot—the last survivor of a godlike race, arriving in an outer space version of a basket sent floating down the river. Think of Marlon Brando intoning, "And so I send them you...my only son." It just doesn't get more messianic than Superman.

THE TWIST

The twist, of course, was that he possessed all these elements of literary and Biblical predecessors, with the gaudy additions of a blue-and-red costume and a cape. No one had ever seen anything quite like it. Sure, the Phantom wore tights and his undershorts on the outside, but he wasn't godlike...just believed to be. Superman was brand-new but familiar at the same time.

WALK THE LINE FOR GREAT CHARACTERS

In crafting characters, that's what you want to aim for. You want to give your own imagination free rein. You want to create something that will not only be unique for the readers, but unique to you as well. Something that doesn't simply regurgitate that which you've already read, but instead sends it off in a new and interesting direction. If you err on the side of conservatism, your character will just be cliché and have a feeling of "been there, done that." But if your entire concept is too outré, you're going to leave your reader behind you. Walking the fine line between old and new, novel and cliché, is not easy.

Worse, what may seem new to you may be old hat to others. Read what's out there. See where you can zig when others have zagged. When I developed *Spider-Man 2099*, I took every aspect of Peter Parker that existed and went in the opposite direction so we'd have someone who was recognizably Spider-Man...but new and different as well.

Superheroes are, almost by their very nature, wish fulfillment. In a world where everything seems to be spiraling out of control, superheroes are capable of taking hold of a situation and making things right in a way that we can only wish that we ourselves could. Combine this primal desire to be able to control one's own destiny with the sort of iconic characters that have been part of legend for as long as there have been legends...and then put your own individual stamp or twist on it.

I can't guarantee that you'll produce the next Superman or Batman. But you'll never know unless you try.

CURES FOR CHARACTER CLICHÉ

- Whatever your first impulse for a character is, dump it. The odds are sensational that your initial direction will stem from that with which you're already familiar. Indeed, it was only after Siegel and Shuster moved Superman away from the obvious inspiration of *Gladiator* that they were able to find a market for it.

- Deconstruct characters who are familiar to you and determine the types of creative decisions that were used to create them. Then go in another direction.

- Add the word "and" to everything you come up with. Don't settle for the easy description. For instance, don't just say, "He's a speedster." There are about a dozen of those running around. Instead, say, "He's a speedster who's recovering from a heart attack and knows that any use of his power might be enough to kill him and still feels compelled to use his abilities to help others, and his doing so makes his wife crazy with worry."

In short, don't settle. Always push yourself and your characters to the next level, and the next, and the next after that.

THE ETERNAL POWER OF MYTHIC ARCHETYPES

If comics are the modern equivalent of ancient myths, do not hesitate to plumb the depths of myth and legend when creating your characters. Sometimes you can do so literally, as Stan Lee and Jack Kirby did to create the Mighty Thor... although notice that they gave him a human alter ego (and human love interest), taking a godly character and providing him ties to Earth (see page 57). As we discussed earlier, giving superheroes mundane problems or human foibles has helped make them accessible and identifiable for the majority of readers who presumably do not have superpowers.

Creating heroes with feet of clay is more than just a clever marketing gimmick. Intentionally or not, it also serves to bring modern superheroes more in line with the classic tradition of making everyone from the greatest heroes to the mightiest gods as capable of screwing up as the lowliest of mortals. This is a time-honored practice. Gods were fine to be instigators and troublemakers, but the memorable heroes were the spawn of dalliances between gods/godlings and men (Hercules, son of Zeus and a mortal woman; Achilles, the son of a king and a water nymph). They had human weakness and mortality as part of their makeup, and Thor was no different.

But you don't have to be a god to have roots in godhood. Consider the Hulk...a combination of Jekyll and Hyde and Frankenstein's monster, the Hulk is truly a modern Prometheus (the Greek god who inspired Zeus' wrath by giving humans the

> "You don't have to be a **GOD** to have roots in **GODHOOD**."

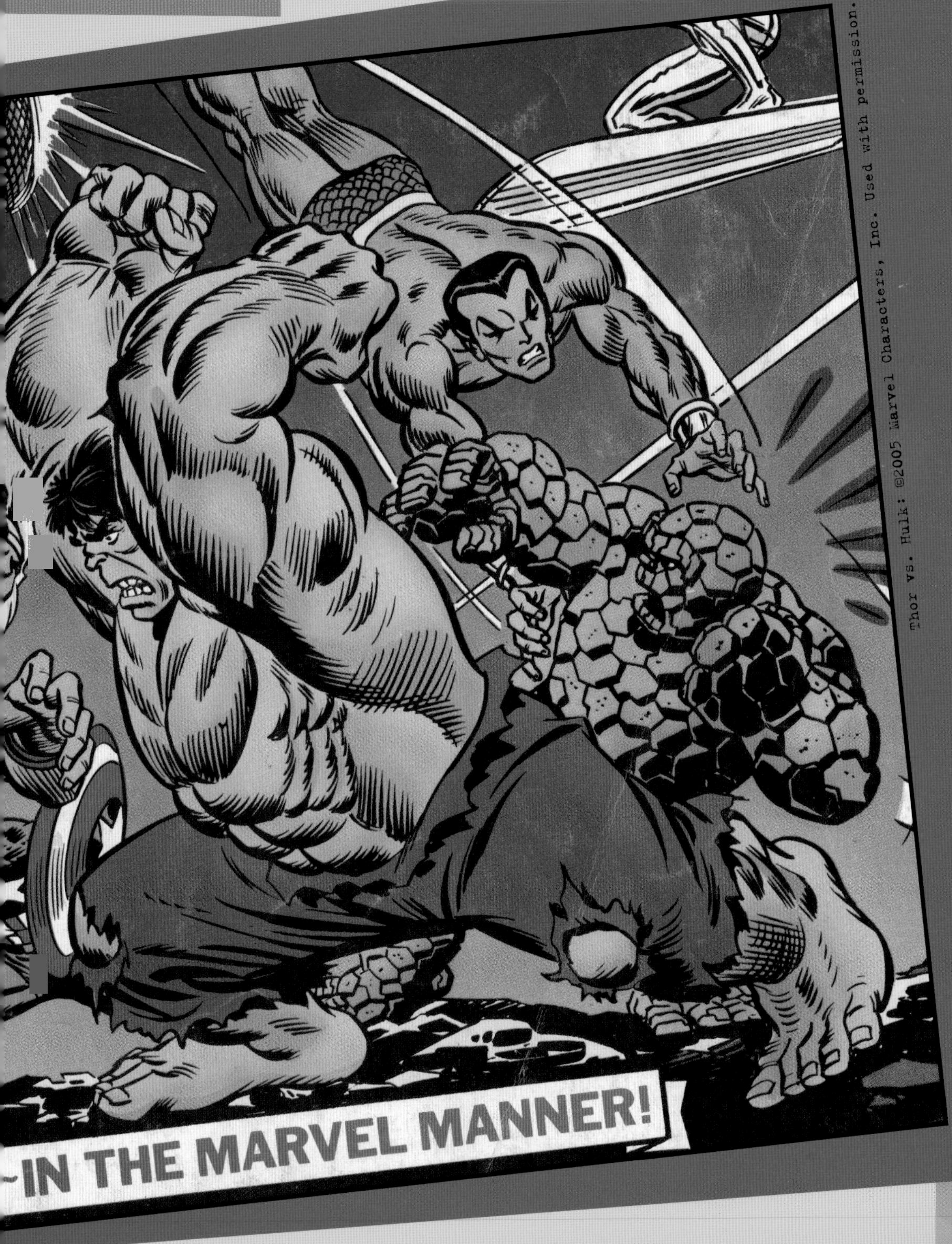
-IN THE MARVEL MANNER!

gift of fire), as Mary Shelley subtitled *Frankenstein*. Bruce Banner attempted to help not only mankind in general, but one human—Rick Jones. But like Prometheus, whose innards were constantly being gnawed out by birds, Bruce Banner brought forward formidable knowledge (in Prometheus' case, fire; in Bruce's, the gamma bomb) and is to be eternally tormented for it. Endlessly wishing, like a gamma-irradiated Greta Garbo, just to be "left alone" and never having that wish fulfilled.

Look to books on mythology and the constant role of the hero and his relationships with gods as a guide to traveling the mythic route. George Lucas would tell you to consult Joseph Campbell's *The Hero With a Thousand Faces* (Pantheon Books, 1949) or *The Power of Myth* (Doubleday, 1988), contending that these books provided the underpinning for *Star Wars*. To that I say Bull... finch.

Specifically, *Bulfinch's Mythology*, by Thomas Bulfinch. It remains, in my opinion, the best source for boning up on pure myth. It can provide everything from notions for new characters to reinterpretations of existing ones that will enable you to tell stories that are new and vibrant...but have the sort of resonance that can only stem from time-tested tales.

But isn't that (I hear you say) just ripping off stories? Only if you consider *West Side Story* to be a rip-off of *Romeo and Juliet*, which in turn can trace its origins all the way back to a 1476 tale of two lovers, Mariotto and Gianozza, written by one Masuccio Salernitano. And God only knows where he got it, although I'd be willing to wager it was the Greeks. It isn't the source that matters; it's what you do with it to make it uniquely yours.

EXERCISE

BUILDING ON MYTH

1 Read up on an ancient pantheon: Egyptian, Norse, Hindu. Select a god who has qualities and/or a personality that appeals to you.

2 Produce a superhero who is a modern-day incarnation of that character.

3 Produce a villain who is either drawn from the same mythology, or from another where he would serve to complement the hero.

4 Work up a story arc that brings the two together in conflict.

TRACING A CHARACTER'S DEVELOPMENT

So I was working on a villain for *Friendly Neighborhood Spider-Man* and decided that I wanted to develop a character who was more than he appeared. He would start out seeming to be little more than a garden-variety bank robber with cybernetic implants, then I would build him up, flesh him out. Drawing on the notions of iconography and mythic archetypes (in this case, classic tricksters such as the Norse Loki or the Native American coyote), I would reveal over time that he was far more than a mere mortal. That he was a sort of "trickster god," taking on a persona that made him seem human when he was, in fact, not. Now of course, if I were working up this villain for an episode of *Law & Order*, the producers would think I was out of my mind. But this was intended

for the Marvel Universe, which is already replete with gods, demons, cyborgs and what-have-you.

The additional twist I decided to go for was that whereas previous gods in the Marvel Universe were worshipped by humans, Tracer would be the beginning of a possible pantheon of machine gods who were worshipped by the increasingly sophisticated array of Artificial Intelligences slowly developing in the Marvel Universe. After all, there had been any number of stories out there detailing how machines gained sentience and, invariably, wanted to overthrow mankind. But I couldn't remember any offhand (although I've no doubt someone will send me samples once they've read this) of stories involving machines imitating

Artist Mike Wieringo's first pass on Tracer. Exactly what I asked for...and it did nothing for me.

HOW TO NAME A CHARACTER

Often-asked question from fans: Where do you come up with names? In the case of Tracer, I named him after part of his weaponry: tracer bullets that would literally be able to follow Spider-Man wherever he went. In terms of names themselves, I highly recommend you don't create a villain (or hero for that matter) and then stare at him and wonder, "Who the heck is this guy?"

Instead, keep a notebook with you, keep your eyes and ears open and as you hear passing inspiration for names—be it from television, newspapers, a sign you notice on your local commute, a trip to the zoo, or something a teacher says in class—jot them down (although, technically, you should be writing down what the teacher says anyway).

See what they suggest to you. Anything from popular sports terminology to scientific terms can provide inspiration.

humanity's desire to worship something greater than themselves...and go up against an enemy in the name of their new deity.

But that's a heck of a lot to dump onto the reader in a new opponent's first appearance. So I knew I'd take my time doing it.

The initial description of Tracer in the script was: "He's wearing a long, black duster, his head is shaved, and he's sporting high-tech-looking goggles. He's holding a Real Impressive Gun in a casual manner."

Artist Mike Wieringo initially crafted a version of Tracer that was precisely what I asked for. Once seeing him visualized, neither Ringo, editor Tom Brevoort nor myself were ecstatic. I wanted him to have some sort of flowing garment so he would look like he was in motion, even when standing still. But the coat was deemed too bulky. In a progression of sketches from Ringo, the coat vanished, to be replaced by a breech cloth modeled on the one worn by Mel Gibson in *Mad Max Beyond Thunderdome*. His weaponry underwent modification, and also he acquired hair to give him a more puckish, tricksterish look.

The final version: More youthful and energetic, more of a smart-alecky appearance that's in keeping with his tricksterish attitude. If you're lucky, you get an artist like Ringo, who's willing to do whatever it takes to get the character as "right" as possible. Not all artists are.

Sometimes artists will give you even more than you bargained for. Neil Gaiman's first description of Death for his *Sandman* series was tall, elegant, icy...very similar to what Desire would become. The character sketches he received instead featured a cheerful, sparky Goth girl, which Neil liked far better than his original incarnation. That's the advantage of working in comics; sometimes you wind up with something superior to what you'd have come up with on your own.

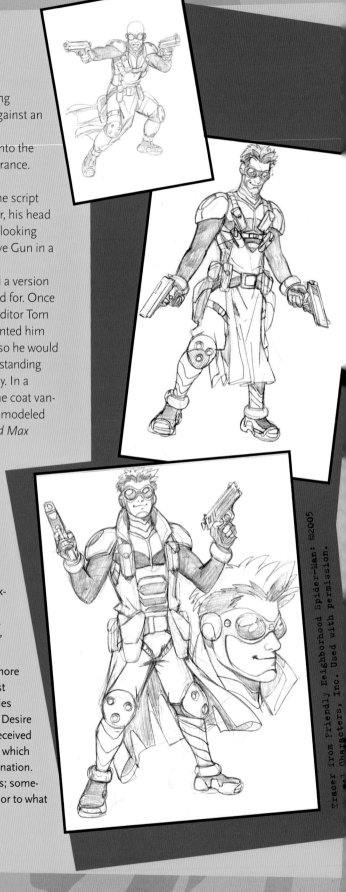

56

PUTTING YOUR OWN SPIN ON ESTABLISHED CHARACTERS

It may well be that you aspire only to creating your own characters, self-publishing or remaining within the realm of creator-owned material. If that's the case and you can make a go of it, by all means do so.

However, sooner or later you may find yourself writing for existing characters in a shared universe. Whether that's a good thing or a bad thing depends on your point of view. But it is, for lack of a better term, a thing. And if it's something you aspire to, there's no harm in looking ahead to how you would deal with it.

When dealing with characters who have been around for a while, you're being handed a certain degree of reader investment up front. That's why it's far easier to sustain and build an audience with established characters rather than start from the ground up with a new one.

TIPS FOR SPINNING ESTABLISHED CHARACTERS

- **Look for patterns.** Pick a character, search out common threads and try to interweave them in ways that other writers haven't yet. Example: I feel safe in saying that Joe Straczynski didn't read forty years worth of *Spider-Man* continuity before he embarked on his run for *The Amazing Spider-Man*. But he knew enough to notice the recurring animal theme of many of Spidey's foes to develop his entire "Spider-totem" concept, which sent Spidey off in a new and different direction.

- **Pull on a single thread.** You don't have to make vast, sweeping changes in order to find effective story lines or character redefinition. Potential can be explored in the most subtle shadings. Example: Alan Moore's acclaimed run on *Swamp Thing* launched with a deceptively simple notion: The Swamp Thing was not a human being who had been transformed into a walking plant. He was, instead, a walking plant who thought it was a transformed human... but wasn't. The result? A complete change in the Swamp Thing dynamic resulted as he first went berserk over the loss of his humanity, then went catatonic, and then gradually discovered and explored his true nature. All from changing a few words.

- **Get into a character's head.** Crawl into his skin and try to perceive things differently than before. Work up dialogues that explore the innermost workings of his mind and break new ground. For instance, although I've never written Thor as an ongoing character, I messed with his head somewhat in *Captain Marvel*. In the midst of a story wherein it seems that Death itself will be destroyed, I wrote this dialogue between Thor and the villainous Thanos to illuminate a previously unexamined aspect of Thor's personality:

THOR: Man need never fear mortality cutting short his aspirations. Need never fear that his accomplishments will be lost to the dust of time, forgotten and pointless. Would that be, in the end... so *terrible*?

THANOS: Death, Thor, defines life. Gives it aim and meaning. Is it that your *own* immortality. *weighs* upon you? Leaves you wondering whether your own existence has *purpose* because it is not *finite*? Answer true, Thunderer... does the end of Death interest you because you fancy mankind would embark on a golden age...? Or does *misery* simply enjoy *company*?

Ooo, ouch, kids. The mad god Thanos has just accused Thor of being fundamentally unhappy. Considering the profoundly depressing nature of much of Norse mythology—the only one I know of offhand that features a scenario describing the death of all the gods in excruciatingly agonizing detail—maybe that's the right attitude for Thor to have.

Worth exploring, don't you think?

That doesn't mean, though, that you can't put your own spin on them. For instance, in *The Incredible Hulk* #373, Bruce Banner and Betty were holed up in a convent, surrounded by the pursuing U.S. Army. I thought it would be fun to have the commanding officer thoroughly cowed by the angry Mother Superior because he'd gone to Catholic school. But since I needed to have the scene move on from that point, I decided to have Doc Samson step in and not be intimidated at all for a simple reason: He is Jewish. Why not? "Leonard," a Jewish-sounding first name, and "Samson," an Old Testament hero. So it didn't seem like a stretch to me.

But it got me a fast, almost panicked call from the assistant editor who said, "Has it been established that Doc Samson is Jewish?" I said, "We're establishing it now." He paused and said, genuinely interested, "Can we do that?" "Why not?" I replied. And lo and behold, Doc Samson became the first Marvel hero that we can reasonably infer is circumcised.

Remember one thing as you're developing notions for how to send established characters off in new and interesting directions: You're only the caretaker of these characters. Is it possible that you may eventually chart wildly new concepts that will irrevocably change them and render them practically unrecognizable? Yes, it's possible…if you're editor-in-chief. There's nothing wrong with aiming high. But since there are a lot fewer editor-in-chief jobs than there are people aspiring to it, let's play the odds and figure you won't be that editor anytime soon, if ever.

On that basis, it makes far more sense to adhere to what Stan Lee referred to as "the illusion of change," or concepts that are novel and exciting but won't irrevocably change the character. Developing the Spider-totem concept, as I mention in the sidebar on page 57, put some additional layers onto the Spider-Man mythology. It gave an elaborate reason for the spider singling out Peter Parker to bite that makes it less an accident than divine scheme. But it doesn't change the fundamental notion that Peter Parker gained his powers from the bite of a radioactive spider. On the other hand, you don't see anyone working up a notion where Spider-Man starts packing guns and killing criminals on sight. That's no illusion of change. That's a change to the core notion of who Peter Parker is, and it's not a change you really want to make.

In other words: You're redecorating the living room, not demolishing the house.

Writers' ideas for characters often become part of the "established" character. No one knew that Doc Samson was Jewish until I established it.

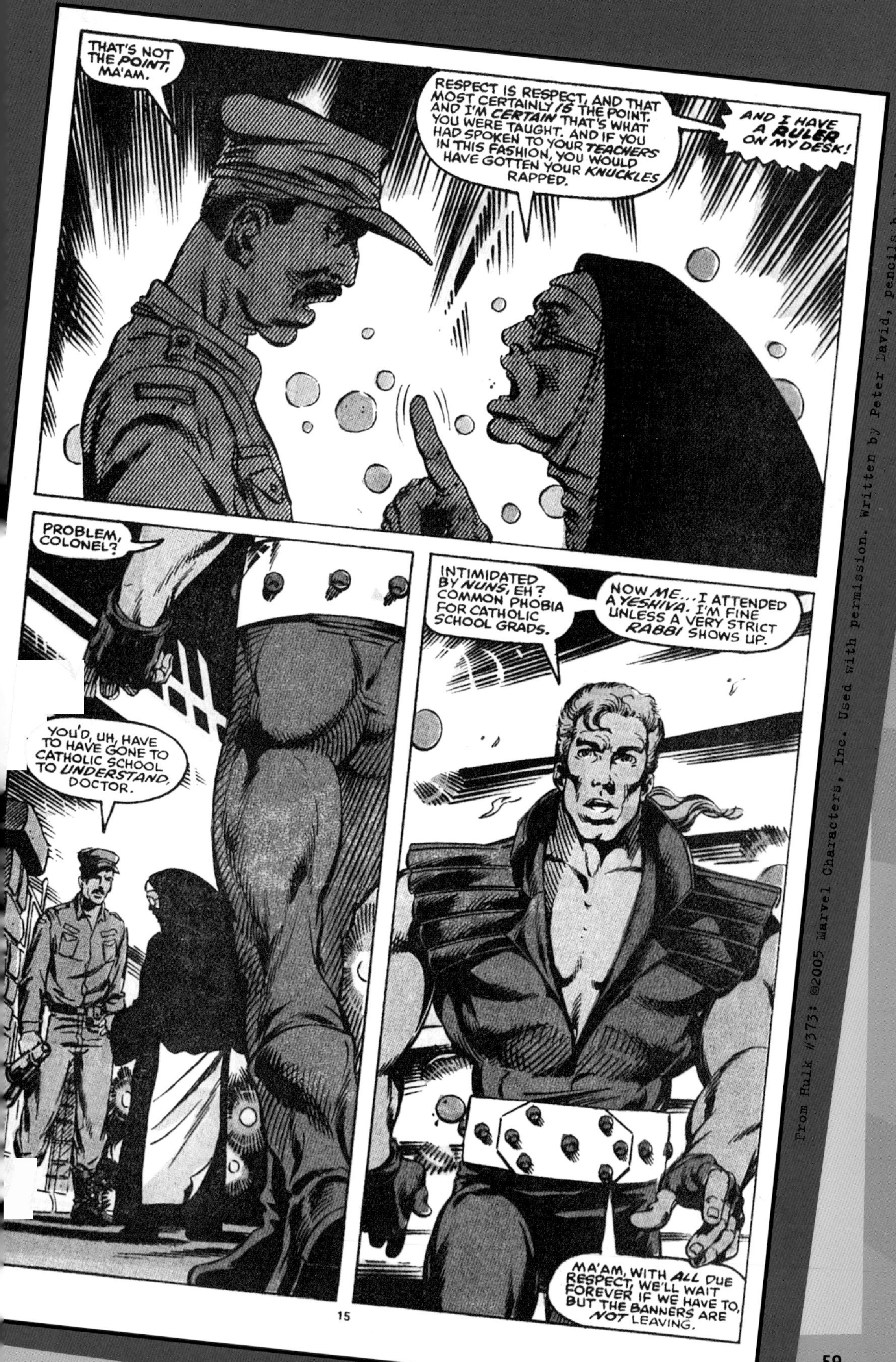
THAT'S NOT THE POINT, MA'AM.
RESPECT IS RESPECT, AND THAT MOST CERTAINLY IS THE POINT, AND I'M CERTAIN THAT'S WHAT YOU WERE TAUGHT. AND IF YOU HAD SPOKEN TO YOUR TEACHERS IN THIS FASHION, YOU WOULD HAVE GOTTEN YOUR KNUCKLES RAPPED.
AND I HAVE A RULER ON MY DESK!
PROBLEM, COLONEL?
YOU'D, UH, HAVE TO HAVE GONE TO CATHOLIC SCHOOL TO UNDERSTAND, DOCTOR.
INTIMIDATED BY NUNS, EH? COMMON PHOBIA FOR CATHOLIC SCHOOL GRADS.
NOW ME... I ATTENDED A YESHIVA. I'M FINE UNLESS A VERY STRICT RABBI SHOWS UP.
MA'AM, WITH ALL DUE RESPECT, WE'LL WAIT FOREVER IF WE HAVE TO, BUT THE BANNERS ARE NOT LEAVING.
15

CONFLICT

I'VE TOUCHED ON THE CONCEPTS OF CONFLICT AND THEME BEFORE, BUT NOW IT'S TIME TO BRING THEM CENTER STAGE IN AN OVERALL DISCUSSION OF PLOTTING.

Many would-be, and even working, writers wrestle with the notion of what the most important aspect of storytelling is. The theme? The central conflict? The plot? The stakes? The characterization? To me, that's like asking what the most important part of the body is: The skin? The heart? The lungs? The blood? The brain?

The bottom line is that every aspect of your story has to be as strong as possible. Any weakness provides a chink in your armor that the sword of audience disbelief can pierce. The stronger every aspect of your story is, the stronger your story will be.

All drama is conflict. All of it—whether it's 10,000 men standing on opposite sides of a field, shaking their spears in preparation for charging each other, a police detective grilling a suspect in an interrogation room or a lone alcoholic staring at a tempting bottle of bourbon that's calling his name.

Your theme is that aspect of the human condition that serves as the spine of your story, and as many elements of your story as possible serve to illuminate that theme. When people say, "What is your story about?" your response as a writer should be the theme. What's *Spider-Man* about? Well, the plot is about Peter Parker getting bitten by a radioactive (or genetically altered, take your pick) arachnid and being transformed into a human spider. But the theme is, "With great power comes great responsibility." It is a theme that *Spider-Man* revisits again and again. The Hamlet of the superhero set, he constantly questions himself. There are times when he wonders if he's doing any good in his efforts. Indeed, there are occasions where he thinks he's doing more harm than good, especially when he's bringing stress and unhappiness to his loved ones through his Spider-Man activities. He's quit any number of times, most memorably in the original *The Amazing Spider-Man* #50 when he dumps his costume in a garbage can and walks away. (A scene lovingly re-created in the film *Spider-Man 2*. I remember being at a Marvel screening of the film and John Romita Sr., seated near me, watched Peter Parker leave his costume behind and said proudly, "I drew that.")

Yet no matter how many times he tries to walk away from his life as Spider-Man, Peter can't bring himself to. Why? Because with great power comes great responsibility, a lesson that, once learned, he can never abandon. It's the core theme of *Spider-Man*, probably the most clearly delineated theme in all of comics: a theme so universally embraced that a Google search for it scores 161,000 hits on articles ranging from church leadership to George W. Bush.

Hulk vs. Leader ©2005 Marvel Characters, Inc. Used with permission.

WHAT IS CONFLICT?

Conflict is what stands in the way of the protagonist accomplishing his goal. It doesn't have to be limited to a single conflict: It can come from within and without. A hero might have to overcome both the obstacles arranged for him by his opponent (vast armies lying in wait; a cave of mind-numbing horror) and from within himself (he's a raging alcoholic; he ran from a challenge years ago and is trying to convince himself he's not a coward).

Conflict consists of individuals in opposition to something. If the individuals aren't interesting enough, it's not going to matter to the reader what the conflict is. Ideally you'll be able to craft a protagonist who will sufficiently engage the attention of your readers so they will become personally invested in your hero's success or failure.

By the same token, if the conflict is not challenging enough, the obstacles the hero must overcome not sufficiently daunting, the readers will feel they have wasted their time. The conflict must be of enough importance, both to your reader's personal frame of reference and to your protagonist himself, that the reader will engage his willing suspension of disbelief.

So, what is the nature of conflict? Well, as I said earlier in these pages, all stories can be boiled down to variations of three conflicts: Man vs. Man, Man vs. Himself, and Man vs. Environment.

CLUE THE READER IN EARLY

Although you don't have to spell out the conflict(s) in detail, it does help to give the reader at least a general idea of what your hero is going to be up against. Wait until halfway through your story to give your reader at least some sense of what challenges await the protagonist and the reader is going to get impatient. For instance, you're a good chunk of the way into *The Fellowship of the Ring* before you know Frodo's full mission. However, it's established quite early on that the ring presents a serious danger to Middle-earth. With Frodo as your clear protagonist, it's easy to intuit that he's going to be the one who has to deal with it. Details such as how can wait until the author is ready to provide them.

The problem is that, when dealing with superheroes and bigger-than-life characters, there's going to be a temptation to make the conflict likewise bigger-than-life. The more you do this, the more likely you are to leave your readers behind.

KEEP THE CONFLICTS SMALL

Although I've written team books in my time (*Young Justice*, *X-Factor*), I've always done everything I can to have the actual conflicts in such titles be as small as possible. Small equals real.

TAP INTO PARENTAL CONFLICT

A staggering amount of literature explores the theme—and conflicts—stemming from father/son or mother/daughter relationships. That, or a child and parent-substitute such as a teacher or mentor.

The core of *Star Wars* is nothing but such relationships: Anakin/Obi-Wan, Luke/Obi-Wan, Luke/Yoda, and finally back to Luke/Anakin (a.k.a. Darth Vader). Even a slam-bang action film such as *Terminator 2* is really about a boy trying to fill an emotional gap in his life due to the absence of a father, and for that matter, a mother who's lost sight of the simple love her son truly needs.

One has to think that parent/child relationships are the single most important aspect of our lives, be it ourselves to our parents or us to our own children. Find new and different ways to tap into this emotional vein, which has been going strong for centuries (it doesn't get more primal than "Father, why hast thou forsaken me?" does it?) and you're certain to connect with your readers on some level.

The conflicts most people have to face on a daily basis involve family, friends and the like. These are the conflicts that have meaning to readers. And the closer to home you can make your conflict, the more resonance it's going to have. That's why in *Young Justice* most of the true conflicts stem from teen angst, while in *X-Factor* the conflicts center on the personal issues between the various team members. There's nothing wrong with huge, slam-bang fights, but the truly successful ones are the ones that have some manner of emotional underpinning. Otherwise it's just drawings of guys smacking each other. And that emotional under-pinning stems from conflict.

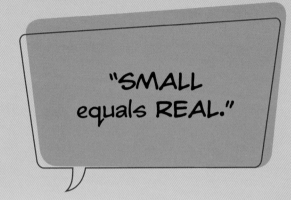

"SMALL equals REAL."

THE ART OF SELF-DENIAL

You've seen it in any number of movies and TV shows (but mostly movies) and probably didn't even realize you were watching a common writer's trick when the plot is just getting way too out there and you're concerned you're going to lose your audience.

Let's say you're watching a science-fiction movie in which strange things are happening. You're likely to hear an exchange along the following lines:

"This is like something out of a science-fiction movie..."

"Yeah? Well, this ain't no science-fiction movie. This is real life."

Except, of course, it is a science-fiction movie. It isn't real life. You want to try and keep the connection with the audience, which is perfectly capable of telling the difference between the two. You want to make sure your audience identifies with your protagonists. After all, the degree to which your story is going to be effective stems entirely from your audience being able to connect with the heroes.

So an occasional trick to use, when your fictional situation is beginning to get

outlandish, is to have your protagonists acknowledge the sheer outlandishness of it by making a clear identification with movies they themselves might have seen. It would seem "unrealistic," after all, for your heroes to encounter truly bizarre happenings and take them completely in stride. Would you? Of course not. If you found yourself suddenly faced with UFOs or monsters or what-have-you, you'd very likely say, "Oh my God, this is like something out of (fill in the blank)." Having your protagonists react in this same way implies two things: First, that they have an entire fictional "life" where they go to the movies for recreation; and second, that they've lived lives no different than those lived by your audience until this sudden avalanche of weirdness cascaded down upon them.

When your heroes openly acknowledge that this is like something out of a horror movie/SF flick/comic book, it's a tactic designed to deny the very medium they inhabit. It's almost a strange form of self-loathing, with characters denying what they are in order to make themselves appear to be something more.

WHAT IS THEME?

If someone asks you about a story, "What's the theme? What are you trying to say?" and you have no answer, there's something wrong with the story. Theme is different from conflict. Your conflict should help to illuminate the theme—that aspect of the human condition upon which you intend to comment that serves as the spine of your story.

The theme may well be the trickiest aspect of storytelling, if for no other reason than that it's difficult to determine just how clear you want to make the theme. Great literature allows the reader to make his own determinations of what the author's intended theme was. This can actually lead to spirited debate in literary circles as one group says, "This was clearly what the author meant to say" while another group aggressively contests the first group.

In fact, science-fiction legend Isaac Asimov once put in an appearance in a classroom where the teacher had ascribed a particular thematic meaning to one of Dr. A's stories. Asimov politely informed the teacher that, no, he had gotten it all wrong. That wasn't Asimov's intent at all. The teacher's response? That author intent isn't always the most correct measure of what a story is actually about!

IT'S A DELICATE BALANCE

However, if you spell it all out, you run the risk of writing dialogue that is "too on-the-nose." See, the fact is that most of the time, people don't really say what's on their minds. They don't speak in flat-out declaratives. They talk around the subject and don't offer specific commentary on what's happening in their lives. When dialogue is "on-the-nose," it means there are no subtleties, no shadings. It's inherently unrealistic. And if you put the themes into captions in omniscient narrative, you run the risk of coming across as condescending to the readers, as if they couldn't figure it out for themselves.

THEME EQUALS CONSISTENCY

Unfortunately, many readers can't figure out the themes for themselves. For instance, the consistent theme of Neil Gaiman's *The Sandman* is finding oneself trapped by circumstances beyond one's control, and the different ways one finds to escape...especially since the desire for freedom is one of the most fundamental human needs. That's what *Sandman* is "about," that's what its theme is. But if you ask the average fan what the theme of *Sandman* is, the odds are tremendous that they won't know what you're talking about, or won't be able to articulate it.

And they shouldn't have to. If they're not of a literary or analytical bent, the sheer existence of a theme will still benefit them. Why? Because it will provide a consistency of tone, style and story execution that they will appreciate, even if they don't know they do.

The theme should be the consistent driving force of the plot. Characterization and plot developments should serve to illuminate the theme whenever possible and find different ways to address it. If your plot seems to be meandering or your characters without focus, ask yourself whether there are moments or sequences in your story that have nothing to do with the theme. If there are, chances are they're slowing down your narrative and should either be reworked or excised.

AGAIN, THERE'S NO ONE WAY

There's no one right way to develop your story. You can start out with the theme, as in, "I want to write a story about a man in conflict with his own faith," and build from there. Or a character could just wander into your head, capture your imagination and demand to have his adventures told. A

> "The **THEME** should be the consistent **driving force** of the plot."

particular plot notion may seize you: Once, a fan came up to me, looking slightly annoyed, and held up the latest issue of *Wolverine*, which I had written. "This whole thing was a twenty-two-page car chase!" he said. "I know," I told him. "Why did you write it that way?" he asked. I replied, "Because I wanted to see if I could write a twenty-two-page car chase." He kind of blinked and said, "Oh. Well...I guess you succeeded then."

"**Characterization** and **plot developments** should serve to ILLUMINATE the theme whenever possible."

But if you start out without the theme—if you jot down some plot notions, if you know you want to do a Man vs. Himself story, if a character is banging to get out of your head—you should still make darned sure that you develop your theme in short order. Once you have a clear idea of what you want to say, it's merely a matter of determining how you're going to say it.

Knowing your theme, and making sure that every major aspect of your story relates to it in some way, is the surest means of making certain your story doesn't go completely off the rails.

CLICHÉS CAN BE YOUR FRIENDS

Readers come to your stories with certain expectations. Everything they read is siphoned through the prisms of their own experiences, and among those experiences is reading stories by other people (not to mention seeing movies, television shows, etc.).

Many of these stories have certain standard tropes that everyone comes to expect. "Clichés," to use a less polite word. The character aspects or story developments that readers have come to know and expect.

So if you want to surprise your readers, to catch them off guard, all you need to do is analyze these clichés and make them work to your advantage. If you do that successfully, the readers will wind up doing much of the work for you. They'll have the cliché in mind already so that, when you zig where they were expecting you to zag, they will bark in surprise and say, "I wasn't expecting that!"

Probably one of the great anti-cliché moments in recent memory was *Raiders of the Lost Ark*, in which Indiana Jones finds himself squaring off against a swordsman. The cliché is that the hero is basically going to be sporting about it, taking on his opponent with either a sword or his own signature weapon, a whip. Instead, defying cliché and expectations, Indy pulls out his gun and shoots the swordsman from twenty feet away. The moment gets a huge laugh and simultaneously feels "right" and "real." There's a reason for that: Harrison Ford, running a fever and suffering from dysentery while they were trying to film the obvious whip vs. sword sequence, just wanted to get out of there and said, "Why don't I just take out my gun and shoot the f---r?" Thus, in one stroke, did Indiana Jones establish himself as a hero who could not be counted on to embrace the cliché.

The moment you find yourself treading familiar ground in a story, take a step back and say, "What would happen if I did B instead of A, D instead of C?" If you can make it work, not only will it be a more stimulating creative challenge, but your readers will gasp and say, "Man! I didn't see that coming!" And isn't that (and not the hokey pokey, as some claim) what it's really all about?

Nowhere have you ever seen Man vs. Man better distilled to its essence than in *Mad Max Beyond Thunderdome*, where an impending battle in the titular arena is announced with the chant, "Two men enter, one man leaves!" Two men in opposition to each other, each with the same basic goal: to stop the other one from accomplishing whatever he's setting out to do.

There are many variations: both seeking the same treasure and trying to stop the other from getting there first. One wants to annihilate innocent people, the other wants to save them and thus must thwart the plan. There are any number of ways to play it, but the bottom line is that when the dust settles, only one can succeed. Ideally, it's the hero. If it is, you have an adventure. If it's not, you've got either tragedy or film noir. Which is fine; if that's what your muse suggests, go for it.

Here we're illustrating an adventure of Man vs. Man, and in comic terms, it doesn't get better than *Fantastic Four #40*. The FF's greatest enemy, Doctor Doom, has taken over the Baxter Building and transformed it into a massive death trap. Unbeknownst to Doom, this is overkill since the FF have lost their powers and could be taken out with nothing more than an AK-47. Upon realizing this, Doom decides to toy with them rather than annihilating them outright.

Big mistake. The FF, aided by Daredevil (the blind leading the powerless; you have to love the Lee/Kirby sense of irony), manage to penetrate their HQ and get their hands on Reed's unfortunately named "electronic stimulator." He uses it to restore their powers...which requires transforming Ben Grimm from his long-wished-for human form back into a monster.

The emotional stakes are now through the roof. Ben has lost his heart's desire, and there are two potential places to lay the blame. The first is on Doom, and the second is on his friends, and the Thing does both in memorable fashion. Particularly note the crumbling of Doom's bravado as he realizes just how completely screwed he is in the face of the Thing's wrath.

Man vs. Man is probably the most ubiquitous of the three principal conflicts. It's the one in which your hero finds himself opposed by someone with a thought process (not found in nature) that is markedly different from his own (not typical for Man vs. Himself...unless he's Dr. Jekyll). It allows for the writer to present the greatest variety of challenges, coming from assorted directions, either singly or all at once. It also enables you to switch points of view to give more shadings of the conflict. For instance, if you're doing a Man vs. Nature story of someone trying to survive a hurricane, it's not as if you can cut to the hurricane's point of view.

Endeavor to avoid the by-now-standardized tropes of Man vs. Man. For instance, the movie *The Incredibles* neatly skewered the comic book convention of having a villain spill his entire plan to the helpless hero in a practice writer Brad Bird referred to as "monologuing." Fans of fantasy and science fiction delight in trading off lists of "Things I will do if I become an evil overlord," which include such solid advice as "Shooting is NOT too good for my enemies," "The hero is not entitled to a last kiss, a last cigarette, or any other form of last request," and "If the beautiful princess that I capture says, 'I'll never marry you! Never, do you hear me, NEVER!!!,' I will say 'Oh well' and kill her."

The stronger and more compelling the personalities of Man vs. Man, the better your story is going to be.

Doctor Doom and the Thing face off in a classic Man vs. Man showdown.

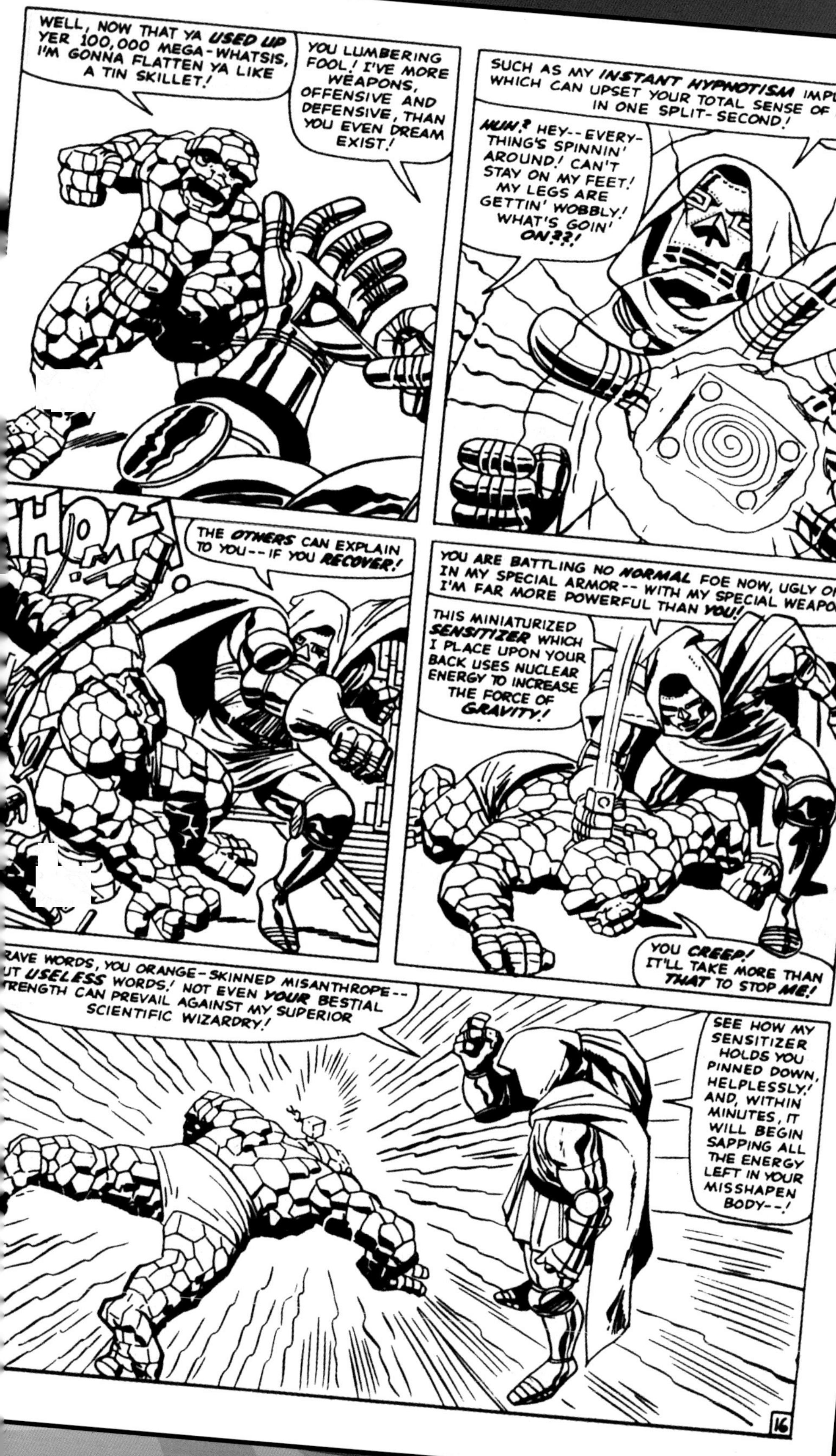
WELL, NOW THAT YA USED UP YER 100,000 MEGA-WHATSIS, I'M GONNA FLATTEN YA LIKE A TIN SKILLET!
YOU LUMBERING FOOL! I'VE MORE WEAPONS, OFFENSIVE AND DEFENSIVE, THAN YOU EVEN DREAM EXIST!
SUCH AS MY INSTANT HYPNOTISM IMPULSER, WHICH CAN UPSET YOUR TOTAL SENSE OF BALANCE IN ONE SPLIT-SECOND!
HUH? HEY--EVERY-THING'S SPINNIN' AROUND! CAN'T STAY ON MY FEET! MY LEGS ARE GETTIN' WOBBLY! WHAT'S GOIN' ON??!
THE OTHERS CAN EXPLAIN TO YOU--IF YOU RECOVER!
YOU ARE BATTLING NO NORMAL FOE NOW, UGLY ONE! IN MY SPECIAL ARMOR--WITH MY SPECIAL WEAPONS--I'M FAR MORE POWERFUL THAN YOU!
THIS MINIATURIZED SENSITIZER WHICH I PLACE UPON YOUR BACK USES NUCLEAR ENERGY TO INCREASE THE FORCE OF GRAVITY!
YOU CREEP! IT'LL TAKE MORE THAN THAT TO STOP ME!
RAVE WORDS, YOU ORANGE-SKINNED MISANTHROPE--UT USELESS WORDS! NOT EVEN YOUR BESTIAL TRENGTH CAN PREVAIL AGAINST MY SUPERIOR SCIENTIFIC WIZARDRY!
SEE HOW MY SENSITIZER HOLDS YOU PINNED DOWN, HELPLESSLY! AND, WITHIN MINUTES, IT WILL BEGIN SAPPING ALL THE ENERGY LEFT IN YOUR MISSHAPEN BODY--!
16

DOCTOR DOOM AND THE THING FACE OFF IN A CLASSIC MAN VS. MAN SHOWDOWN. SEE PAGE 66.

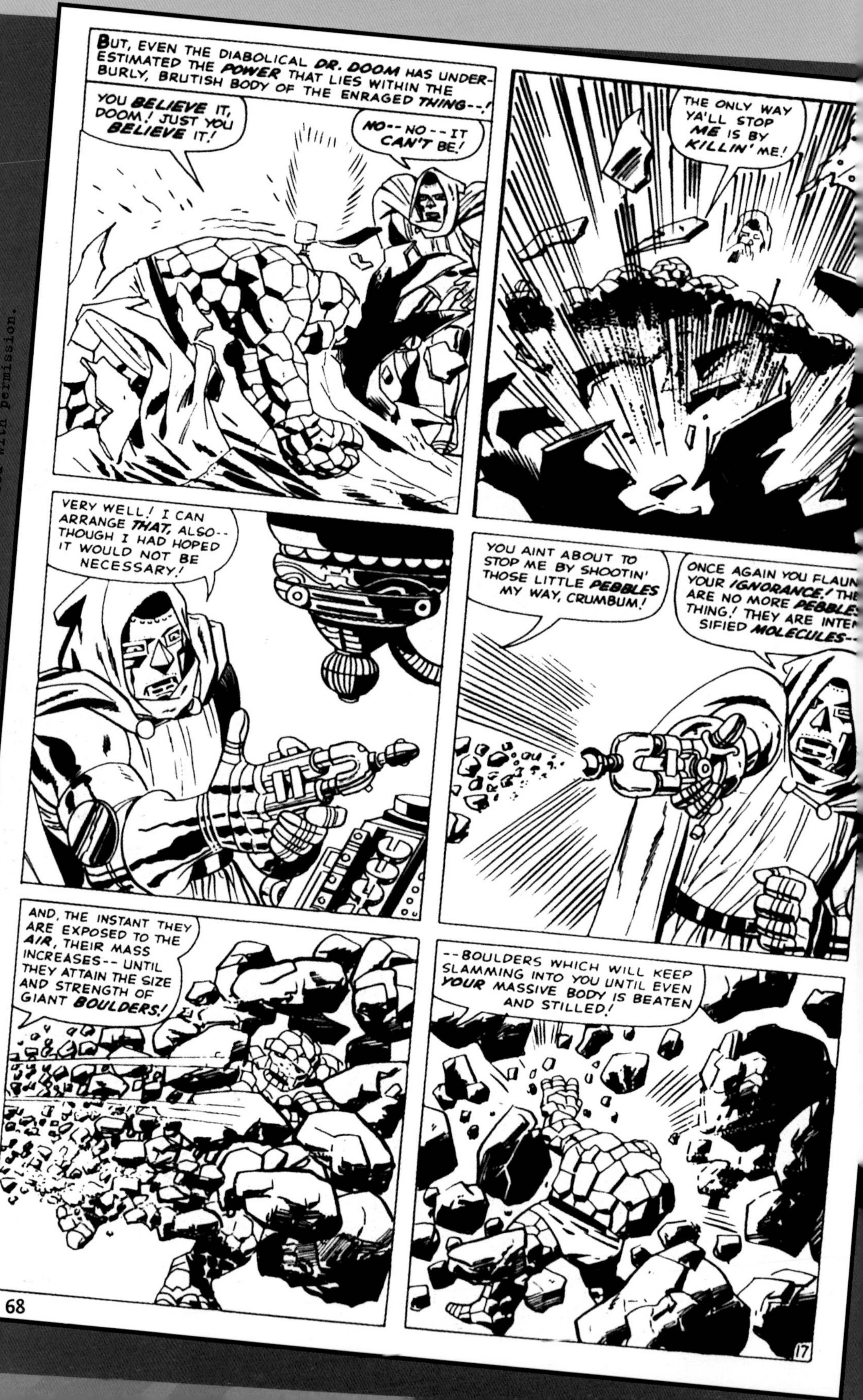
BUT, EVEN THE DIABOLICAL DR. DOOM HAS UNDER-ESTIMATED THE POWER THAT LIES WITHIN THE BURLY, BRUTISH BODY OF THE ENRAGED THING--!
YOU BELIEVE IT, DOOM! JUST YOU BELIEVE IT!
NO-- NO-- IT CAN'T BE!
THE ONLY WAY YA'LL STOP ME IS BY KILLIN' ME!
VERY WELL! I CAN ARRANGE THAT, ALSO-- THOUGH I HAD HOPED IT WOULD NOT BE NECESSARY!
YOU AINT ABOUT TO STOP ME BY SHOOTIN' THOSE LITTLE PEBBLES MY WAY, CRUMBUM!
ONCE AGAIN YOU FLAUN YOUR IGNORANCE! THE ARE NO MORE PEBBLES THING! THEY ARE INTEN SIFIED MOLECULES--
AND, THE INSTANT THEY ARE EXPOSED TO THE AIR, THEIR MASS INCREASES-- UNTIL THEY ATTAIN THE SIZE AND STRENGTH OF GIANT BOULDERS!
--BOULDERS WHICH WILL KEEP SLAMMING INTO YOU UNTIL EVEN YOUR MASSIVE BODY IS BEATEN AND STILLED!
17

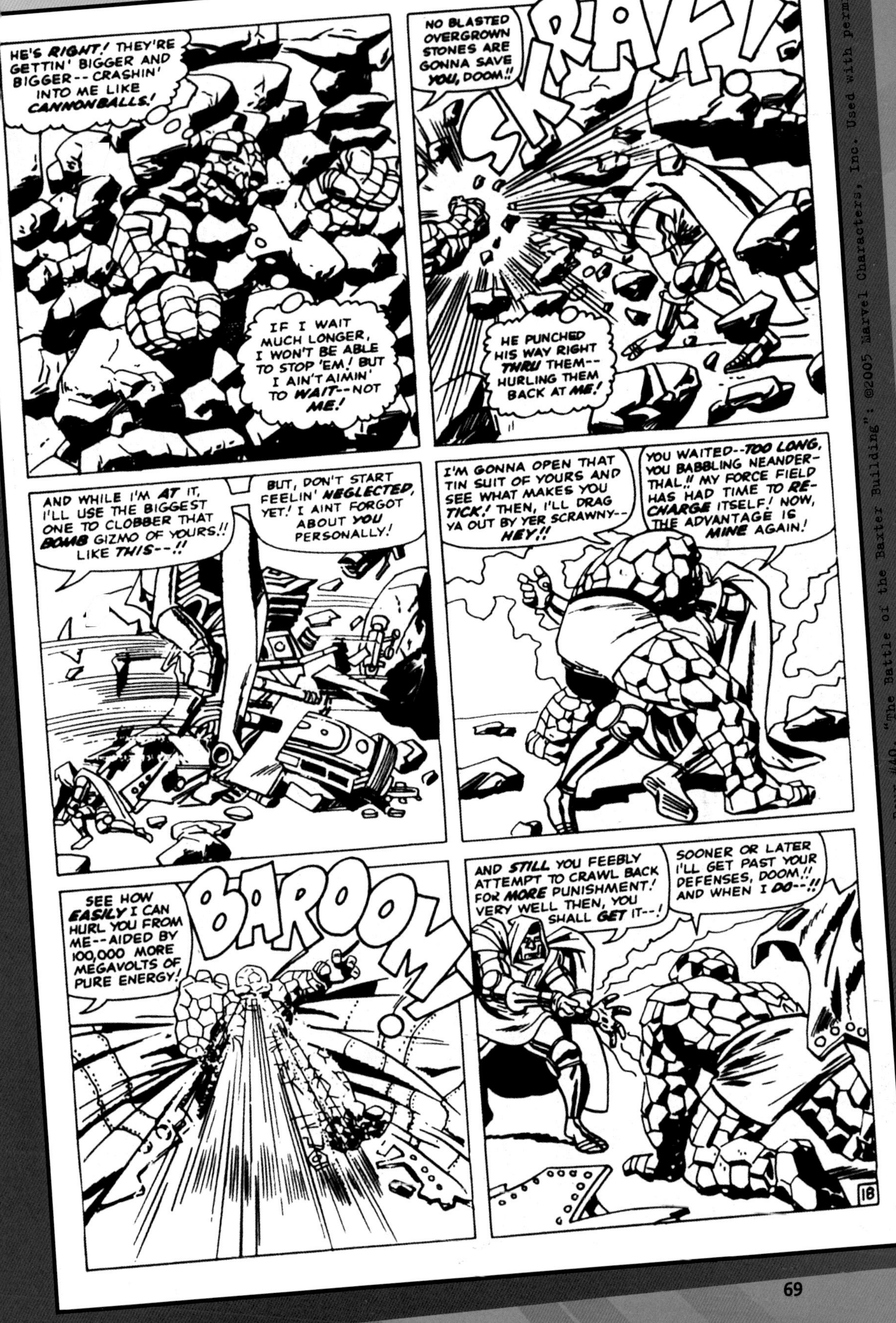
HE'S RIGHT! THEY'RE GETTIN' BIGGER AND BIGGER--CRASHIN' INTO ME LIKE CANNONBALLS!
IF I WAIT MUCH LONGER, I WON'T BE ABLE TO STOP 'EM! BUT I AIN'T AIMIN' TO WAIT--NOT ME!
NO BLASTED OVERGROWN STONES ARE GONNA SAVE YOU, DOOM!!
SKRAK!
HE PUNCHED HIS WAY RIGHT THRU THEM--HURLING THEM BACK AT ME!
AND WHILE I'M AT IT, I'LL USE THE BIGGEST ONE TO CLOBBER THAT BOMB GIZMO OF YOURS!! LIKE THIS--!!
BUT, DON'T START FEELIN' NEGLECTED, YET! I AINT FORGOT ABOUT YOU PERSONALLY!
I'M GONNA OPEN THAT TIN SUIT OF YOURS AND SEE WHAT MAKES YOU TICK! THEN, I'LL DRAG YA OUT BY YER SCRAWNY--HEY!!
YOU WAITED--TOO LONG, YOU BABBLING NEANDERTHAL!! MY FORCE FIELD HAS HAD TIME TO RE-CHARGE ITSELF! NOW, THE ADVANTAGE IS MINE AGAIN!
SEE HOW EASILY I CAN HURL YOU FROM ME--AIDED BY 100,000 MORE MEGAVOLTS OF PURE ENERGY!
BAROOM
AND STILL YOU FEEBLY ATTEMPT TO CRAWL BACK FOR MORE PUNISHMENT! VERY WELL THEN, YOU SHALL GET IT--!
SOONER OR LATER I'LL GET PAST YOUR DEFENSES, DOOM!! AND WHEN I DO--!!
18

Fantastic Four #40, "The Battle of the Baxter Building": ©2005 Marvel Characters, Inc. Used with permission.

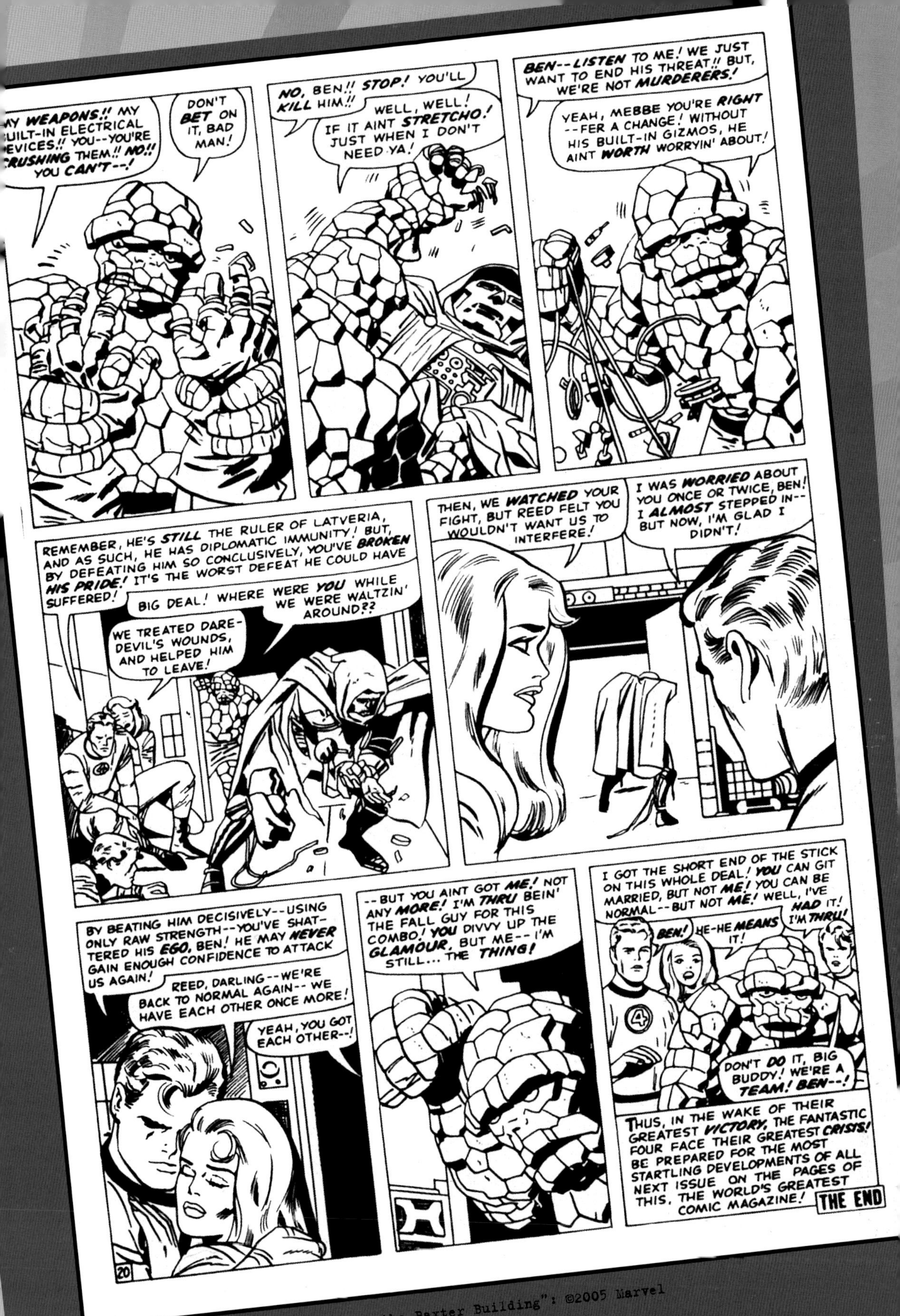

MY WEAPONS!! MY BUILT-IN ELECTRICAL DEVICES!! YOU--YOU'RE CRUSHING THEM!! NO!! YOU CAN'T--!
DON'T BET ON IT, BAD MAN!
NO, BEN!! STOP! YOU'LL KILL HIM!!
WELL, WELL! IF IT AINT STRETCHO! JUST WHEN I DON'T NEED YA!
BEN--LISTEN TO ME! WE JUST WANT TO END HIS THREAT!! BUT, WE'RE NOT MURDERERS!
YEAH, MEBBE YOU'RE RIGHT --FER A CHANGE! WITHOUT HIS BUILT-IN GIZMOS, HE AINT WORTH WORRYIN' ABOUT!
REMEMBER, HE'S STILL THE RULER OF LATVERIA, AND AS SUCH, HE HAS DIPLOMATIC IMMUNITY! BUT, BY DEFEATING HIM SO CONCLUSIVELY, YOU'VE BROKEN HIS PRIDE! IT'S THE WORST DEFEAT HE COULD HAVE SUFFERED!
BIG DEAL! WHERE WERE YOU WHILE WE WERE WALTZIN' AROUND??
WE TREATED DARE-DEVIL'S WOUNDS, AND HELPED HIM TO LEAVE!
THEN, WE WATCHED YOUR FIGHT, BUT REED FELT YOU WOULDN'T WANT US TO INTERFERE!
I WAS WORRIED ABOUT YOU ONCE OR TWICE, BEN! I ALMOST STEPPED IN--BUT NOW, I'M GLAD I DIDN'T!
BY BEATING HIM DECISIVELY--USING ONLY RAW STRENGTH--YOU'VE SHAT-TERED HIS EGO, BEN! HE MAY NEVER GAIN ENOUGH CONFIDENCE TO ATTACK US AGAIN!
REED, DARLING--WE'RE BACK TO NORMAL AGAIN--WE HAVE EACH OTHER ONCE MORE!
YEAH, YOU GOT EACH OTHER--!
--BUT YOU AINT GOT ME! NOT ANY MORE! I'M THRU BEIN' THE FALL GUY FOR THIS COMBO! YOU DIVVY UP THE GLAMOUR, BUT ME--I'M STILL... THE THING!
I GOT THE SHORT END OF THE STICK ON THIS WHOLE DEAL! YOU CAN GIT MARRIED, BUT NOT ME! YOU CAN BE NORMAL--BUT NOT ME! WELL, I'VE HAD IT! I'M THRU!
BEN!
HE-HE MEANS IT!
DON'T DO IT, BIG BUDDY! WE'RE A TEAM! BEN--!
THUS, IN THE WAKE OF THEIR GREATEST VICTORY, THE FANTASTIC FOUR FACE THEIR GREATEST CRISIS! BE PREPARED FOR THE MOST STARTLING DEVELOPMENTS OF ALL NEXT ISSUE ON THE PAGES OF THIS, THE WORLD'S GREATEST COMIC MAGAZINE!
THE END
20

Fantastic Four #40, "The Battle of the Baxter Building": ©2005 Marvel Characters, Inc. Used with permission.

As the so-called masters of this planet, we're always so impressed by what we ourselves create. The buildings, the monuments, the ingenious devices.

And then, every so often, our world decides to show us who's boss.

You think our buildings are mighty? Watch an earthquake level them in about ten seconds, or a tsunami wash over and annihilate them. You think the bombs we create are impressive? Check out what tornadoes can do without even trying. Someone built a boat that was declared unsinkable? Right. One iceberg later, 1,500 innocent people died in service of that little display of hubris.

Man vs. Nature is the only conflict in which Man is consistently outmatched. Nature doesn't strap the hero down to a table, send a laser heading toward the hero's privates and say, "No, Mr. Bond, I expect you to die!" when asked if the hero is expected to talk. Nature doesn't care if the hero dies, lives, talks or cries like a baby. Nature is unknowable, unstoppable, and the hero basically just tries to stay the hell out of nature's way...or else pay the price (just ask Captain Ahab). The hero cannot really defeat nature, but instead simply hope to survive to fight another day.

In *Aquaman #3*, written by yours truly and penciled by Marty Egeland, Aquaman goes to Pearl Harbor to get into the face of a Navy officer, only to find Superboy blocking his way. Superboy is dismissive of Aquaman's long hair and newly acquired harpoon, declaring, "The new [hair]do and the pigsticker? Not impressed." He sends the sea king packing, figuring he and Aquaman aren't in the same league. He's right, but not in the way he expects. For Superboy believes that he's in a Man vs. Man scenario. Aquaman proves that Superboy is actually in a Man vs. Nature scenario by becoming a figurative (if not literal) force of nature that cannot be stopped. Worse... it's a bizarre instance where a force of nature is being propelled by wounded pride, upping the consequences for the arrogant Superboy.

THEY ARE SUPERHEROES, AFTER ALL

When I was working up the opening of *The Incredible Hulk #77*, the first part of the "Tempest Fugit" story line, I considered the fact that the Hulk himself is more than a man. He is himself almost a force of nature. Most of the time, Man vs. Nature is overmatched. So I figured, let's see what happens if nature winds up face-to-face with something almost as powerful as nature itself. Turn the tables a bit on one of the classic conflicts.

So I began with a sequence that was inspired by the moment in *Pirates of the Caribbean* when the skeletal pirates are slogging, slowly but steadily, across the ocean floor. I imitated the sequence for *The Incredible Hulk #77* (minus the pirates, of course). Instead it is the Hulk trudging determinedly across the ocean bottom, as unstoppable and inevitable as a riptide.

The first order of business the Hulk encounters is a gigantic shark. The most formidable predator in the ocean comes straight at the Hulk...and gets torn in half for its efforts. It's the Hulk's, and my, way of telling nature there's a new sheriff in town.

The opening pages generated some degree of controversy, by the way. I chose not to put any dialogue in the sequence. Not so much as a single caption. Some fans complained it was too quick a read. But I really couldn't think of any dialogue or captions I could have come up with that would have improved the sequence. There's not going to be any chitchat since the Hulk's alone and underwater. Narrative thought captions? Whose? The Hulk doesn't make his appearance until several pages in. Putting in narrative captions would have blown the reveal. Omniscient narrator? What could I have said narratively that would have improved the sequence?

Despite the criticism I received, I remain convinced that I handled it in exactly the right way. That's going to happen sometimes: People are going to complain loud and long that you messed up. Don't let it get you down. If you feel critics have a point, try and learn from it for next time. If you feel they've missed the point...the heck with 'em.

So, anyway...the Hulk continues his long, slow trudge along the ocean floor. As he does so, he suddenly finds himself face-to-beak with a sea creature that borders on the mythic: a giant Kraken. This presents a considerably greater challenge for the Hulk, but he is able to overcome it because, well, he's the Hulk. Those pages are reproduced here.

While Man vs. Man may allow you more latitude, Man vs. Nature lets you kick the odds skyward (literally) and can serve as a truly humbling experience for your protagonist, provided you think he needs it. Some of the best Superman stories have involved the Man of Steel up against some major natural disaster and finding a way to minimize or eliminate the danger entirely. It's a nice bit of comforting fantasy, to imagine having a protector so powerful and ingenious that he'll come up with some astoundingly clever method of countering whatever nature can attempt to throw at us. This is as opposed to having mere humans slugging it out with nature, which usually results in stories wherein the protagonists are just trying to stay alive until nature gets done slapping them around.

HANDS OFF!

The Hulk engages in a classic struggle of Man vs. Nature as he battles a giant Kraken in this issue. Of course, the Hulk holds up better than most, because, after all, he's no ordinary man.

73

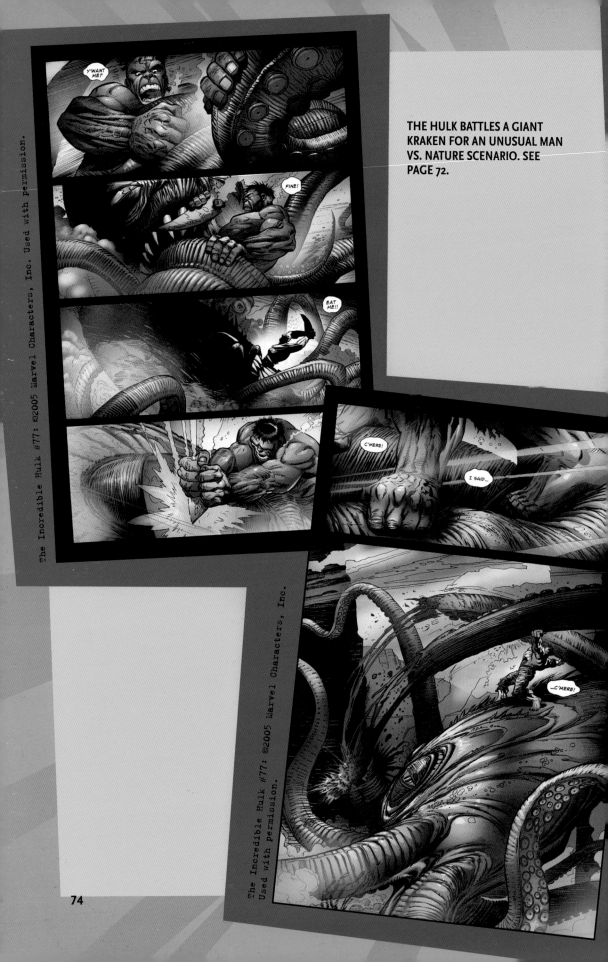

THE HULK BATTLES A GIANT KRAKEN FOR AN UNUSUAL MAN VS. NATURE SCENARIO. SEE PAGE 72.

The Incredible Hulk #77: ©2005 Marvel Characters, Inc. Used with permission.

The Incredible Hulk #77: ©2005 Marvel Characters, Inc. Used with permission.

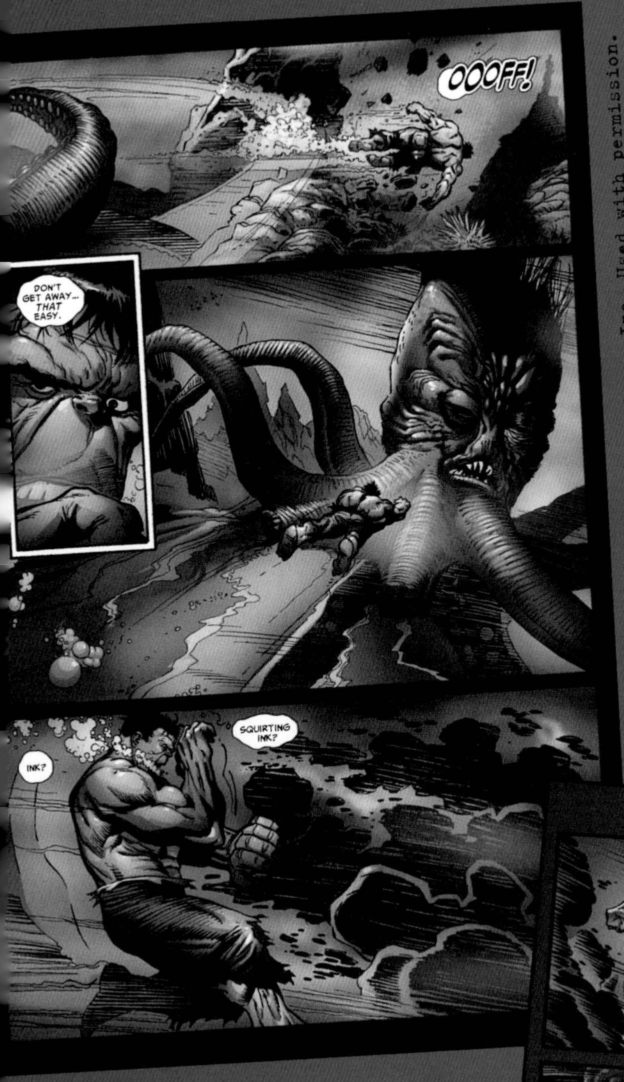
OOOFF!
DON'T GET AWAY... THAT EASY.
INK?
SQUIRTING INK?

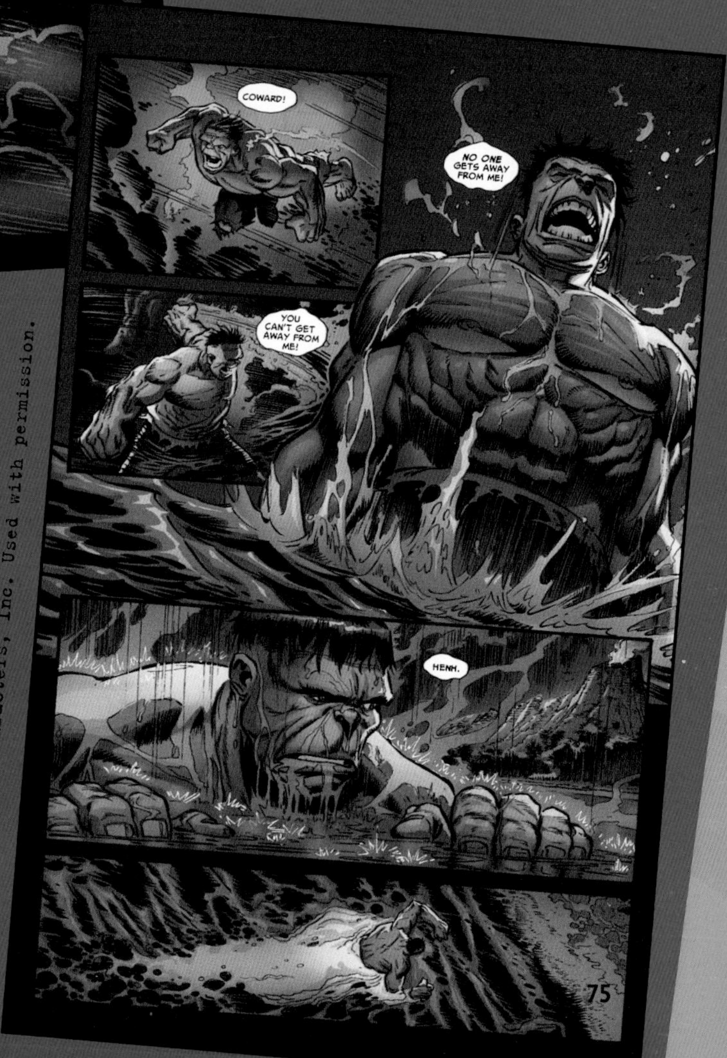
COWARD!
NO ONE GETS AWAY FROM ME!
YOU CAN'T GET AWAY FROM ME!
HENH.

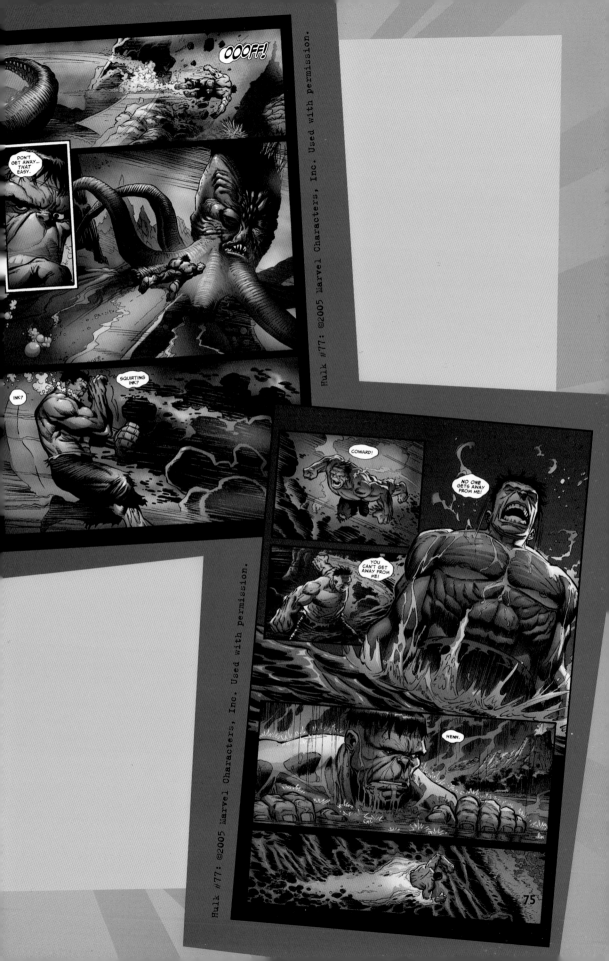

CONFLICT: MAN VS. HIMSELF

In his first inaugural speech, President Franklin Delano Roosevelt addressed the uncertain times in which the United States found itself, with its economic back breaking under the weight of the Great Depression. FDR was certain the Depression could be turned around (perhaps a little orphan girl had convinced him; I couldn't say). But he knew that the first and greatest stumbling block toward financial recovery was convincing the poverty-weary citizens—afraid of what new calamity each day would bring—that such a recovery was possible. Roosevelt uttered the words that Americans would seize hold of as a clarion cry toward making things better: "So, first of all, let me assert my firm belief that the only thing we have to fear is fear itself—nameless, unreasoning, unjustified terror which paralyzes needed efforts to convert retreat into advance."

A hero's greatest opponent can often be himself. Overcoming some sort of weakness, be it fear of failure, fear of death, alcoholism, drug addiction or a gamma-powered monster living inside him (don't you just hate when that happens?). In order to fulfill his destiny, the hero can find himself struggling against seductive evil, seductive women or—worst of all—seductive evil women.

The comic book poster boy for battling his own demons is probably the Hulk, but instead let's focus on the single most memorable instance of a hero triumphing over inner doubt and fear of failure: the sequence fondly remembered as Spider-Man lifting the hunkajunk off himself, the absolute high point of the Stan Lee/Steve Ditko run on the series.

In this three-parter, Aunt May is desperately ill, her blood cells deteriorating because nephew Peter was boneheaded enough to give her a transfusion some issues earlier of his radioactive blood. Trying to undo the damage he has done, he seeks out Dr. Curt Connors, who in turn sends for a serum called ISO-36, which could theoretically undo the damage. As Peter's typical bad luck would have it, the serum is stolen by the "Master Planner," a pseudonym adopted by Doctor Octopus for no apparent reason. Spider-Man goes in pursuit of the serum and defeats Doc Ock, bringing Doc's HQ crashing down in the process.

Unfortunately, Spidey is now trapped under massive fallen machinery, unable to escape from beneath it, with the needed serum sitting twenty feet away, proving yet again that, when he wants to be, God can be a funny guy.

Now this may sound like Man vs. Nature, but it's not. No matter how much he wills it, Spider-Man can't beat (for instance) a tornado. In this case, he does have the ability to remove the machinery. What he must overcome is his fear of failure, his fear that he cannot move it. And this he does, in an emotionally charged sequence that's a brilliant combination of visuals and pep talk.

Be cautious, though: Man vs. Himself is the trickiest path to walk because you have to be completely candid in presenting your hero's weakness in such a way that he doesn't simply seem like an indecisive whiner. In trying to tell a compelling tale, you run the risk of losing the reader's sympathy for your character. His doubts have to arise honestly out of his experiences and seem reasonable rather than out of proportion. Hamlet dithers and second guesses over what he should do; however, he's been visited by the ghost of his father, who reveals he was murdered and his mom has wed the murderer. So Hamlet's taken a few emotional kicks to the head that make his uncertainty understandable. Even Hamlet eventually decides upon a course of action and, once committed to it, pursues it with homicidal intensity.

Sometimes the greatest triumph that people can achieve is overcoming their own weaknesses. Just be sure to give that weakness a solid support. You want a hero with weakness...not a weakling.

> "A **HERO'S** greatest **opponent** can often be **HIMSELF**."

What makes this particular sequence work so well is that
Spider-Man overcomes his doubts in order to triumph.

ONE OF SPIDER-MAN'S MOST LEGENDARY MAN VS. SELF SITUATIONS. SEE PAGE 76.

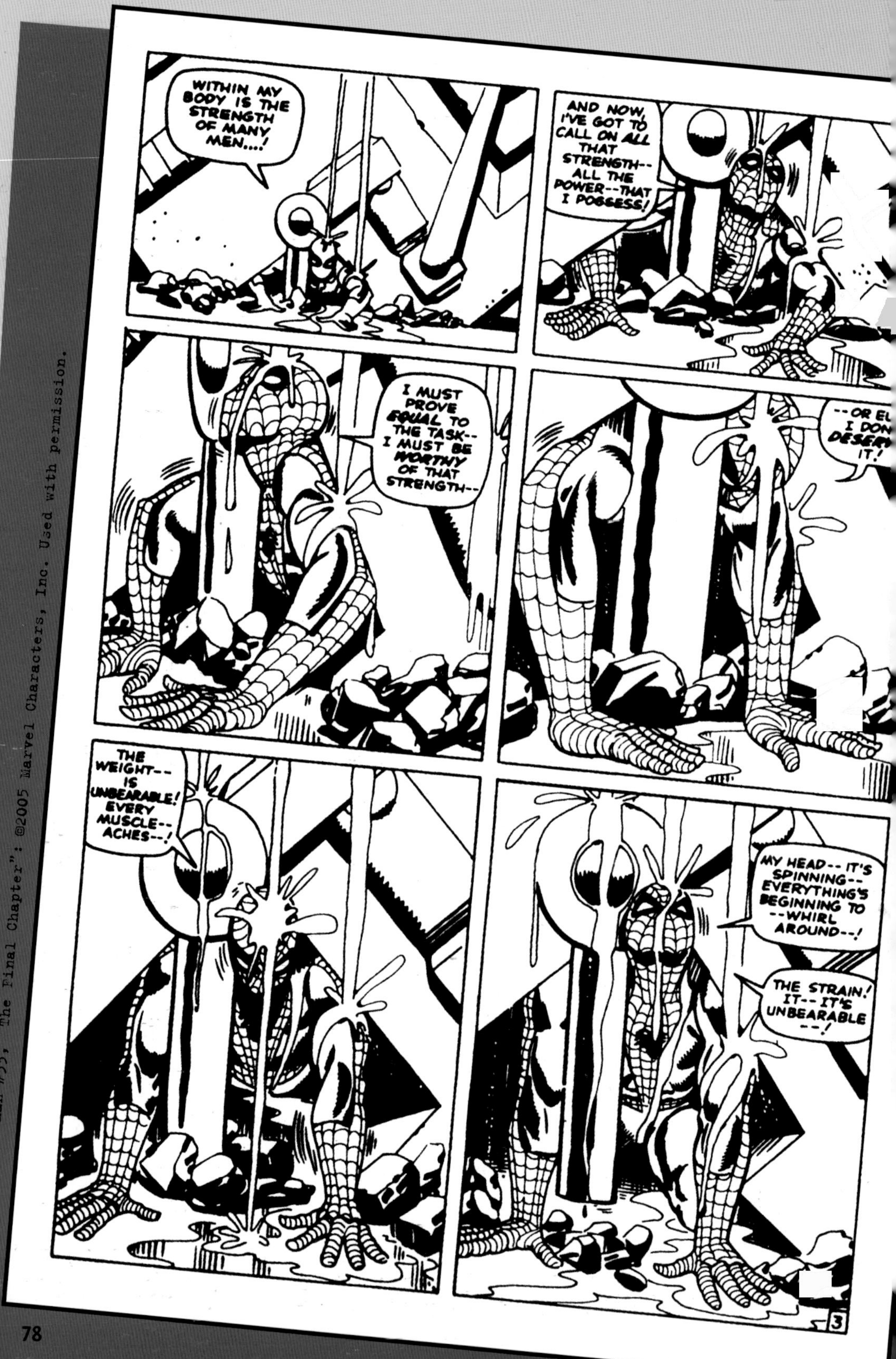
WITHIN MY BODY IS THE STRENGTH OF MANY MEN...!
AND NOW, I'VE GOT TO CALL ON ALL THAT STRENGTH-- ALL THE POWER--THAT I POSSESS!
I MUST PROVE EQUAL TO THE TASK-- I MUST BE WORTHY OF THAT STRENGTH--
--OR EL I DON DESERV IT!
THE WEIGHT-- IS UNBEARABLE! EVERY MUSCLE-- ACHES--!
MY HEAD-- IT'S SPINNING-- EVERYTHING'S BEGINNING TO --WHIRL AROUND--!
THE STRAIN! IT-- IT'S UNBEARABLE --!
3

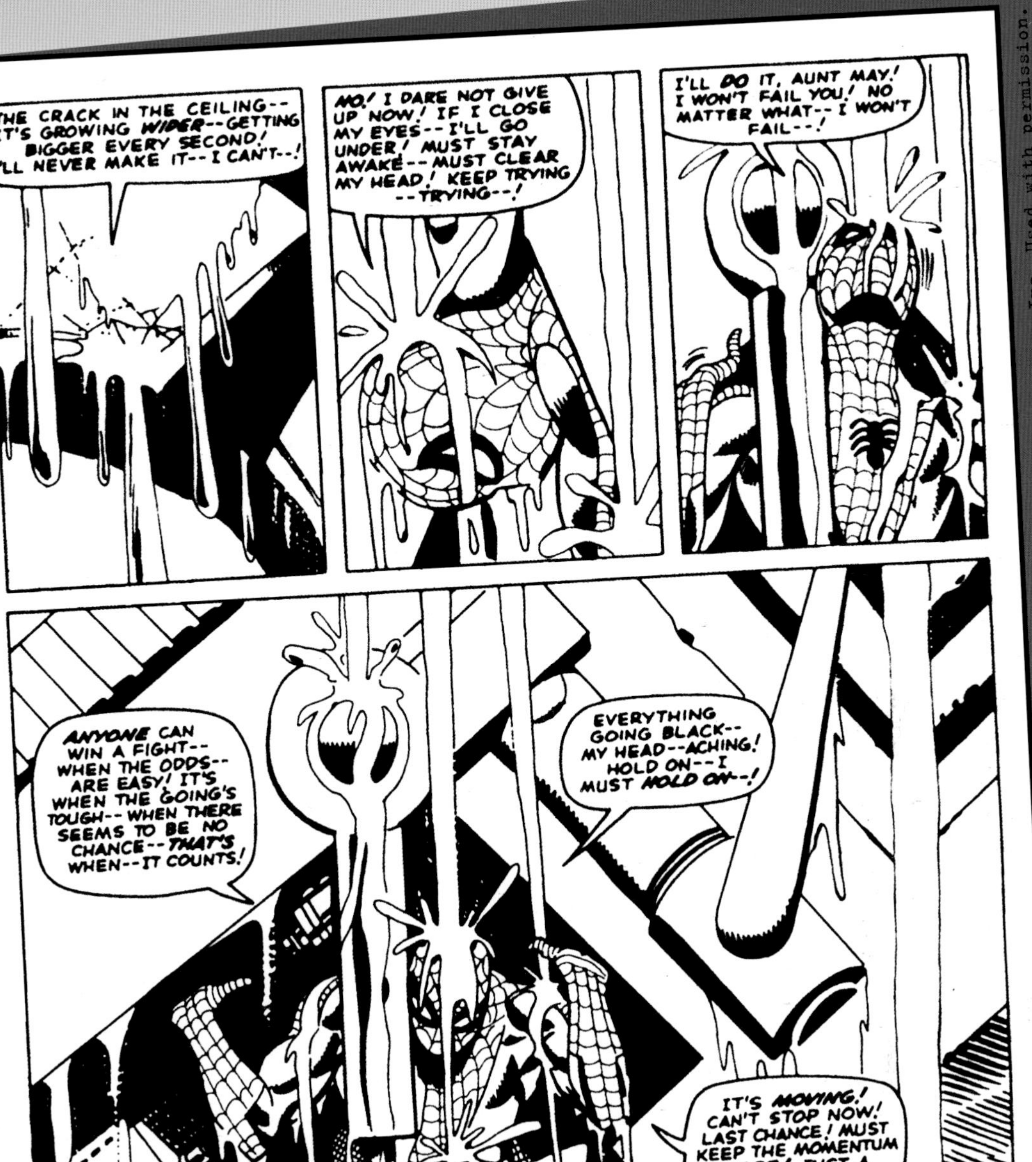
THE CRACK IN THE CEILING-- IT'S GROWING WIDER--GETTING BIGGER EVERY SECOND! I'LL NEVER MAKE IT-- I CAN'T--!
NO! I DARE NOT GIVE UP NOW! IF I CLOSE MY EYES--I'LL GO UNDER! MUST STAY AWAKE--MUST CLEAR MY HEAD! KEEP TRYING --TRYING--!
I'LL DO IT, AUNT MAY! I WON'T FAIL YOU! NO MATTER WHAT-- I WON'T FAIL--!
ANYONE CAN WIN A FIGHT-- WHEN THE ODDS-- ARE EASY! IT'S WHEN THE GOING'S TOUGH-- WHEN THERE SEEMS TO BE NO CHANCE--THAT'S WHEN--IT COUNTS!
EVERYTHING GOING BLACK-- MY HEAD--ACHING! HOLD ON--I MUST HOLD ON--!
IT'S MOVING! CAN'T STOP NOW! LAST CHANCE! MUST KEEP THE MOMENTUM --MORE! JUST A LITTLE MORE--!
4

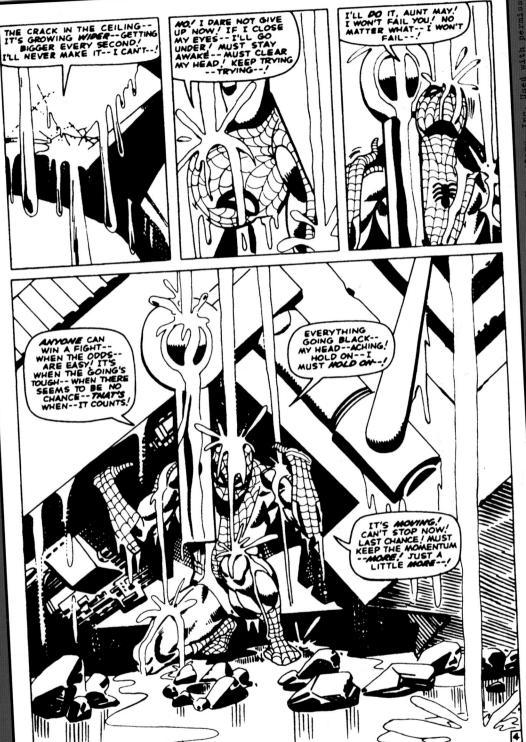

ONE OF SPIDER-MAN'S MOST LEGENDARY MAN VS. SELF SITUATIONS. SEE PAGE 76.

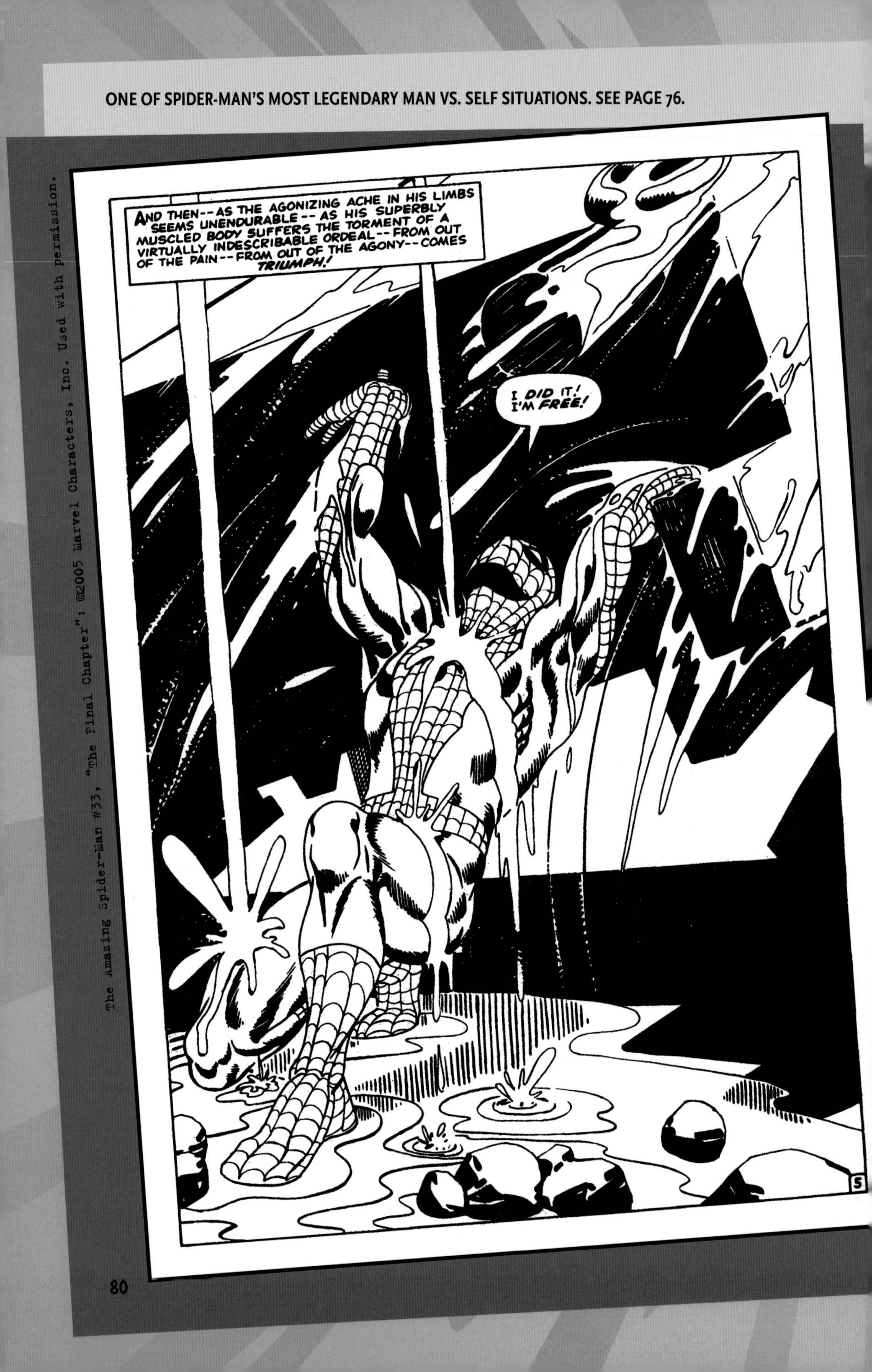
AND THEN--AS THE AGONIZING ACHE IN HIS LIMBS SEEMS UNENDURABLE--AS HIS SUPERBLY MUSCLED BODY SUFFERS THE TORMENT OF A VIRTUALLY INDESCRIBABLE ORDEAL--FROM OUT OF THE PAIN--FROM OUT OF THE AGONY--COMES TRIUMPH!
I DID IT! I'M FREE!
5

In exploring basic themes and the inherent conflicts, no one story has to restrict itself to only one of them. You can work it in combination. Indeed, that's the typical approach taken by, for instance, the average disaster movie. Against a backdrop of, say, an impending asteroid that's going to strike the Earth, different people react to the coming doomsday in different ways, and those ways wind up bringing the people into conflict with each other.

You can have Man vs. Man as people struggle with one another to board a lifesaving space ark or find sanctuary in a specially built bunker that can only house a hundred people. You can have Man vs. Himself as one protagonist who has always been selfish or self-centered overcomes that selfishness by giving his seat on the space ark to someone whom he comes to believe needs it more than he, and is more worthy of it.

The more variety you have, the more that's at stake for your heroes, the more depth your story will have and the bigger the payoff. The one thing you don't want to do is throw in everything that occurs to you with no thought as to how it fits together. If you do that, your story is going to wander around, unfocused and getting underfoot and getting hurt, like a blind long-tailed cat in a room full of rocking chairs. You must remember to develop your more narrow, single, overarching theme ("Disaster can bring out the best and worst of people") and try to make sure that every story development ties to that in some way.

If you have some particular bit of business that you like but that doesn't attach to the theme, don't be afraid to dump it. As Sir Arthur Quiller-Couch said, "Murder your darlings." That which doesn't make the story better makes it worse.

The old romantic saw is that opposites attract.

No. They don't. Only in romantic comedies do a woman and man who are nothing like each other fall madly in love with one another. In real life, should such a coupling occur, in short order each of the couple will be trying to get the other one to be more like him or her.

OPPOSITES CREATE CONFLICT

What opposites do attract, however, is friction. Arguments. Mutual frustration. Since the essence of drama is conflict, that's essential for storytelling.

Let's start with teams. Since we were speaking of *Buffy the Vampire Slayer* before, consider that the entire group is made up of opposites. Each person has someone who's a polar opposite. There's Buffy, the promising but flighty student, vs. Giles, the worldly and barely patient teacher. Willow, the emotionally in-touch, academically gifted student, as opposed to Xander, the emotionally discombobulated, academically challenged student. Even the "outsider" characters are opposites: The beautiful Cordelia, the self-adoring social butterfly who says whatever's on her mind, compared to the handsome Angel, the self-loathing social outcast who initially speaks cryptically or not at all. No wonder that when Angel was spun off into his own series, Cordelia came along for the ride.

LOOK FOR REAL DIFFERENCES

As for the Fantastic Four, consider the fundamental differences between the key players...differences that long ago elevated the FF beyond simply a buncha guys with super-abilities. The powers themselves weren't anything wildly original. Both Plastic Man and Elongated Man were stretching before Reed Richards as Mr. Fantastic. And Ben Grimm as the Thing was just the latest in a line of Kirby-esque monsters. Invisibility? Please. And Marvel had already produced a "Human Torch" decades earlier, albeit an android one.

What makes the FF different—what makes them classic and what's kept the book going for four decades—is not just the powers but the personalities, and how they interact and contrast, with each other.

Reed Richards is cerebral, thoughtful, intellectual and settles problems with the power of his mind. Ben Grimm, his friend and opposite, is gruff, despises big words and settles problems with his fists. Reed's body is fluid and shifting like water... Ben's body is solid and unyielding, like the ground.

Sue Storm Richards is the caring, nurturing mother figure of the group, worrying about everyone's safety. Her brother, Johnny, is the impetuous teen in relation to the mother-surrogate of his sister, living only for practical jokes and taking point in every dangerous situation. Sue's power of invisibility is like the air, enabling her to hide. Johnny's power is fire, which has a love/hate relationship with air (can't survive without it, but can be extinguished by it) and by its nature demands notice and attention.

Each of them, in short, are defined by their opposite numbers.

Perhaps that's the reason their son, Franklin Richards, has gone through so many changes. Without an ongoing member of the series to be his opposite, he continues to remain undefined, confusing and at the mercy of whoever the latest writer is to inherit him and wonder what the heck to do with him.

KEEP IT SIMPLE

If you want to start producing your own team of heroes, start small and simple. There are certain traits, certain forces, that are simply always in opposition to each other. Cheerful vs. dour. Modest vs. boastful. Short-tempered vs. calm. Impulsive vs. deliberate. Optimist vs. pessimist. Old vs. young. Vain vs. self-deprecating.

REED RICHARDS
Scientific. Polysyllabic. Pliable.

MISTER FANTASTIC

BEN GRIMM
Unscientific. Monosyllabic. Rock solid.

THE THING

INVISIBLE GIRL

SUE STORM RICHARDS
Maternal. Fades into the background...literally.

HUMAN TORCH

JOHNNY STORM
Showy. Demonstrative. Can blind you with his presence...literally.

Start with these fundamental character aspects. Decide that you're going to have a cheerful individual vs. a downbeat individual. Develop the characters and the reasons that they are the way they are. For example, look at the movie *Finding Nemo*. Dory the blue tang fish is teamed with Marlin the clownfish in search of Marlin's missing son. Dory is perpetually upbeat; Marlin is

---

X-FACTOR PROPOSAL

Notice how, in the selection from my proposal below, I stressed the character interaction and conflict, both with each other and internally:

JAMIE MADROX: Team leader and boss who will, in the course of the series, discover things about himself that he had not remotely suspected. Someone who will not hesitate to skirt the edge of the law or even skip over the edge if it means accomplishing what he believes to be a greater good—especially since, by his very nature, he can see all sides of a situation.

RAHNE SINCLAIR: Wolfsbane, serving as the conscience to Madrox. She's no angel herself (and therein lies her own internal conflict), but she will often be the one to call Jamie on anything he does that is skidding off the path of morality.

GUIDO: Philosophically somewhere between the two (and often serving as mediator in an agreement), Guido is the wisecracking, streetwise muscle of the group. Supposedly cavalier about the world in general and himself in particular, Guido will nevertheless fight like a wildman if he thinks that anyone in his odd little "family" is threatened.

MONET: Sharp, intelligent, sophisticated. Jamie actually develops a romantic interest in her, but it manifests itself in sharp, scathing, Hepburn/Tracy-esque exchanges. Monet also tends to regard Rahne as something of a hick, causing sparks to fly.

RICTOR: The James Dean of the group. If you need someone to go roust a stoolie, intimidate people, etc., Rictor's your guy. He's got a ground-shaking ability, a boatload of anger and personal issues, and he's not afraid to let people know he's the toughest mofo around. On again/off again relationship with Rahne. Monet will make a play for him just to piss Rahne off.

SIRYN: When you need a "bad girl" to seduce/entice a male suspect (or even a female suspect, for that matter) into cooperating with you 110 percent, you send in Siryn. She has learned to modulate her voice so that—in addition to the hammering scream effect—she can also make it sound mellifluous and enticing to her potential victim. Her Achilles' heel is that she's an alcoholic, and a hard-drinking outing with Rictor is going to make her fall off the wagon, hard.

perpetually downbeat. Why? Dory has perpetual short-term memory loss. She has no worries because she can't remember anything, and thus is perpetually upbeat. Marlin, by contrast, lives with the loss of his wife and family to a ravenous barracuda, and thus sees potential disaster around every corner. Yet they learn from each other over the course of the film. By the end Dory has become more grounded in the concept of a consistent life lived with a family (although she still has a mental block about Nemo's name) while Marlin has lightened up somewhat and learned not to worry so much.

That's what you need to do in creating teams: Create characters in sets of two to be in opposition to each other so you'll always have some element of conflict in the interpersonal dynamics.

WORKING WITH EXISTING CHARACTERS

If you're putting together a team consisting of already existing characters, select those whose already established traits may provide interesting fodder for stories. For instance, when I was determining which characters to go with for the new *X-Factor* series (based on the list of available mutants provided me by editor Andy Schmidt), I did so with an eye toward who would present viable conflict with each other.

EXERCISE

CREATE YOUR OWN DISASTER COMIC

It's fun! It's easy! It's entirely conflict driven! And best of all... it's simply an exercise. It will, however, help you prepare for a career as a writer. There will be any number of times where you will be required to "pitch" as many as half a dozen possibilities in order to land one story assignment. Every proposal has to be as cogent and thought out as possible to increase the odds that whoever is doing the reading will consider your proposal workable. Making certain you've got your fundamentals lined up—particularly a clear conflict—will go a long way in that regard. So...

1 Come up with three internal conflicts that represent Man vs. Himself. Example: A hero struggling with drug addiction; a hero who has left behind his street gang origins but feels pulled back to them; a hero who has crippling agoraphobia and can't set foot outside.

2 Come up with three conflicts representing Man vs. Man. Example: A couple locked in a bitter divorce battle; a frustrated writer who discovers a book he was developing was ripped off by another writer; a hero who discovers his long-lost brother is actually a supervillain aimed at world domination.

3 Come up with three conflicts representing Man vs. Nature. Example: A hurricane is bearing down upon a small town; a villain has tampered with the San Andreas Fault and earthquakes are ripping through Los Angeles; global warming is melting the polar ice caps.

4 Mix and match what you've come up with to see if you can create a six-sentence precis of a story from it. It doesn't matter if the story is over-the-top. The point is to force yourself to think in story structure within a short descriptive passage. That way, when you're developing story springboards and proposals for real, you'll be in the habit of hitting the major bullet points that will elevate your story above a simple string of happenings to specific conflicts to make your vision clear.

Ideally, of course, your heroes won't be spending all their time at odds with other members of the team or supporting cast. Heroes need their villains because one side helps define the other. The best sort of hero/villain match-ups are those in which the villain, using his power, abilities, origin or personality, or some combination of the four, provides a direct contrast to the hero. He is the hero gone wrong, the hero who is sent off the rails somehow.

It was perhaps best stated by the villainous Belloq in Lawrence Kasdan's script for *Raiders of the Lost Ark*. In a memorable confrontation in a bar, Belloq tells the slightly drunk Indiana Jones, "We have always done the same kind of work. Our methods have not differed as much as you pretend. I am a shadowy reflection of you. But it would have taken only a nudge to make you the same as me, to push you out of the light." Kasdan's own scene description notes: "There's a certain amount of truth to this; the recognition of it flickers across Indy's bleary eyes."

It's the same with heroes and their arch-enemies. More often than not, they both work at the outer edges (or beyond) of the law. Their goals are self-appointed: World Saver vs. World Destroyer. In the old days, the main way of distinguishing the good guys from the bad guys was that the former would refrain from a killing stroke. With the onset of dubious heroes such as Wolverine and the Punisher, even that line of demarcation has been erased. When heroes pound on bad guys, like as not, they're trying to put down their opposite numbers.

AND WE'RE BACK TO CONFLICT

When you get down to it, the entire hero/villain dynamic culls two aspects of the conflicts we discussed earlier.

First there is the obvious: Man vs. Man. The villain wants to accomplish certain goals; the hero wants to stop him.

But then there is the less obvious: Man vs. Himself. If you've pulled off your hero/villain conflict properly, at least in some measure the villain reflects aspects of the hero that the hero would rather not address. In working to overcome the villain, the hero is battling his own darkest impulses.

In *Future Imperfect*, I made that contrast as literal as possible, putting the Hulk in opposition to a future version of himself called the Maestro who was thoroughly evil. Yet the second half of that story was largely a psychological battle as the Maestro basically tried to bring the Hulk over to his way of thinking. What made the conflict so

BATMAN VS. THE JOKER

1   They both wear masks (one painted, the other cloth) that not only define their personalities, but have consumed them. Spider-Man is Peter Parker with a costume on, but Bruce Wayne is simply Batman with his mask off. He's Batman 24/7, with Bruce Wayne merely the disguise that Batman hides behind during the day. The Joker is likewise the Joker every waking moment... presuming he ever sleeps.

2   They're both mad geniuses, one using his ingenuity for death, murder and mayhem, and the other using it to prevent death and murder while engaging in mayhem. How far this analogy goes for you depends on whether or not you think Batman is nuts. Is dressing up like a bat really that different from dressing up like a character from a card deck? What makes the Batman/Joker dichotomy work so well is that certainly Batman himself doesn't think he's insane... but every time he looks at the Joker, he can't help but wonder just a little bit.

REED RICHARDS VS. DOCTOR DOOM

1 Both of them are brilliant scholars and explorers who seriously botched their initial major ventures but went in drastically different directions afterwards. Victor Von Doom was embarking on a bold experiment to communicate with another dimension when the machine went awry and blew up, ruining his face. And for the record, no, I don't buy into the notion that it simply left a little scar. His face was savaged in the explosion, end of discussion. Reed, meantime, hauled his pilot friend Ben Grimm (along with, inexplicably, his girlfriend and even more inexplicably, her kid brother) on a space voyage to beat out the Russians, only to ignore Ben's cautions about sufficient shielding to keep out cosmic rays. However, Reed and company rose above this unexpected development to become heroes, while Von Doom was dragged down into villainy by his mishap.

2 Both of them have inflated egos. Von Doom's ego was so massive that, rather than acknowledge that he'd screwed up in his calculations in creating the dimension-hopping machine that blew up, he decided to blame Reed Richards for the accident even though Reed in fact tried to prevent it. As for Reed...c'mon. Guy named himself Mr. Fantastic. That's even more egotistical than calling yourself "Doctor" Doom without ever actually having gotten a doctorate of any kind.

daunting for the Hulk was that he knew that the potential for becoming the Maestro was already within him. The evidence that he'd already gone down this path once was right there in front of him. So he had to battle not only his internal doubts, but also the crushing weight of future history.

Not every villain needs to be a spot-on reflection of the hero. But he shouldn't be interchangeable with someone else's opponent, either. Both in terms of personality and power level, he should tie in thematically with the hero so that he is unique to the hero he opposes. Granted, there are some villains who transcend that. Doctor Doom is the specific nemesis of Reed Richards, but he's gone up against everyone from Spider-Man to Thor with facility. If your villain has that kind of crossover power, that's great. To start out, though, it's best to think about how the villain can best serve in conflict to your main hero.

HULK VS. LEADER

1 Both of them were guys with alliterative names who were affected by gamma rays. Bruce Banner was struck with gamma radiation while trying to save Rick Jones. Sam Sterns was an ordinary laborer who was exposed to gamma rays while moving a load of radioactive waste.

2 Bruce Banner was a brilliant scientist who, after his accident, transformed into a being of limitless strength but virtually no intellectual capacity, with no desire except to be left alone. Sam Sterns was a high school dropout who, as a result of his mishap, acquired limitless intelligence and a desire to be surrounded by followers—a clear necessity when you've dubbed yourself "the Leader." A leader with no one to lead is just a guy standing around. Both of them are capable of destructive acts, but the Hulk is always the one who is provoked while the Leader is the one doing the provoking. In other words, the Hulk is the hornet's nest and the Leader is the stick.

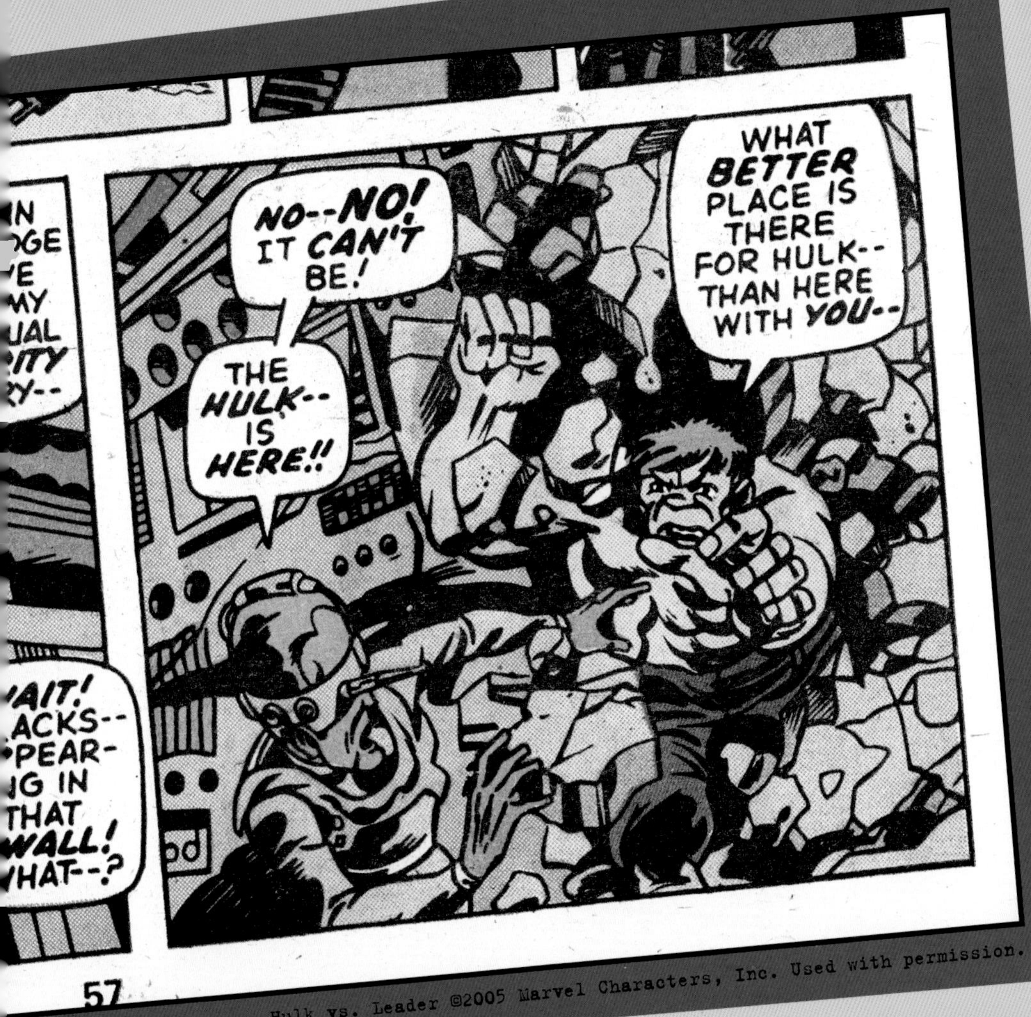
NO--NO! IT CAN'T BE!
THE HULK-- IS HERE!!
WHAT BETTER PLACE IS THERE FOR HULK-- THAN HERE WITH YOU--
57

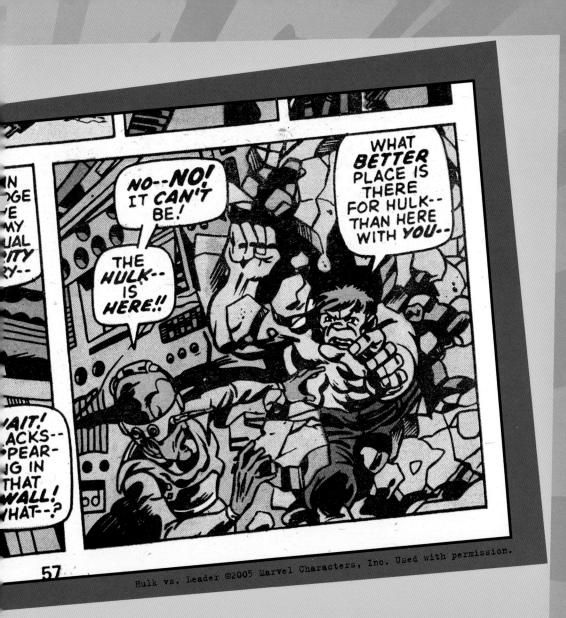

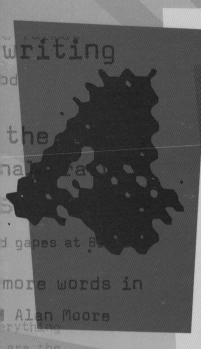

writing

the

gapes at B

more words in

Alan Moore

logue

PLOT AND STORY STRUCTURE

THERE ARE TWO ASPECTS OF STRUCTURE IN A STORY. THE FIRST IS THAT OF THE HERO'S DEVELOPMENT AS AN INDIVIDUAL. ULTIMATELY, AT THE END OF THE STORY, YOUR HERO SHOULD UNDERGO A *CHARACTER ARC*—HE SHOULD BE DIFFERENT IN SOME WAY, SHAPE OR FORM THAN HE WAS IN THE BEGINNING. HE HAS TO BE, FOR IF HE LEARNS NOTHING FROM HIS ADVENTURES, WHAT WAS THE POINT OF EMBARKING ON THEM IN THE FIRST PLACE?

The second aspect is how your hero undergoes his voyage and how his personal arc progresses. This is the *function* of the plot and the pacing thereof.

Unless, of course, you're making the latest in a series of generic action thrillers featuring a single protagonist who is pretty much the same from one adventure to the next. In that event, since the audience can't be fulfilled by experiencing the character's growth, you have to substitute bigger and louder challenges to make up for it. Sooner or later, though, you're going to run into the law of diminishing returns as audiences get more jaded and tougher to impress.

Basically, both the characters and the plot have their individual arcs and are specifically intertwined. Think of the plot as an automobile and the character as the passenger. The plot drives the character through his arc so that he goes through various experiences in his journey and winds up a different person when he turns off the car and steps out than he was when he first climbed behind the wheel.

Pacing is the speed with which the car makes the journey. It's knowing when to hit the gas, when to ease up, when to slam on the brakes and then how fast to accelerate once more.

"I'M DEAD, BUT I GOT BETTER"

In classic fiction, in a normal drama, dead is dead. Death is a real hazard, and if a character succumbs, that's pretty much it for that character. But in stories set in the worlds of comic books or fantasy or science fiction, death doesn't necessarily mean the end. Heck, in horror fiction, death is often the beginning.

Stories conceived with fantastic elements can go in many more directions than something more down-to-earth. The problem is that it takes one of the ultimate "stakes" out of the writer's tool box. A life-or-death situation is difficult to sell in comics when most fans will read that as "life-or-death-until-we-bring-them-back."

This is particularly the case when discussing characters of truly long standing, who date back to the 1960s or more. Kill off a supporting or even lead character with that sort of history, and the fan reaction will be jaded, thus making your story less effective.

The more general world doesn't understand this. When DC undertook its famed "Death of Superman" story line, many noncomic readers took the story at face value. I personally heard some nonfans discussing it at a local eatery, saying things like, "Yeah, they've really killed Clark Kent. There's going to be some new guy as Superman now." The average fan could have told them that it was merely a matter of time until Kal-El returned from the dead, but people who don't read literature of the fantastic simply can't comprehend that. They're anchored in real life where dead is dead.

For that matter, I once encountered a woman on an airplane who asked me what I did for a living. When I told her that, among other things, I wrote *The Incredible Hulk*, she looked bewildered and said, "I thought the Hulk was dead." She was referring, of course, to the 1990 TV movie, *The Death of the Incredible Hulk*, in which the Hulk is depicted as falling to his death from a departing helicopter. I tried to explain to her that the "real" Hulk could fall from orbit, and the only result would be an annoyed Hulk climbing out of a Hulk-sized crater, dusting himself off and going on about his business. But she literally couldn't understand what I was talking about. She couldn't grasp the concept of two different incarnations of the Hulk, and besides, she'd seen him die. Dead is dead.

So how do you have death have any meaning in comics you write?

- **Don't kill off your protagonists unless it's part of an ongoing story line** in which you make it clear that they're not really dead, or that their return from the dead is part of the plot. Otherwise you're simply not going to make anyone believe they're really dead, no matter how hard you try.

- **Kill off incidental or secondary characters.** Characters who might have a fighting chance of staying dead, even in the hands of subsequent writers.

- **Use the most mundane means of death as possible.** Knife. Shotgun at close range. Beheading. Don't have your character vanish into the ether after being hit with a blast from an Illudium Q-36 Explosive Space Modulator and expect your readers to believe that your guy is dead. When I decided to kill off a major character in *Fallen Angel*, I had him shot six times at close range including a bullet through the head, and threw him off a high balcony besides, and still fans wrote in and asked if he was really dead.

- **Be consistent within the context of the series you're writing.** I will never, ever bring back a character who was killed in *Fallen Angel* because I don't want the series to have that sense of "death is transient" that can torpedo any feeling of genuine life-or-death jeopardy. The moment you bring back a dead character in a series, that's it for all time: Death will never again have a true meaning of finality.

Is it worth killing off characters at all if readers are so skeptical of such an action? Definitely, especially if you can convince the reader of its gravitas. In order to do that, remember it depends on whom you kill, how you kill them and what happens afterwards.

A good litmus test to know if you have a shot with your reader? Your own reaction as you're writing it. On a few occasions, I've killed off characters and the mere act of writing it was so upsetting to me that I started crying while I was doing it. If your story hits such emotional depths that you yourself are grieving, you've got a good chance of getting to your reader.

RAIDERS OF THE LOST CHARACTER AND STORY ARCS

A classic character arc gives us a young innocent from a rural area who winds up going on an adventure with an assortment of colleagues, undergoes traumas, learns great and amazing things and finally returns to his home, sadder but wiser and more worldly. Think of Frodo from the Shire in *The Lord of the Rings*, Dorothy Gale in *The Wizard of Oz* or Harry Potter in *Harry Potter and the Sorcerer's Stone*. Plus there are infinite variations on the formula, if one considers, say, Ebenezer Scrooge. Not a young innocent, to be sure, but nevertheless a famed voyager who underwent a journey of personal discovery and transformation so accessible that everyone from Quincy Magoo to Bill Murray has taken the trip.

As mentioned, there is no one way to pace a story. No definitive means by which every story can and should be told. And whenever you do try to carve absolutes into concrete, you're going to wind up with a cracked sidewalk.

For instance, one editor often said that the poem "Little Miss Muffet" was ideal from a storytelling point of view because it had all the elements.

* The set-up ("Little Miss Muffet sat on a tuffet, eating her curds and whey")

* Followed by an action setting the story into motion ("Along came a spider and sat down beside her")

* And the reaction which resolved it ("And frightened Miss Muffet away.")

The problem is...okay, actually, there are two problems. The first is, what's a tuffet? The answer is, a low seat.

The second problem is, although the structure is there, it's really not much of a story. There's no character arc. Miss Muffet doesn't really learn anything, unless one assumes that she suddenly discovers she has arachnophobia. And all she does is run away. She does nothing to direct the story, doesn't take any initiative, doesn't affect the outcome in any way except to absent herself from it.

Then again, when you consider it purely from a story point of view, *Raiders of the Lost Ark* is abysmal. Indiana Jones accomplishes nothing. He's perpetually one step behind the bad guys. Whenever he gets his hands on anything, he loses it. At the climax of the story, he attempts a bluff that doesn't work, has no plan B, gets tied to a stake, and God has to save his butt.

For that matter, Marv Wolfman pointed out that if you remove Indy from the story, there is no difference. If Indy isn't there, the Nazis go to Marion and get the headpiece of the Staff of Ra. They take the headpiece, use it to find the Ark because they're digging in the right place this time, put it on the sub, bring it out to the island to open it and they all die. The end.

The much-despised *Indiana Jones and the Temple of Doom* featured Indy as a far more proactive hero who made a tremendous difference and saved the day. But *Raiders* is a more successful movie...which just goes to show that the way you tell the story is as important, and sometimes even more so, than the story being told.

In *Temple of Doom*, the pacing was way off as endless amounts of time were spent in pointless scenes designed to get us to like supporting characters whose personal journeys were simply of no interest to us. In fact, the supporting characters were a large part of where the script let the filmmakers and audience down. Indy's character arc was rock solid, but it was really the only thing in the film that was. As lively as the action set pieces were, it's hard to become involved in them when we really don't care if Indy's companions live or die.

CLIMACTIC DECISION POINT

The same editor who revered "Little Miss Muffet" for its perfect structure also had an ironclad rule when it came to storytelling: In every story, the hero must face a climactic decision point. He must find himself saying, "I can do this or I can do that, oh my god, which one should I do?" The movie *Spider-Man* is textbook of this method: The Green Goblin tells Spidey that he can either save MJ or the tram full of nameless extras. It should be a no-brainer, but hey, Spider-Man saves both of them because he's Spider-Man. *Raiders*, for that matter, also has a decision point as Indy has to choose between Marion or the Ark. And he chooses the Ark...although, really, it was a pretty crappy choice situation, because if he does blow up the Ark, the Nazis will just kill Marion and he winds up with neither. Then there's *The Lord of the Rings*, with Frodo in Mount Doom, struggling with the decision to toast the ring or not...and he decides not to. Essentially, Frodo is a failed hero, and it's Gollum who actually saves the day, albeit unintentionally.

But this editor's dictate was so rigid that it drove many writers to distraction, because although it's a valid way to tell a story, it's not the only way to tell a story.

For instance, a hero can never waver in his determination, and the story focuses on how he manages to accomplish his goal rather than trying to decide which goal he should pursue.

Consider *The Karate Kid*. Technically, yes, Daniel has to decide whether to allow his injured leg to prevent him from going out for the final confrontation, but it's really never an issue. To his mind there's simply no choice; it's just a matter of convincing Mr. Miyagi to aid him in getting back on his feet.

Or think of *The Terminator*. At no point does Sarah really have a choice in her actions: She's just trying to stay alive. The film isn't about her deciding to become the woman she's capable of being; it's about the circumstances that put her back against the wall so that she has no choice but to become the kick-butt freedom fighter she eventually morphs into.

Or, again, there's *The Lord of the Rings*, where Frodo does indeed have a decision point...but utterly fails in his decision as he succumbs to the blandishments of the ring, with the result that Gollum leaps in and inadvertently saves the day.

> "There is only **ONE WAY** to tell a story badly: bore **THE READER.**"

THE WRITTEN-IN-STONE RULE

In short: There is no one way to tell a story well. There is, however, only one way to tell a story badly: bore the reader. You might bore him because the character is flat, or the prose is impenetrable or the pacing is leaden, but the result is the same. To quote Howard Beale in Paddy Chayefsky's *Network*, "We're in the boredom-killing business." First and foremost, grab and keep your reader's attention. What you do with it once you've got it is the measure of your quality as a writer.

Pacing is a completely different matter from story structure. Story structure remains remarkably consistent in terms of how stories are put together, as we will see later in discussion of three-act structure. Pacing relates to how briskly and efficiently you tell the story, and it can make all the difference in the world.

You've certainly experienced good and bad pacing when you've gone to the movies. A movie such as *Titanic* weighs in at three hours, yet it practically seems to fly by. By contrast, there are movies where you check your watch five times in the course of a mind-numbing eighty-eight minutes. It's easy to say that the plot is inferior or the characters aren't engaging. But it's just as likely that you've got a pacing problem.

PACING ESSENTIALS

Every scene should serve to move along either the plot or the character arc or, ideally, both. Trim scenes down to the information that is essential to be imparted to your audience. For example, there's nothing more boring than showing a character entering or exiting a room. Start sequences with scenes already in progress. You want the readers to pick up speed to keep up with you, not be made to feel that they have to slow to a saunter lest they run past your story.

START SCENES AS CLOSE TO THE ACTION AS POSSIBLE

By action I don't simply mean punching. I mean the point of conflict that propels the scene. For example, a couple going through a divorce meets for lunch, which dissolves into an argument. You could begin the sequence with the two of them arriving at the restaurant. They park their respective cars, turn them off, put the keys in their pockets, go in, check their coats, wait to be seated, get seated, get the menus, order drinks, make chitchat, start talking in general terms and then get into a furious argument, which winds up with

her throwing her drink on him, she storms out, he follows her into the street shouting at her. Sounds riveting, doesn't it? Well, not so much. Instead, start the scene when she's throwing the drink on him. The whys and wherefores of the scene are then handled in one line of dialogue: Her saying, "I don't know why I agreed to meet you in this restaurant; I should have known you'd just throw the same old accusations in my face." She bolts, he follows her, they argue on the street. It's faster, tighter and has heat to it.

CROSSCUT BETWEEN CONCURRENT STORY LINES

Don't give a scene a chance to taper off or become boring. Cut to something else happening elsewhere...one of the advantages to having a supporting cast or writing a team book. It gives you somewhere else to go.

USE PARALLEL PHRASES OR OVERLAP CAPTIONS

When you're changing airplanes on a lengthy trip, it's entirely possible to miss your connection and get left behind. Same thing with scene transitions: If you don't make the connection easy and smooth, you risk leaving your reader behind. There are several tricks you can use to make transitions painless.

* Have the last words of the previous scene be the same words as the next scene so there's a thematic connection. Example: Madrox looking at a dead body at the end of one scene saying, "He's dead. I don't believe it." Next scene, cut to an establishing shot of X-Factor Headquarters (i.e., an exterior shot of a place positioned mainly to give the reader a sense of where the next scene is going to be set) with someone inside saying, "I don't believe it!" followed by cutting to the interior where Siryn is looking angrily at an empty coffee pot and complaining, "I just don't believe it! We're out of coffee again?!"

* Begin a line of dialogue at the end of one scene and end it in the next scene, either to continue a thought or, even more fun, to provide contrast and a change of mood. Example: Madrox facing a grieving widow, saying, "I know we promised to protect him. I don't know what else to say except..." and we cut to the next scene where Guido, watching television, is shouting, "The Yankees suck!"

* Continue a conversation or narration from dialogue at the end of one scene as a caption in the next. Example: Madrox walking down the street with Rahne by his side. Rahne is saying, "It's going to get out that Mr. Smith is dead. But don't worry. No one will blame you for it." Madrox replies, "Oh really? Well..." CUT TO Siryn looking at a newspaper headline that reads "MR. SMITH FOUND DEAD." The caption—which finishes Madrox's dialogue line in quotes so as to distinguish it from narrative—reads, "I sure hope you're right." And Siryn, reading the paper, is shouting, "Madrox blew it! Smith is dead, and I had to find out in the morning news! Plus I still have no coffee!"

* Try to end a scene at the bottom of a page. Scene transitions in the middle of a page can be jarring. Best instead to aim for ending scenes right when the reader is about to turn the page. The ideal means of moving your story along is having a mini cliffhanger at the end of every single page. Nothing hugely dramatic, just some moment, some line of dialogue, some anticipated character reaction to information just revealed that will make the reader feel as if he can't turn the pages fast enough to keep up with what's going on.

A FINAL WORD ON PACING

There are some who complain that the overall pacing of many comic book stories has slowed to a crawl thanks to what's referred to as *decompressed storytelling*. Frequently it's ascribed to laziness on the part of the writers, a desire to produce a story long enough to be collected as a trade paperback or just a blatant attempt to get readers to pick up the next issue.

Personally, I don't think it's any of those. I think it's simply that, more and more, we've become a nation where more emphasis is placed on telling a story visually than orally. As opposed to the Golden and Silver Age of comics where each and every caption was packed with words, modern readers have grown up in a world that prefers images to words. Heck, the advent of Windows over DOS was hailed as making computers accessible to so many more people because everything keyed off pictures, when all we've really managed to do is reinvent Egyptian hieroglyphics.

So it only makes sense that comic books would emulate the sort of storytelling that leans heavily on visuals. And while you may think that one picture is worth a thousand words, it can sometimes take a thousand pictures to do the job that a hundred words would have.

BASIC STORY STRUCTURE

Anyone who's ever taken a creative writing course has, at some point or another, seen a graph similar to the one on this page. The basic concept is simple: A story is a slowly moving roller coaster. It starts up, then down, then up, then down, in a progressively higher series of peaks and valleys until you get to the highest peak. This is theoretically the most exciting part of the story, at which point the story drops off and you finish your tale.

It's right as far as it goes, but it doesn't go very far, and it doesn't go far enough. Over the next pages I'll walk you through some standard concepts for plotting, using a classic story as an illustration, and then show you the chart with which we end up. It's a story structure that is fairly popular in Hollywood and is espoused by a variety of people including, most prominently, screenwriting guru Robert McKee. It is one that many movies and TV shows are built upon. If you become conversant enough with it, you'll find it quite useful and infinitely malleable. You'll also dazzle your friends as you realize you can predict most studio films while watching them. The downside is, do this too much and no one will want to watch movies with you.

Some of you may be more familiar with the "single hump" version of this chart. Events build steadily, peak, then tail off. Which is perfectly fine for, say, a short story or perhaps a single issue of a comic book. But if you're looking at the long form—a novel or movie or six-issue story arc—you're really looking at a series of ups and downs, peaks and valleys, in order to tell your story. This is workable, if simplistic. If you're looking for something more challenging, however, keep reading.

> You've got me? Who's got you?!?

Lois Lane's response to Superman's airborne rescue in SUPERMAN: THE MOVIE

> If thou didst ever thy dear father love, Revenge his foul and most unnatural murder.

HAMLET, Act I, Scene V

> My father is no different than any powerful man, any man with power, like a president or senator.

Michael Corleone describes his dad in THE GODFATHER

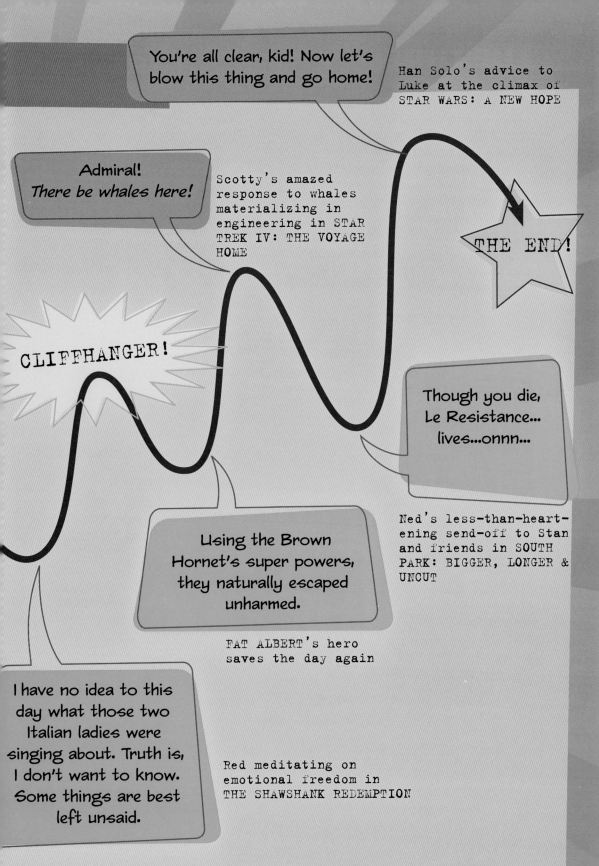

You're all clear, kid! Now let's blow this thing and go home!

Han Solo's advice to Luke at the climax of STAR WARS: A NEW HOPE

Admiral! There be whales here!

Scotty's amazed response to whales materializing in engineering in STAR TREK IV: THE VOYAGE HOME

THE END!

CLIFFHANGER!

Though you die, Le Resistance... lives...onnn...

Ned's less-than-heart-ening send-off to Stan and friends in SOUTH PARK: BIGGER, LONGER & UNCUT

Using the Brown Hornet's super powers, they naturally escaped unharmed.

FAT ALBERT's hero saves the day again

I have no idea to this day what those two Italian ladies were singing about. Truth is, I don't want to know. Some things are best left unsaid.

Red meditating on emotional freedom in THE SHAWSHANK REDEMPTION

Most stories are divided into three parts. These are usually referred to as the first, second and third acts (and for those theatergoers out there, it has nothing to do with first and second act divisions with intermission for going to the bathroom).

The reason I believe the diagram on the previous page is insufficient for a writer's needs is because it doesn't readily apply to the three-act structure. The three-act structure has twists, turns and specific moments in which certain things should be unfolding at certain times. A series of increasingly high peaks and valleys isn't a story; it's a roller coaster. I assure you, there's nothing wrong with roller coasters. And you can even write a story that is something of a roller coaster in and of itself. But that alone doesn't make it a story. The story has to be more than that; it has to have specific twists and turns at specific points in the narrative, all designed to have a particular emotional impact.

THE ESSENTIAL PARTS

I will break down the three-act structure over the next pages. But just to give you a general sense of footing, below are the essential ingredients. Since I brought it up earlier, consider *The Karate Kid*.

* **The first act.** The introduction of the cast of characters.

* **The first-act turning point.** The moment when Mr. Miyagi kicks the crap out of the guys who wanted to beat the snot out of Daniel, because it's at that moment that you fully understand what the film is about: Mr. Miyagi is going to teach Daniel how to defend himself.

* **The second act.** Everything that leads up to the karate tournament and Daniel's fast-approaching final confrontation with the Cobra Kai.

* **The second-act turning point.** When Bobby of the Cobra Kai kicks Daniel in the knee, disabling him. This propels us into...

* **The third act.** Wherein everything comes to a head, and...

* **The climax.** In which Daniel uses the crane kick to take down Johnny. (Which is strange since it was a kick to the face and should have been illegal, just as Johnny's punch to Daniel's face moments before was. But never mind.)

IT'S NOT A NEW IDEA

It's not as if someone recently invented the three-act structure and all new stories are adhering to it. Rather, the fundamental concept has existed for decades and is simply a sound way of telling a story. Aristotle said that dramas consisted of three parts: a beginning, a middle and an end. That may seem self-evident, but remember, the Greeks invented drama, and what we take for granted now was groundbreaking a couple thousand years ago.

For instance, the first time a Greek dramatist, Aeschylus, introduced the concept of two actors on the stage talking to each other—as opposed to one actor interacting with a chorus—that was a huge deal. Until that point, a drama consisted of one guy on stage talking to the audience. How in the name of the gods could anyone top such an innovation?

Hang on: Sophocles introduced the concept of three characters to the mix. This dramatic one-upsmanship kept on until the era of Cecil B. DeMille and his casts of thousands, at which point it kind of leveled off.

In recent years, Aristotle's simple observation of beginning, middle and end has been codified, institutionalized, some might say mummified. You will frequently find that editors, producers, etc., will be analyzing your story based on whether they see the beats of the three-act structure present. So it will be helpful to know what they're looking for so you can be sure to accommodate them.

I should emphasize that this is a *structure*, not a *formula*. A *formula* results in a sameness that makes everything seem overly familiar and predictable. But films ranging from *Air Force One* to *Casablanca* all hinge on three-act structure, and no one can say those films—or the vast array between them—are all the same.

The pages to follow present you with a simple demonstration of the three-act structure in action. In this case, we'll examine *Fantastic Four* #51 by Stan Lee and Jack Kirby. Although I doubt writer Stan Lee was deliberately following the three-act structure, the story is a stellar example of the technique.

HAPPY ENDINGS: THE GREAT CURE-ALL

It is said, correctly, that real life makes lousy fiction. You can have a chance encounter with someone in the street that you haven't seen in years, and it can lead to a whole new chapter in your life. But in fiction, that chance encounter will seem manufactured and lame. So just what will readers forgive when it comes to telling your story?

In my experience, you'd be amazed how much slack fans will cut you if the result is a happy ending. The simplest litmus test is you yourself. Ask yourself how much YOU would be willing to accept for the sake of your payoff.

This was driven home to me when I wrote the conclusion of *The Incredible Hulk #372*, which is easily the shakiest, most unlikely ending I've ever written. Here's the setup: Bruce Banner has managed to track down wife Betty to a convent where she has taken refuge. But Bruce arrives right after Betty has headed off for a train station to parts unknown. He now has mere minutes to catch up with her and get to a train station. So what happens? Naturally an opponent gets in his way, just enough to slow him down.

We cut to Betty with the vague feeling that perhaps she shouldn't go, that she's overlooking something...but then she gets on the train. The train rolls off just as Bruce gets there (the Hulk having fought off the opponent). Bruce chases on foot down the track and then sinks to his knees, sobbing and in despair (not angry, because anger triggers the Hulk). Convinced that he's lost Betty again, this time forever, we go to a series of higher and higher shots, a "pull-back," which audiences are trained to know means that a scene is ending. The reader, sharing Bruce's agony, is now praying right along with the frustrated Bruce.

Turn to the next page, and we're suddenly back in close-up as Bruce reacts with shock to Betty's voice. Angle around and there she is, standing on the train track, her suitcase by her side. She's telling him that something made her get off the train. They run toward each other, leap into each other's arms and kiss passionately. The end.

It's preposterous.

I'm asking the reader to believe that Betty not only "sensed" that Bruce was near but that she stopped the train (presumably by pulling the emergency brake), grabbed her suitcase, forced her way off the train, climbed down onto the tracks (since the train was gone from the platform) and then hotfooted it, complete with her bags, down the tracks on the off chance that Bruce might be standing there.

Fan response? Uniformly positive. "I was so relieved! Betty and Bruce are together again! Thank you, Marvel!" No one, not a single person, complained that it was—to put it mildly—unlikely.

Give your audience a strong beginning and they'll follow you anywhere. Give them a kick-butt or satisfying ending and they'll go home happy. So just don't mess up the middle and you're golden.

FIRST ACT

The first act is info-dump time. You present the audience with the basic setup. You introduce the characters, you provide as much data as they will require in order to understand the particular situation they're expected to become involved with. Generally you try to be subtle about it...although, for my money, the best use of first act was in *The Great Muppet Caper*, wherein Lady Holiday is going on at length about her relationship with her family. The recipient of this apparently pointless recitation is a bewildered Miss Piggy, who asks, "Why are you telling me all this?" It's a question that's often posed in such fictional situations, and there's usually some self-conscious rationalization presented for it. But in this instance, Holiday simply fixes her a look and says matter-of-factly, "It's exposition. It has to go somewhere."

A truism by which comic writers and editors abide is that every comic is someone's first issue. Going on the assumption, Stan Lee deftly provides the novice reader all the information he requires in the first act of this issue. All of the major protagonists are introduced in the first few pages.

INTRODUCE THE HERO

We meet Ben Grimm, the tragic hero—or, even more accurately, victim—of our piece. There's no better way to quickly and visually show that someone is completely bummed out than to depict him as just standing out in the rain all alone. So we know where Ben's head is at.

INTRODUCE OTHER PERTINENT CHARACTERS

In short order, two more characters are introduced. First is the unnamed individual who offers Ben a place to get in out of the rain. And the second is Reed Richards. Although Reed does not visually appear in this sequence, his name is mentioned repeatedly. We don't have to see Reed to know, thanks to the first-act exposition, that he is brilliant...a scientist...Ben's friend...and the object of much frustration for the nameless guy.

WHO YOU CAN LEAVE OUT

We haven't met Sue or Johnny or even Wyatt Wingfoot yet, but that's okay. Sue is basically a bystander in this story, and Johnny and Wyatt don't intersect with the main plot at all. So they can be introduced a bit later and not present confusion.

USE THE SETTING

This sequence is a sound reminder that you should utilize the environment whenever possible. The visual surroundings can have a tremendous effect on your presentation. If the Thing were presented standing around on the street in broad daylight, there's no sense of mood. He might just as well be waiting for a bus to a baseball game. If he's there at night with a streetlight shining down on him, he might be on his way home from a bar, or perhaps about to launch into a stirring rendition of "One for My Baby." But no: He's standing there alone in the rain. There's no other way to read it, even without the captions: The guy's depressed.

So always keep a clear focus of when and where your story is taking place. If you just say, "day," that's neutral. It can be a scalding day and everyone's sweating (well, not the Thing, but...). It can be a freezing day and everyone's bundled up with mist coming out of their mouths. A rainy day, a snowy day. Buildings could be filthy and you can have someone lean against one and come away with dirt on his hands or clothes. Particularly in the beginning of your story, establish a genuine sense of place. Remember, comics is a silent medium, and you don't have sound effects, actors or music to add depth to the visuals. So add as much sense of "reality" as possible.

The first act is the time to set up your
story and the characters involved.

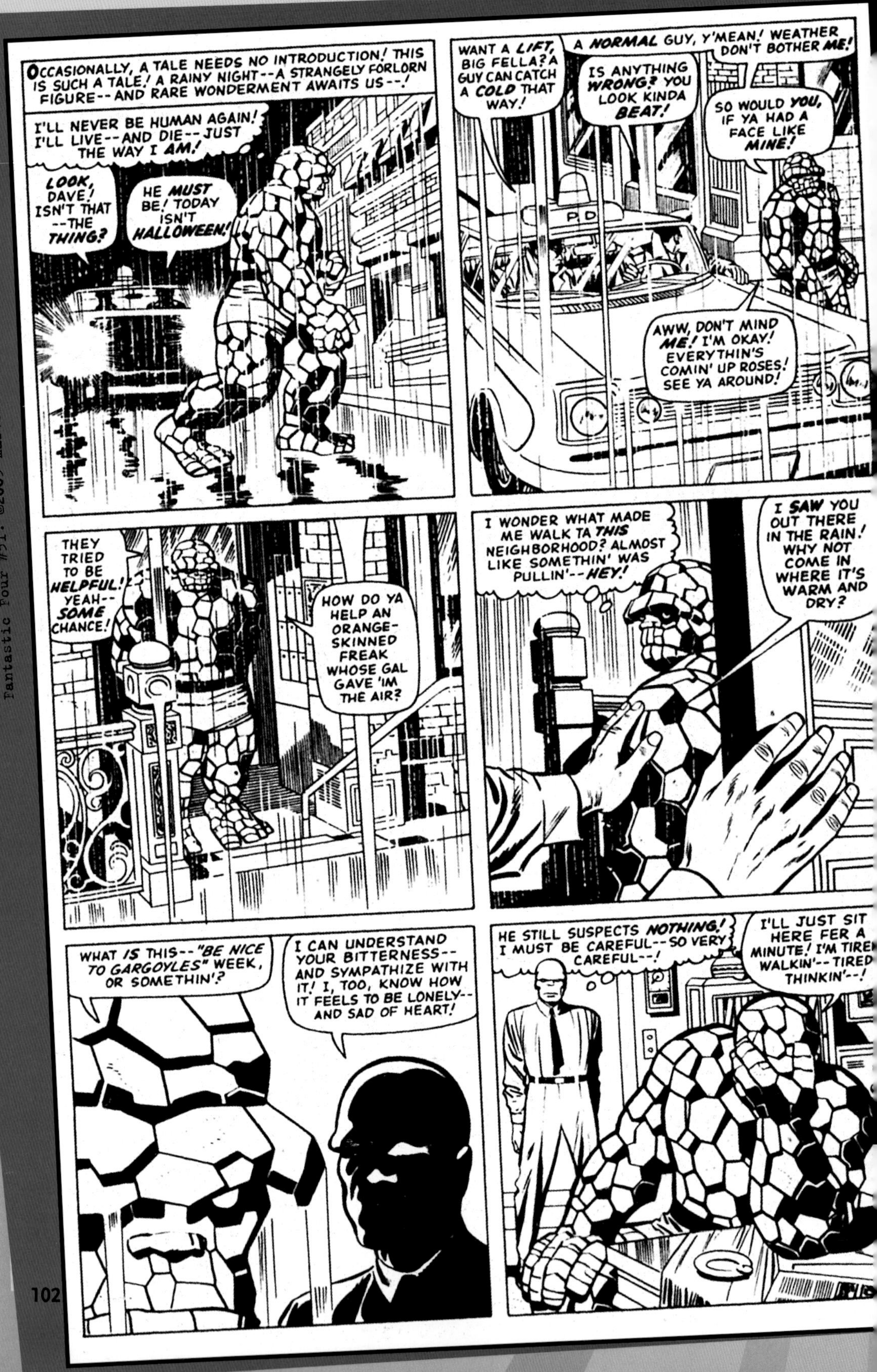
OCCASIONALLY, A TALE NEEDS NO INTRODUCTION! THIS IS SUCH A TALE! A RAINY NIGHT--A STRANGELY FORLORN FIGURE--AND RARE WONDERMENT AWAITS US--!
I'LL NEVER BE HUMAN AGAIN! I'LL LIVE--AND DIE--JUST THE WAY I AM!
LOOK, DAVE! ISN'T THAT --THE THING?
HE MUST BE! TODAY ISN'T HALLOWEEN!
WANT A LIFT, BIG FELLA? A GUY CAN CATCH A COLD THAT WAY!
A NORMAL GUY, Y'MEAN! WEATHER DON'T BOTHER ME!
IS ANYTHING WRONG? YOU LOOK KINDA BEAT!
SO WOULD YOU, IF YA HAD A FACE LIKE MINE!
AWW, DON'T MIND ME! I'M OKAY! EVERYTHIN'S COMIN' UP ROSES! SEE YA AROUND!
THEY TRIED TO BE HELPFUL! YEAH--SOME CHANCE!
HOW DO YA HELP AN ORANGE-SKINNED FREAK WHOSE GAL GAVE 'IM THE AIR?
I WONDER WHAT MADE ME WALK TA THIS NEIGHBORHOOD? ALMOST LIKE SOMETHIN' WAS PULLIN'--HEY!
I SAW YOU OUT THERE IN THE RAIN! WHY NOT COME IN WHERE IT'S WARM AND DRY?
WHAT IS THIS--"BE NICE TO GARGOYLES" WEEK, OR SOMETHIN'?
I CAN UNDERSTAND YOUR BITTERNESS--AND SYMPATHIZE WITH IT! I, TOO, KNOW HOW IT FEELS TO BE LONELY--AND SAD OF HEART!
HE STILL SUSPECTS NOTHING! I MUST BE CAREFUL--SO VERY CAREFUL--!
I'LL JUST SIT HERE FER A MINUTE! I'M TIRED WALKIN'--TIRED THINKIN'--!

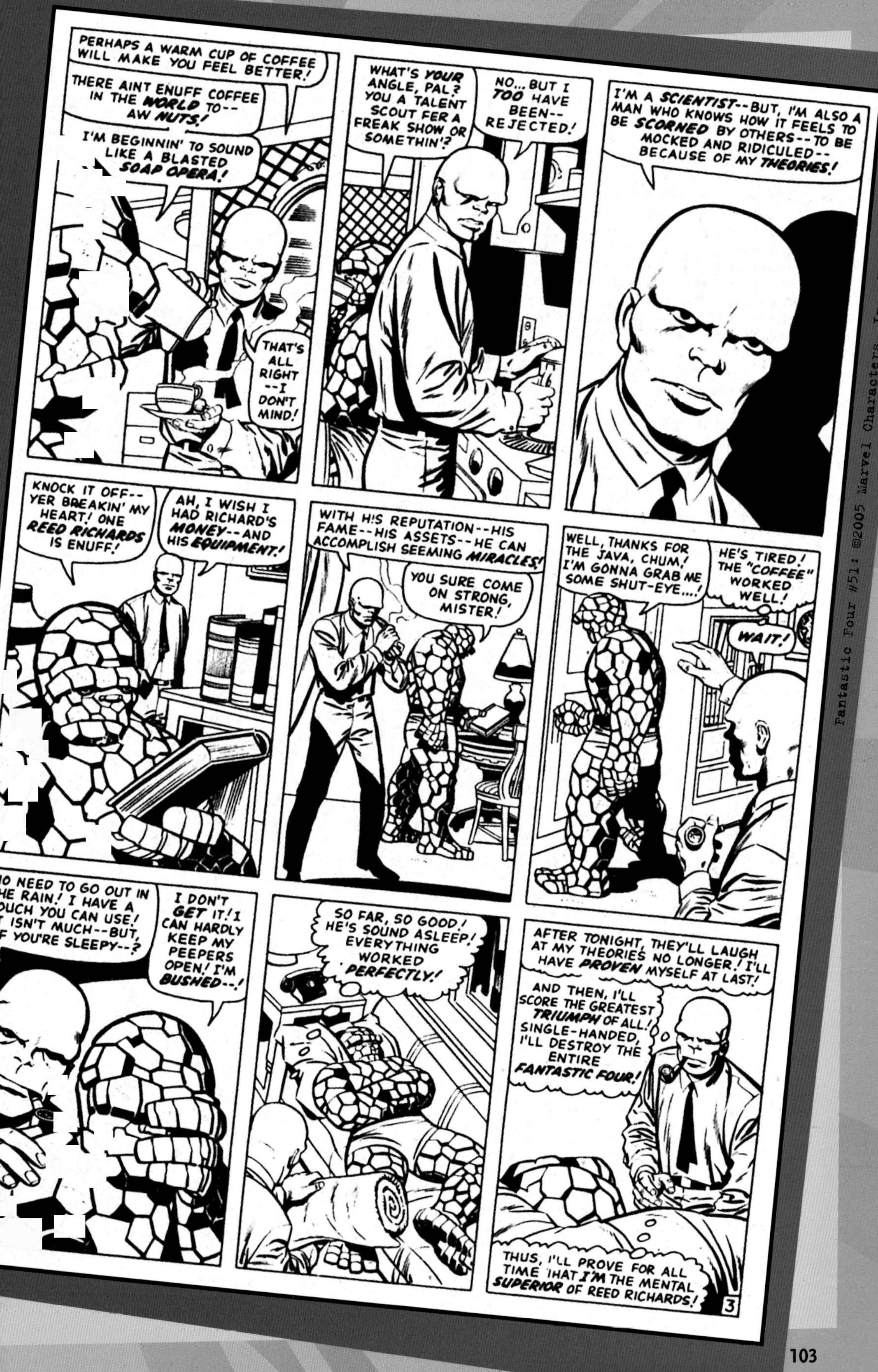
PERHAPS A WARM CUP OF COFFEE WILL MAKE YOU FEEL BETTER!
THERE AINT ENUFF COFFEE IN THE WORLD TO-- AW NUTS!
I'M BEGINNIN' TO SOUND LIKE A BLASTED SOAP OPERA!
THAT'S ALL RIGHT --I DON'T MIND!
WHAT'S YOUR ANGLE, PAL? YOU A TALENT SCOUT FER A FREAK SHOW OR SOMETHIN'?
NO... BUT I TOO HAVE BEEN-- REJECTED!
I'M A SCIENTIST--BUT, I'M ALSO A MAN WHO KNOWS HOW IT FEELS TO BE SCORNED BY OTHERS--TO BE MOCKED AND RIDICULED-- BECAUSE OF MY THEORIES!
KNOCK IT OFF-- YER BREAKIN' MY HEART! ONE REED RICHARDS IS ENUFF!
AH, I WISH I HAD RICHARD'S MONEY--AND HIS EQUIPMENT!
WITH HIS REPUTATION--HIS FAME--HIS ASSETS--HE CAN ACCOMPLISH SEEMING MIRACLES!
YOU SURE COME ON STRONG, MISTER!
WELL, THANKS FOR THE JAVA, CHUM! I'M GONNA GRAB ME SOME SHUT-EYE...!
HE'S TIRED! THE "COFFEE" WORKED WELL!
WAIT!
IO NEED TO GO OUT IN HE RAIN! I HAVE A OUCH YOU CAN USE! T ISN'T MUCH--BUT, F YOU'RE SLEEPY--?
I DON'T GET IT! I CAN HARDLY KEEP MY PEEPERS OPEN! I'M BUSHED--!
SO FAR, SO GOOD! HE'S SOUND ASLEEP! EVERYTHING WORKED PERFECTLY!
AFTER TONIGHT, THEY'LL LAUGH AT MY THEORIES NO LONGER! I'LL HAVE PROVEN MYSELF AT LAST!
AND THEN, I'LL SCORE THE GREATEST TRIUMPH OF ALL! SINGLE-HANDED, I'LL DESTROY THE ENTIRE FANTASTIC FOUR!
THUS, I'LL PROVE FOR ALL TIME THAT I'M THE MENTAL SUPERIOR OF REED RICHARDS!
3

FIRST-ACT TURNING POINT

Once the audience has its footing, you then present the first-act turning point. A catalyst occurs that sets your story into motion. It could be any number of things.

* A body is discovered.

* A man overhears something he wasn't supposed to overhear.

* A woman tells her husband the marriage is over.

* Government men show up and tell the hero his help is required to save the world.

Now your audience knows where you're going. Ideally, you don't tip your hand. You don't want to show them all your cards...just enough to lure them in. We now have a basic idea of who our characters are. The first-act turning point comes as our heroine learns who her client is and what her needs are. This is the information that will set the story into motion and send us into the second act.

THE CATALYST

Let's take a look at the first-act turning point of this story. The nameless guy who has taken pity on Ben seems decent enough, albeit a bit obsessed with Reed, so we're left wondering where Stan is going with this...

Holy crap, kids! Check out this action! In a shocking turn of events, the nameless guy—whom we will henceforth refer to, for the purpose of this story, as the Changeling—has used a high-falutin' machine to trade off physical appearance with the Thing! At first glance, it appears the Changeling really does have a legitimate gripe. Without breaking anything resembling serious sweat, the Changeling has managed to accomplish in four panels what Mr. Fantastic has been unable to achieve in four years: permanently transforming the Thing back into Ben Grimm. Yet he's living in a crummy apartment while Reed is a hotshot residing in the top ten floors of the Baxter Building.

WHAT THE STORY IS ABOUT

Now, though, his plan is clear. He's no longer just going to sit around and be jealous. Instead he's going to head to the Baxter Building, impersonate the Thing and put himself in a position where he can vent his by-now-homicidal jealousy and dispose of Reed Richards once and for all.

So, now we know what the story is going to be about, and we are propelled into the second act.

The first-act turning point is when you reveal the catalyst that gets your story moving.

I'VE SPENT A *LIFETIME* CREATING MY *DUPLICATION APPARATUS!*

AND, IT'S TAKEN LONG MONTHS OF PATIENT PLANNING TO LURE THE *THING* INTO THIS ROOM, BY USING MY SHORT-RANGE SUBLIMINAL INFLUENCER!

BUT NOW, ALL THE LABOR, ALL THE WAITING, ALL THE SCHEMING, WILL PAY OFF AT *LAST!* I'M *THRU* BEING A *LOSER*-- *THIS* TIME I'VE GOT THE *WINNING HAND!*

AS FOR THE *THING*--- THERE'S *NO WAY* HE CAN EVER *STOP* ME!

WAS THE ERFECT ICE FOR MY PERIMENT, CAUSE OF R SLIGHT KELETAL EMBLANCE...

THAT FACT WILL MAKE THE *DUPLICATION PROCESS* ALL THE MORE EFFECTIVE!

AND NOW--LET IT *BEGIN!*

WORKING--AS I IT WOULD! I CAN E IT-- I CAN *FEEL* IT--!

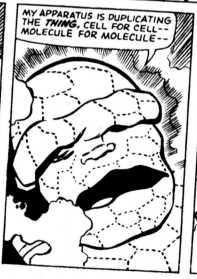

MY APPARATUS IS DUPLICATING THE *THING*, CELL FOR CELL-- MOLECULE FOR MOLECULE--

IT'S *OVER!* I'M AN EXACT *REPLICA* OF HIM!

NOW, ALL HIS *FAME*--AND HIS *POWER*--ARE *MINE!*

4

The first-act turning point propels you into the second act. The second act is where the majority of the story will be told. Knowing that your hero is at point Alpha to start out, the second act should drive him, slowly but inevitably, toward point Omega. Ideally you will present the audience with enough twists and turns to keep their attention engaged. Even more ideally, the journey becomes increasingly grueling.

WITHIN AND WITHOUT

Although many obstacles can be presented in your hero's journey, they basically boil down to two types: from within and from without. Look at Frodo: He faces both. Not only does he have to contend with Orcs, Cave Trolls, Nazgûl, and everyone and their brother (literally) trying to get the ring, but the ring works its way into his mind and soul, sending him spiraling toward inner darkness, despair, temptation and damnation. It's that multileveled challenge that elevates a story from the merely ordinary to a classic that speaks to generations.

THE MAIN PART OF THE STORY

So...the second act of this issue of *Fantastic Four*. Our story unfolds as the Changeling is accepted as the real item without question. So convincing is the duplication, in fact, that

when the genuine Ben shows up to try to alert Reed and Sue to the danger, they don't believe it's really him. Which, let's face it, is a bit curious. Perhaps Reed's ego is so monumental (as noted earlier, he does call himself "Mr. Fantastic," after all) that it literally never occurs to him that someone other than he might have found a way to change Ben back to human form.

Fantastic Four #51; ©2005 Marvel Characters, Inc.
Used with permission.

In any event, the story unfolds apace as Reed reveals to the Changeling his new endeavor: He's going to explore the mysteries of an alternate dimension called Sub-Space. (Curiously enough, some issues earlier, a race called the Inhumans sealed themselves off from humanity through the creation of a barrier called the Negative Zone. In issues after #51, Reed would revisit Sub-Space, except for no discernible reason Stan Lee started referring to it also as the Negative Zone...presumably because he got the two confused. Eventually the Inhumans barrier was destroyed, leaving Sub-Space with sole title to the name.)

Anyway, Reed explains to the Changeling that he requires the Thing to anchor him by holding onto a tether line...because apparently Reed can invent a gateway to another dimension, but he can't whip up a winch. But that gap in Reed's ingenuity plays right into the rocky hands of the Changeling. All he has to do is let go at the right time, and Reed goes floating away into Sub-Space, never to be seen again.

ANOTHER CHARACTER ARC

Now something interesting is occurring: The Changeling, it turns out, has his very own character arc. Beginning with a deep-seated hatred for Reed, he slowly starts to develop genuine respect and admiration for the leader of the Fantastic Four. So much so that he's wavering on his plan to dispose of Reed, and mulling it over. We have a brief cutaway to a "B" plot (not shown here) involving a coach who wants Johnny's pal, Wyatt Wingfoot, to play college football.

And then the time for mulling is over, because it's time for the second-act turning point.

The majority of your story should happen in the second act.

Finally you arrive at the second-act turning point, which should ideally then drive you into the third act. At the second-act turning point, you have to take all the story development, all the threads you've presented thus far, and then have something happen—set some sort of ticking clock into motion—that does two things:

1 Sends your story off in an unexpected, yet logical direction.

2 Provides a sense of immediacy for the solution. A state of affairs has been reached wherein the hero is running out of time. He's been presented with a major kick in the teeth, but he has to overcome it because the problem has to be solved now. It could be that an actual bomb has been found and is ticking down. It could be the Wicked Witch turning over the hourglass while sneering, "This is how long you have to live!" Whatever.

This is the most problematic aspect of fiction writing. Why? Because life is messy. Life is ongoing. Life is unfinished. If the first rule of writing is "Write what you know," you know that life doesn't tend to have third acts. Which means that a second-act turning point followed by a dramatic third act is intrinsically unrealistic, but necessary, because otherwise you can't end your story or provide your audience with a sense of closure.

In this particular instance, Stan's second-act turning point is a doozy. It is unveiled in two "beats," or two separate moments that combine to present us with the turning point.

The second-act turning point should create a defining crisis that propels the story toward the climax.

* The first beat is Reed's discovery that he's drifting toward the explosive center of Sub-Space. The ticking clock has been put into motion: Reed now has to get the heck out of Dodge pronto before he winds up as random floating bits of matter.

* The second beat of the second-act turning point is the snapping of the tether. Not only is the clock ticking, it's ticking down faster, because Reed's lifeline has literally broken. There's no more time for the Changeling to muse on the situation. If the Changeling doesn't act instantly—instantly—Reed's a goner.

We are now propelled directly into the third act and climax.

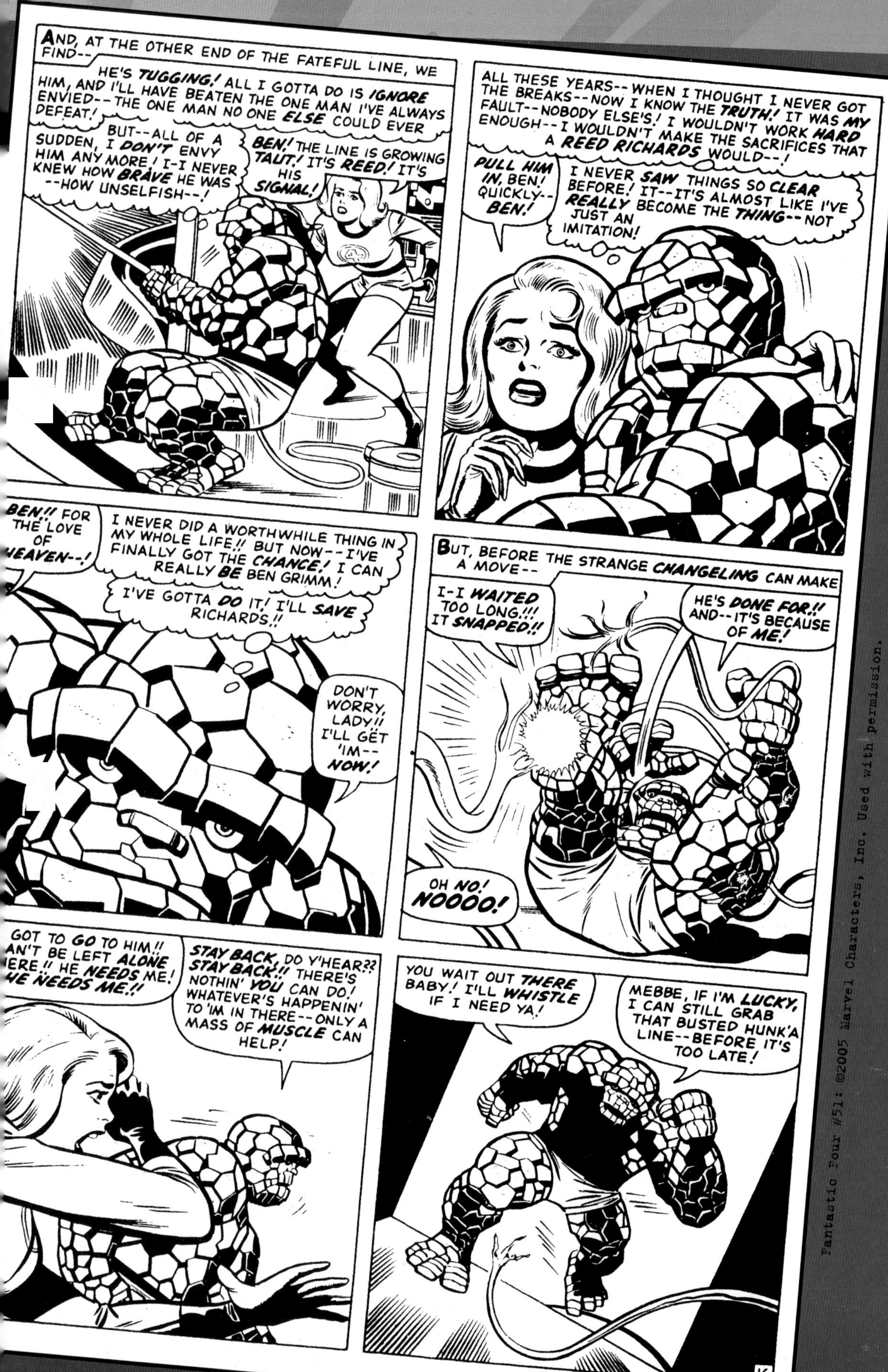
AND, AT THE OTHER END OF THE FATEFUL LINE, WE FIND--
HE'S TUGGING! ALL I GOTTA DO IS IGNORE HIM, AND I'LL HAVE BEATEN THE ONE MAN I'VE ALWAYS ENVIED-- THE ONE MAN NO ONE ELSE COULD EVER DEFEAT!
BUT--ALL OF A SUDDEN, I DON'T ENVY HIM ANY MORE! I-I NEVER KNEW HOW BRAVE HE WAS --HOW UNSELFISH--!
BEN! THE LINE IS GROWING TAUT! IT'S REED! IT'S HIS SIGNAL!
ALL THESE YEARS-- WHEN I THOUGHT I NEVER GOT THE BREAKS--NOW I KNOW THE TRUTH! IT WAS MY FAULT--NOBODY ELSE'S! I WOULDN'T WORK HARD ENOUGH--I WOULDN'T MAKE THE SACRIFICES THAT A REED RICHARDS WOULD--!
PULL HIM IN, BEN! QUICKLY-- BEN!
I NEVER SAW THINGS SO CLEAR BEFORE! IT--IT'S ALMOST LIKE I'VE REALLY BECOME THE THING--NOT JUST AN IMITATION!
BEN!! FOR THE LOVE OF HEAVEN--!
I NEVER DID A WORTHWHILE THING IN MY WHOLE LIFE!! BUT NOW--I'VE FINALLY GOT THE CHANCE! I CAN REALLY BE BEN GRIMM!
I'VE GOTTA DO IT! I'LL SAVE RICHARDS!!
DON'T WORRY, LADY!! I'LL GET 'IM-- NOW!
BUT, BEFORE THE STRANGE CHANGELING CAN MAKE A MOVE--
I-I WAITED TOO LONG!!! IT SNAPPED!!
HE'S DONE FOR!! AND--IT'S BECAUSE OF ME!
OH NO! NOOOO!
GOT TO GO TO HIM!! CAN'T BE LEFT ALONE HERE!! HE NEEDS ME! HE NEEDS ME!!
STAY BACK, DO Y'HEAR?? STAY BACK!! THERE'S NOTHIN' YOU CAN DO! WHATEVER'S HAPPENIN' TO 'IM IN THERE--ONLY A MASS OF MUSCLE CAN HELP!
YOU WAIT OUT THERE BABY! I'LL WHISTLE IF I NEED YA!
MEBBE, IF I'M LUCKY, I CAN STILL GRAB THAT BUSTED HUNK'A LINE--BEFORE IT'S TOO LATE!
16

THIRD ACT, CLIMAX AND ANTICLIMAX

In your third act, you build your story to a climax, have the payoff...and then, ideally, get off the stage as fast as possible. Why? Because anything that happens after the climax is by definition an anticlimax.

The third act contains the final beats of your story. Every element should now come smoothly together, driving you hard and fast to the story's climax—the emotional high point. This is the moment in *The Karate Kid* when Daniel wins the tournament, when Sarah Connor (with the aid of a curse word we can't say here) informs the Terminator that he himself is terminated, when Rick insists that Ilsa gets on the plane and then faces off against Major Strasser in *Casablanca*. It is where all your story elements, your character arcs, are resolved in one stroke of brilliance.

THE THIRD ACT PROPELS YOU TO THE CLIMAX

In the case of this issue of *Fantastic Four*, the Changeling's character arc and the salvation of Reed Richards are the climax of the issue and come together in one amazing two-panel sequence. The Changeling, no longer caring about himself, picks up Reed and chucks him in the opposite direction. Having done a complete one-eighty from his original mindset, the Changeling has willingly sacrificed his own life in order to save the man he started out despising.

THE BIG WRAP-UP

Everything from this point on is the anticlimax. It's the wrap-up. Stan and Jack, professionals that they are, dispose of it as quickly and briskly as possible. Ben transforms back into the Thing and turns up for a showdown with his impostor that will never occur. In a sort of epilogue, Reed muses on the Changeling's actions and the worthy way in which he died.

End of story. Fade out.

The crisis-point of your story should resolve with the climax.

THEN, SUDDENLY--

MEBBE WE **DON'T** HAVETA **BOTH** DIE, MISTER!

BEN! WHAT ARE YOU **DOING**--?

THE ONE **WORTHWHILE** THING I EVER DID IN MY WHOLE, WASTED LIFE.!!

EVEN THE STRENGTH WHICH I NOW **POSSESS,** I STOLE FROM **ANOTHER!**

BUT, MAYBE I CAN **USE** THAT STRENGTH-- TO EVEN THE SCORE-- SOMEHOW!

I TOSSED HIM **BACK** IN EXACTLY THE SAME DIRECTION I **CAME** FROM! HE'S OUTTA SIGHT NOW-- SO, I'LL NEVER KNOW--!

SO LONG, RICHARDS! I HOPE YOU **MAKE** IT!

AS FOR **ME,** I'M NOT GONNA FEEL SORRY FOR MYSELF! NOT **MANY** MEN GET A SECOND CHANCE-- TO MAKE UP FOR THE ROTTEN THINGS THEY'VE DONE IN THEIR LIFETIME!

I GUESS I'M **LUCKIER** THAN MOST--! I **GOT** THAT CHANCE!

FOR, I FINALLY LEARNED--WHAT IT MEANS TO HAVE-- A **FRIEND!**

AND, AT THAT MOMENT, IN ANOTHER SECTION OF OUR VAST, UNFATHOMABLE UNIVERSE--UNAWARE OF THE DIRE DANGER CONFRONTING REED RICHARDS, THE **REAL** BEN GRIMM PREPARES TO PAY A CALL--

MY ONLY HOPE IS THAT ALICIA WILL BE ABLE TO TELL WHO I AM!

BEING BLIND, SHE'S MORE SENSITIVE TO A PERSON'S TRUE SELF THAN ANYONE WITH **SIGHT** COULD BE!

EVEN THOUGH SHE CAN'T **SEE**-- I'M **STILL** KINDA NERVOUS-- TO BE FACING HER LIKE A NORMAL MAN!

IT'S WHAT I ALWAYS **WANTED** --ALWAYS **DREAMED** OF! IF ONLY IT HAD HAPPENED SOME OTHER WAY!

I **CAN'T** LET THAT **PHONY** TAKE MY PLACE IN THE F.F.! THERE'S NO TELLIN' **WHAT'LL** HAPPEN IF HE **DOES!**

ALICIA MA

18

THE REAL ARC

The three-act structure doesn't have to be limited to a single issue of a comic. I've developed story arcs that cover years' worth of issues that hinge on the three-act structure. Furthermore, you can do main story arcs and develop separate story arcs that have their own first-, second- and third-act structures that intersect with the main arc at key

MULTIPLE PLOT WARNING

Keep in mind that the more ambitious you get, the more important it is not to lose track of where you are. A story can be like a charging horse, and if you let it get away from you, you can wind up on your back with no story and a major headache.

points. In instances such as this, the main story arc is referred to as the "A" plot, the secondary as the "B" plot and however many additional layers you care to add as the "C," "D" and so on.

Remember that chart we began with? The one that was the slow roller coaster ride?

The chart on this page is, by me, a bit more accurate. Stories shouldn't simply ebb and flow. They should zigzag, go off in unexpected directions, twist and turn back on themselves. This flow chart incorporates the three-act scenario while at the same time suggests just how unexpected the paths of a story can be.

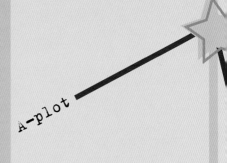

ACT 1

Act
turnaro

A-plot

B-plot

> "Stories shouldn't simply **EBB AND FLOW.** They should **zigzag,** go off in **unexpected directions, twist and turn** back on themselves."

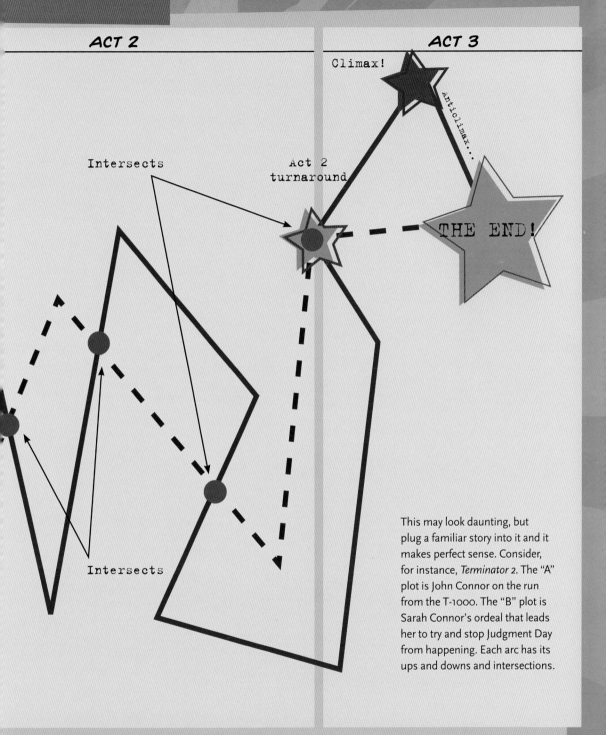

ACT 2

ACT 3

Climax!

anticlimax....

Intersects

Act 2
turnaround

THE END!

Intersects

This may look daunting, but plug a familiar story into it and it makes perfect sense. Consider, for instance, *Terminator 2*. The "A" plot is John Connor on the run from the T-1000. The "B" plot is Sarah Connor's ordeal that leads her to try and stop Judgment Day from happening. Each arc has its ups and downs and intersections.

CONTINUITY, RETCONS AND STETCONS

The following is obviously more of a consideration for those of you who not only wind up having a regular gig, but are doing so within someone else's comic book universe (Marvel, for instance). Still, we here at Impact University want to take the long-term and positive approach, so we might as well address matters that you'll be facing in your upcoming insanely successful writing career! Besides, this is a topic you'll see discussed endlessly—indeed, *ad nauseam*—on any number of computer boards or panels at conventions. So this is as good a time as any to discuss the pros and cons of continuity.

Continuity, quite simply, is that which has gone before. The events, both major and minor, in the history of your hero and your supporting cast. These events inform how your character reacts to the new situations that are presented to him. They are his learning curve, the things he has absorbed that will enable him to handle whatever it is you're tossing him with your story.

For instance, if your hero is facing a villain who, in previous stories, has proven that he laughs off bullets, your hero is going to look like three kinds of an idiot if he stands there and tries to empty a revolver into him. Curiously, villains never seemed to tire of trying to put a cap in Superman as Superman would just stand there with arms akimbo, looking smug...although it's been noted by fans and comedians that George Reeves, in the old TV series, would always duck out of the way when the villains then threw the emptied guns at him. Indeed, in one issue of *Supergirl*, I had the maid of steel withstand a barrage of bullets, and then collapse when the bad guy bounced the empty gun off her skull. Then she got up, grinned and said, "Kidding."

CONTINUITY AND SUSPENSION OF DISBELIEF

If a character has a genuine history, refers to it, acknowledges it and "learns" from past mistakes or altercations, it all goes toward helping convince the reader that the characters are real. For a writer, that's absolutely vital. Moreover, if the character does not learn from previous encounters, that can cripple suspension of disbelief. And trust me, you'll hear about it from the fans. "Why was it that Captain Cunning was totally surprised when the Green Evil shot him with a stun ray? Why didn't he remember that the Green Evil used a stun ray on him in issue #153 nine years ago?"

CONTINUITY STORIES

You can even make entire stories out of a continuity point. This should be done with caution, however. You only want to do this if you feel there's a real need for it, especially since such stories can wind up as genuine flashpoints. So you want to be sure you're willing to deal with the potential fallout/aggravation.

To my mind, these types of stories fall into two different categories; The Retcon and the Stetcon. A Retcon is short for "retroactive continuity." You've heard of "Defcon 1" and so on, depending on severity of the threat? Same thing.

RETCON 1

Retcon 1 takes disparate story elements and ties them together in such a way that it gives the impression the conflict was not a mistake but was, in fact, intentional.

The absolute master of Retcon 1 is Roy Thomas. Roy could take a story element from the Silver Age of comics that was at odds with some aspect of a Golden Age story that no one except Roy remembered and turn it into a three-part mini-epic. In today's editorial climate where the emphasis is on trying to make each issue as humanly accessible as possible, editors are slow to embrace stories that demand intimate knowledge of story points from two generations ago. Still, for those types of tales, no one can top the eternally boyish Roy.

A Retcon I instituted wound up addressing snarled continuity in *The Incredible Hulk* while I was writing *Captain Marvel*. At the time, Hulk writer Bruce Jones was writing versions of such characters as the Absorbing Man that didn't remotely match up with the AM's history, not to mention even recent stories about him. His take on the characters was interesting, but the fact that nothing was jibing was making fans nuts. Meanwhile, I was doing a story line in *Captain Marvel* that involved Marv not only going insane, but essentially destroying and then re-creating the entire universe in association with a being known as Entropy. So, in the course of the story line, I revealed that Marv hadn't quite gotten the job right and had created small pockets of "discontinuity" where contradictory versions of characters co-existed side by side. The notion was that eventually, as the new universe settled in, those pockets of discontinuity would go away. Believe it or not, this pleased fans because it served as a stopgap "in-universe" explanation, rather than something as mundane as that the Hulk team was ignoring past stories.

RETCON 2

Retcon 2 inserts some sort of modern spin to something that's gone before so what's already established now has a totally different subtext.

A perfect example of Retcon 2 was John Byrne's take on Lockjaw. In an issue of Byrne's short-lived Thing solo book, Byrne offered fans a startling revelation about Lockjaw, the massive dog who serves as the Inhuman's pet. The revelation was that Lockjaw was in fact, like the Elephant Man, not an animal but a grotesquely deformed Inhuman. This revelation made for a powerful story since the character of Quicksilver was about to

roll the dice on his daughter's future by exposing her to mists that would give her powers, and Lockjaw's dismal state served as a cautionary tale that brought Quicksilver up short. Why hadn't Lockjaw said a word in the past thirty-some years? Like Toto, who it turned out was perfectly capable of speech while in Oz, he just hadn't had all that much to say.

RETCON 3

Retcon 3 flat-out changes what's gone before and says that this is now the new continuity.

The most legendary and ambitious example of Retcon 3 would be Marv Wolfman and George Pérez's *Crisis on Infinite Earths. Crisis* was itself a response to one of the oldest Retcons in comics history: The Golden Age characters that the Silver Age Flash read about in comic books were not comic book characters but actually still active in a parallel world called Earth-2, while "our" Earth, where the modern Flash was, was actually Earth-1. In the intervening decades since the Earth-1 and -2 notion was introduced, the entire concept had become hopelessly snarled, ranging from revelations that "our" Earth was actually Earth-Prime, to a highly publicized story in which Superman married Lois Lane. This actually got some serious press coverage...except reporters and "outsiders" were left scratching their heads at the final page revelation that it wasn't "our" Superman that had gotten married but instead the Superman of Earth-2 (and considering we're Earth-Prime, "we" don't really have a Superman at all when you get right down to it).

With DC continuity hopelessly ensnared in bewildering continuity that gave potential new readers intestinal cramps every time they tried to parse it, *Crisis on Infinite Earths* was a twelve-issue megaseries designed to simplify and streamline the entirety of the DC Universe by collapsing everything down to one world instead of a confusing multiverse and essentially reboot the origins of all the major players who were left. Nowhere was this more conspicuous than in the Superman line, where Superman's origin was overhauled. Gone was the lush green Krypton of some forty years' standing, replaced by an icy, dispassionate world clearly influenced by the Superman motion picture. To my mind, this was no improvement. The tragedy of Krypton's destruction was that it was a flourishing, sylvan world cut short in its prime. The dispassionate, detached Krypton of the Retcon was so unappealing, you didn't give a damn when it blew up. More of an improvement, however, was Ma and Pa Kent still being alive at the time of Superman as an adult, serving as a useful grounding element for the bigger-than-life super-hero (a change maintained in TV's Lois & Clark).

STETCONS

The term *Stetcon* derives from the proofread-ing mark "stet," meaning "let it stand." When a change has been made by a copyeditor that the author strongly disagrees with, the author can write "stet" in the manuscript, which means "let the original version stand," or "ignore the change." A Stetcon essentially erases a previous Retcon and puts things back the way they were. Why? Usually because someone in authority hated the previous story (which may have simply slipped by, or was done under a previous regime) and wants to make it go away.

The most notorious example of a Stetcon I was ever involved with was John Byrne's Lockjaw story (see page 115). Several editors and at least one writer despised the story because it was felt

that—although no one was denying the emotional punch of the revelation—it ran counter to thirty years' worth of Inhuman's continuity in which the Inhumans clearly treated Lockjaw like, well, a dog. It was a particularly puzzling move for Byrne, who repeatedly advocated honoring the intent of the original creators of a character, since it was abundantly clear that Stan Lee and Jack Kirby had intended for Lockjaw to be a dumb animal.

I was about to embark on *X-Factor*, and the editors and writer asked me to reverse Byrne's revelation as quickly and cleanly as possible. So I did, by "revealing" that Lockjaw's talking to Ben Grimm was simply a practical joke on the part of a couple of the Inhumans. The thing is, this information was relayed by Quicksilver. Thus did I go for what I felt was an elegant solution: For those people who hated Byrne's Retcon, that was that. For people who didn't want to embrace the Stetcon, it could easily be argued that Quicksilver was lying because he wanted to save face in front of the X-Factor folks, since he pretty much came out looking like a jerk in the telling of it should Lockjaw really be a grotesque Inhuman instead of an animal.

Poor Byrne's Retcons have also been targeted by DC, where it was finally decided that they, like me, preferred the original Krypton vs. the passion-less ice world. And so DC did a whole story line in which it was revealed that the ice-world version was in fact false memories (or something like that) and restored the verdant Krypton to continuity.

So, embark on Retcons at your peril, because you never know who down the line is going to hate what you did and Stetcon it. But if it does happen, you can at least know not to take it personally. Instead, you're simply part of a grand tradition of being second-guessed.

IT'S A TOOL, NOT A HANDCUFF

With that said, don't feel that you need to be a slave to continuity. Naturally you must be attentive to the big things. Don't suddenly turn Peter Parker into a criminal because it suits your story, and if you're bringing back a villain, it behooves you to check his most recent status to make sure he's not, y'know...dead. Comic book heaven may have a revolving door rather than pearly gates, but you should perform at least some element of due diligence.

At the very least, you should stay consistent with your own continuity. If you established something, you should try to avoid violating it yourself...unless, of course, you've got some sort of loophole you can slide through that makes it look as if you had it planned the entire time.

However, if you've got a brilliant *Batman* story idea, and then realize it conflicts with a minor story element from a twenty-five-year-old *The Brave and the Bold* story, I say, "Go for it." Will some fans remember? Yes. But most won't, and ultimately your emphasis has to be on trying to tell the best story possible. Continuity should be a tool, not a handcuff.

Besides, worst comes to worst, you can always claim it was Pre-Crisis and doesn't count.

CONTINUITY CONUNDRUMS

Characters with lengthy histories can be daunting to take on. You might find yourself becoming paralyzed over various stories or concepts because you're worried about violating continuity. There are several ways to avoid this:

1 **Read** every single issue of the book you can get your hands on. This, of course, may not be practical. But at the very least, if you're taking on a long-running character, try to read the last three years' worth of stories so you can see the stuff that's of most recent vintage.

2 **Count on your editor** to steer you away from serious gaffes. Unfortunately, some editors may be newer to the game than you are and will be of little help.

3 **Ask the fans.** Seriously. See, writers tend to write stories and then expunge them from their heads to make room for new ideas and new stories. But fans have memories that border on the encyclopedic. To say nothing of the copious websites that exist on even the most obscure characters. If you have some major story point you're concerned about, try to find your answer on one of those websites or, if worst comes to worst, go online to a popular comic book website such as Newsarama.com or Comicon.com and post your question there. Chances are you'll get your answer within minutes, provided by sources ranging from fans calling themselves by names like "Spiffy182" to professional trivia mavens such as Kurt Busiek or Mark Waid.

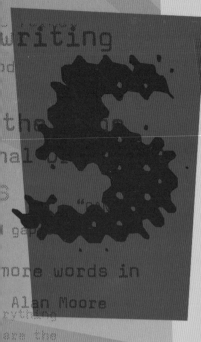

SCRIPTING

THE JOB OF SCRIPTING IS DECEPTIVELY SIMPLE: TO CONVEY VERBALLY THAT WHICH THE ARTIST DOES NOT, OR CAN-NOT, PUT ACROSS VISUALLY. DIALOGUE, CAPTIONS AND SOUND EFFECTS ARE ALL THE WRITER'S CONTRIBUTION. THE SPECIFIC STYLE OF COMIC SCRIPTING, HOWEVER, HAS CHANGED DRASTI-CALLY OVER THE YEARS.

Look at a standard *Superman* comic from the 1960s and you'll see something like this: A panel caption that reads, "And so the Man of Steel flies deep, deep into space...but as he approaches the planet Foobar 4, he finds a most unexpected reception committee!" The artwork then shows Superman approaching a planet and flying men coming through space at him. And Superman is thinking, "A squad of men! Flying toward me! And they can survive in space as easily as I!" Next panel: "A half hour later, after an exhausting struggle, Superman is finally overwhelmed by his assailants, placed in manacles fashioned from kryptonite and brought before the queen, Dyspepsia...who has plans of her own for him!" The artwork shows a manacled Superman standing at the throne, looking bewildered, while the queen says, "So, Superman! You have trespassed into our space for the first and last time!" while she's thinking, "This Superman is far more handsome than I would have thought! Perhaps I have found my true love at last!"

That's two panels. Two panels to convey what would, these days, require an entire issue to project the sort of visual impact modern readers expect. Probably one of the reasons Will Eisner was a grandmaster of comics is that his emphasis on visual storytelling was ahead of its time, and his work of years past remains as vital and powerful as ever.

Comic book storytelling has married the verbal to the visual in ways never before utilized. Granted, we don't have the use of movie aids such as music, sound effects and actors, but clever writers can use the "static" aspect of comics to put across certain sequences in more powerful ways than any film can.

SCRIPT FORMAT

Comic book scripting doesn't follow a rigidly standardized format in the way that, say, movie scripting does. If you're writing a screenplay, you can do so with such popular software as Final Draft and be assured that your film script will appear, on the surface, no different than that of a professional.

Not so with comic books. Talk to a dozen different writers and you could well get a dozen different formats. All of them are perfectly legitimate; writers simply develop a format that works for them. By "works for them," what I really mean is it's a method of storytelling that conveys to the artist what the writer wants on the page with maximum clarity and minimal chance of misinterpretation.

Broadly speaking, there are two "accepted" styles of presenting a script. It is within the parameters of those styles that you will find tremendous variation. One is referred to as *Marvel style*, and the second is called *full script*.

MARVEL STYLE

In the days when Stan Lee was writing ten Marvel Comics a month, naturally he didn't have the time to produce all the scripts. So he would discuss the stories in general terms with the artists, who would take copious notes, go to their studios and—because they were the geniuses they were—return with twenty-two pages of brilliant storytelling, which Stan would then dialogue. Eventually other writers produced stories the same way, and over time these formerly orally delivered stories were written down so editors could read them over and artists had something other than scribbled notes to read.

Marvel style presents the story in a general manner, like a short story written in present tense. It includes some, but not necessarily all, dialogue and gives the artist much latitude in how he visually paces the story.

Once the art pages come back, the writer is sent a photocopy of the pages (or, in some instances, computer files of them). The writer then scripts each panel, adding in the dialogue, captions and sound effects.

Following are sample script pages from *SpyBoy* #2, written in Marvel style. This is what I sent to Pop Mhan, who then made all the choices about how many panels each moment should occupy and what panel composition should consist of. Here we see SpyBoy, very early in his career, slugging it out with his archenemies, the S.K.I.N.S.

CINEMATIC STORYTELLING

It has become popular in recent years to "reboot" the origins of assorted characters and retell them with the current hot writers and artists at the helm. It's not as if this, in and of itself, is a particularly new development. Years ago, it was generally assumed that the readers of comics at any given time were boys aged eight to twelve. The further assumption was that, when the current generation of readers discovered girls, comic books would be left behind along with their bags of marbles and their baseball cards. The notion that readers would stick around into their teens and beyond would have been considered ludicrous. Consequently, every few years publishers would retell the origins of their heroes for the presumed new audience of readers who might be wondering how Bruce Wayne became Batman or how Superman could fly.

The difference between those days and now is that the origins would be told within stories of six pages. Nowadays, however, those same origins can wind up taking six issues. Fans refer to this as "decompressed" storytelling, as if the story is just being expanded for the sake of expansion.

It's not "decompressed" storytelling; it's cinematic storytelling.

SPYBOY SCRIPT PAGES, MARVEL STYLE

PAGES 7 TO 9

SpyBoy then runs in the direction of his gun, which is still lying on the ground. But as he approaches it, several SKINS suddenly charge in from all sides. SpyBoy skids to a halt. He's got a problem, caught flatfooted by the SKINS who are heavily armed and aiming their weaponry straight at our hero, standing in a roughly half ring formation.

"Down!" a voice behind SpyBoy suddenly shouts. Obeying automatically, SpyBoy drops, and suddenly there is an explosion directly behind the SKINS, who are propelled forward and sent flying over SpyBoy's head.

ANGLE ON the magnum opus as a female hand reaches in and picks it up. "Here...I think this is yours," and WE SEE Bombshell, tossing the gun over to SpyBoy. He catches it and looks at her with a fair amount of both suspicion and confusion. "Who are you?" he demands.

"I'm the Bombshell," she says. "There: I know who I am. Do you know who you are?"

He looks at her askance.

We CUT BACK TO Derrek, Butch and Schweitzer. Schweitzer has a large bruise on his head and still has the toilet seat ringed around his neck. He looks woozy, but he's just hauled Derrek out from under the junk and is now pulling Butch out. Suddenly Chinn steps INTO PANEL, shoves Schweitzer aside and yanks Butch to his feet while putting a knife to his throat. "SpyBoy!" shouts Chinn. "I have something that might interest you!"

"Guys! Guys, help me!" screams Butch. Schweitzer and Derrek take one look at each other...and then turn and bolt, ignoring Butch's screams for aid.

Bombshell and SpyBoy step into view some feet away and look at Chinn with his knife to Butch's throat. "Put down the gun, SpyBoy, lie flat both of you and surrender, or else I gut your little friend here from sternum to crotch."

"Go ahead," says SpyBoy, and he aims his gun squarely at Chinn. "Kill him. I couldn't care less. He's a bully and a creep. What happens to him is of no consequence to me."

Tight on Chinn's face, eyes narrowed as he contemplates the situation. Similar shot of SpyBoy, but his face is impassive. He'd be a superb poker

Page 7 from SpyBoy™ #2 ©1999
Dark Horse Comics, Inc.

TAKE YOUR *GUN*, SPYBOY. THE "*MAGNUM OPUS*," I BELIEVE YOU CALL IT.

...SHELL.

...: I AM. ...OW WHO ...RE?

MAN, LET'S GET *OUT* OF HERE ALREADY.

I'VE SEEN DRUG BUYS GO *BAD* BEFORE, BUT THIS IS AN ALL-TIME HIGH FOR SUCKINESS.

HEY! CHWEITZER! HELP!

GUYS! GUYS, *HELP* ME!

I ONLY NEED *ONE* HOSTAGE, BOYS. LEAVE OR I'LL KILL YOU.

SPYBOY! I HAVE SOME-THING THAT MIGHT *INTEREST* YOU!

YOU CREEPS! GET *BACK* HERE! GUUYYYS!!

SHUT UP, BOY!

PUT DOWN THE *GUN*, SPYBOY, BEFORE I GUT YOUR LITTLE FRIEND HERE FROM STERNUM TO CROTCH.

HIS NAME IS *BUTCH*, AND HE'S A BULLY AND A CREEP. WHAT HAPPENS TO HIM IS OF *NO* CONSEQUENCE TO ME.

KILL HIM. SEE WHAT *I* CARE.

121

FULL SCRIPT

When you write full script, you're telling the artist everything that's going to be on the page. If the comic book is like a film, you are the director. Each panel is an individual shot. You're telling your artist (your director of photography) what you want.

* How do you want it framed?

* What angle should it be?

* How many characters are in it?

* What's going on in the background?

* Is it day or night?

* Is it raining, snowing or clear?

* What are your characters' expressions?

* Are their hands in their pockets, hanging at their sides or scratching their heads?

* Is their hair in disarray, or hanging in front of their faces, or are they pushing it away from their eyes?

You don't have to tell all of this, obviously. You'll make yourself nuts and your artist won't be far behind. But the more detail you can provide that's appropriate to the scene, the more you're enabling your artist to tell the story you want to tell and convey the mood you want to get across to the reader.

If I say, "PANEL A: Rick Jones looks at Bruce Banner," I'm giving the artist nothing to work with. If I say, "PANEL A: Rick Jones leans back against the wall, his arms folded, and gapes at Bruce Banner incredulously," the panel's going to have more emotional impact.

Once you've described the contents of the panel, you then write the dialogue. I number each line of dialogue as I break it down into individual balloons. Lettering the panels and numbering the dialogue prevents confusion and simplifies balloon placement, since balloon placement is done by numbering (see page 148).

SPYBOY: THE M.A.N.G.A. AFFAIR SCRIPT PAGES

SCRIPT PAGE 1

PANEL A: Exterior, dressing room of "SpyGIRL" from her TV series. An errand guy carrying an assortment of props is passing by, glancing in the direction of the dressing room in confusion.

FROM WITHIN 1: What in the--?!?

PANEL B: The door suddenly flies open and SpyGirl dashes out of it, knocking the guy on his ass as she runs past. She is carrying an envelope, legal size.

Sfx: WAAAAM

PANEL C: SpyGirl shouts over her shoulder.

SPYGIRL 2: Sorrreeeeee....!!!

PANEL D: The errand guy, buried under an assortment of stuff that he'd been carrying, but which has now fallen upon him.

ERRAND GUY 3: Don't mention it, Spy-Girl.

ERRAND GUY 4: To anyone.

ERRAND GUY 5: If that wouldn't be too much trouble.

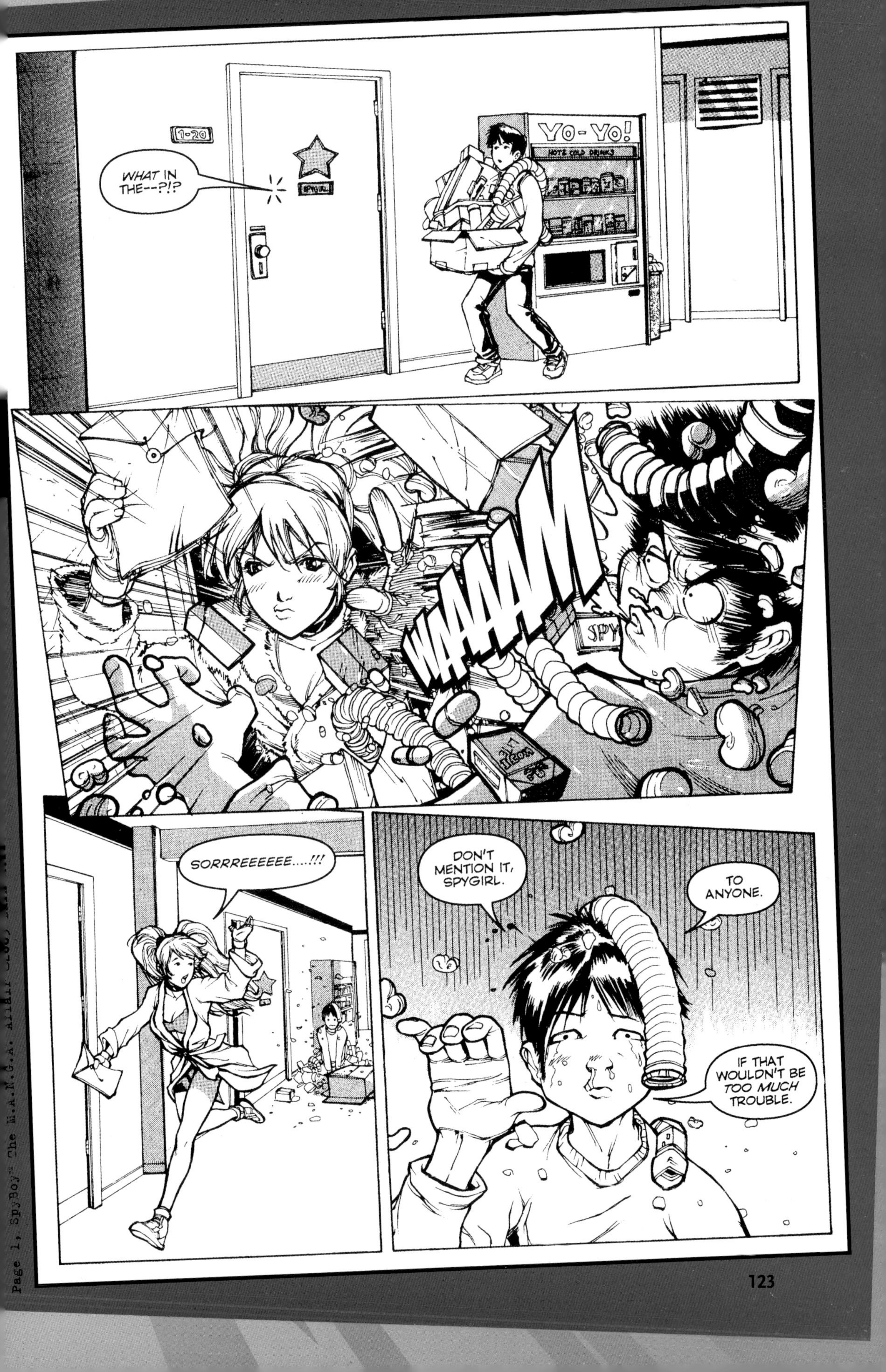
1-20
WHAT IN THE--?!?
SPYGIRL
YO-YO!
HOT & COLD DRINKS
WHAAAM
SPY
SORRREEEEEE....!!!
DON'T MENTION IT, SPYGIRL.
TO ANYONE.
IF THAT WOULDN'T BE *TOO MUCH* TROUBLE.

I prefer full script. It gives me control over the pacing of the story. It forces me to think in a more visual fashion and avoids my tendency to overplot the story while thinking that, hey, it's okay because the artist will figure out how to make it all fit. It's my story, after all, and if I can't figure out how to make it fit into twenty-two pages, it's

SPYBOY: THE M.A.N.G.A. AFFAIR Script Pages

SCRIPT PAGE 2:

PANEL A: Interior, TV studio. A director is talking to four stunt guys who are dressed as Ninjas. They are listening tentatively. Other crew members in view are on break.

DIRECTOR 1: Okay, boys, we'll be filming the big fight scene after lunch. Now you've all been over the choreography, and—

NINJA 2: Are we going to have a chance to rehearse with SpyGirl?

PANEL B: The director suddenly sees SpyGirl barreling toward them.

DIRECTOR 3: Oh yes. Yukio didn't become the premiere comic actress in Japan without paying attention to the details. She never does a fight scene without plenty of—

DIRECTOR 4: Ah. Here she comes now!

PANEL C: And the Ninjas leap at her. The director looks alarmed.

NINJA 5: Get her, boys!

DIRECTOR 6: No, wait!

PANEL D: Tight on SpyGirl, gritting her teeth, looking pissed.

SPYGIRL 7: Grrrr...

SCRIPT PAGE 3

FULL PAGE as SpyGirl, a multi-image blur, clobbers the ninjas.

TITLE: THE M.A.N.G.A. AFFAIR, Part 1

Page 2, SpyBoy™ The M.A.N.G.A. Affair
2003 Dark Horse Comics, Inc.

better I rethink the presentation rather than fob the problem off on someone else. Also, since I used to put so much dialogue into my Marvel-style plots, turning around and writing only the dialogue was a duplication of effort.

Page 3, SpyBoy™ The M.A.N.G.A. Affair
©2003 Dark Horse Comics, Inc.

DIALOGUE BALLOON RULES

When it comes to how many panels to a page, how many words to a dialogue balloon, there are no absolutes. For myself, I try to have:

- No more than twelve to fifteen words in a balloon
- No more than thirty words in a panel
- No more than six panels per page

MORE LIKE GUIDELINES

But, like the rules of piracy, these are more guidelines than rules. If I'm doing a major action sequence, I'll open it up and keep it to two, three panels... but I can always put a lot more words in. If I'm doing an extreme close-up on someone, I'm not going to put more than four or five words in the balloon. On the other hand, Alan Moore and Dave Gibbons in *Watchmen* or Stan Lee and Steve Ditko in *The Amazing Spider-Man* can do nine to twelve panel pages, packed with dialogue, and not make it seem the least bit cluttered.

On a month-to-month basis, I tend to learn my artists' strengths and weaknesses. The longer I work with someone, the more I can tailor stories to hit his strengths and avoid his weaknesses.

I've reproduced here a few pages of full script from *SpyBoy: The M.A.N.G.A. Affair*, also with Pop Mhan, which you can then compare to the final version. Notice that I boldface the panel descriptions and letter them while numbering the dialogue and captions and set them in normal type. It makes it easier to distinguish one from the other and avoid confusion.

DIALOGUE

Dialogue is conversation between two or more characters and serves two basic functions: Either it moves the plot along ("Nine companions. Very well! You shall be...the Fellowship of the Ring!"), or it serves to reveal things about the characters themselves ("*Great!*...Where are we going?").

Within those parameters is a vast range for you to explore. Some writers see dialogue as purely utilitarian. It is the means to the end, the end being to get the story told. Their mastery of dialogue consists solely of enabling characters to convey necessary information and minimal personality (Tom Clancy's dialogue, for instance, does very little for me, his books being mostly plot driven). Some use almost no dialogue at all. Instead they content themselves to tell the story through the force of their prose, with page after page of narrative and only a few lines of dialogue strewn throughout to provide some character illumination (check out Isabel Allende's *Zorro* novel for a recent example). And some tell their stories almost entirely through dialogue, as if they were writing a screenplay with nominal acknowledgment of the novel form (see Robert B. Parker's Spenser novels for use of that technique). Some writers even have dialogue that borders on pure poetry (Ray Bradbury comes to mind).

DIALOGUE AS A NARRATIVE TOOL

Once upon a time, comic books were combinations of dialogue, thought balloons and captions. Over time, as comic books have tended to imitate television and movies in terms of their execution, captions are now usually only used in cases of first-person narrative ("I'm Wolverine. I'm the best there is at what I do. And what I do is fill up page after page with my internal thought process, so I can be strong and silent and yet still never shut the hell up."), while thought balloons have largely been relegated to the dust heap.

So, dialogue is no longer simply one of several narrative tools in comics, but for all intents and purposes your only narrative tool (after all, narrative captions are just running monologues, like some-

A DIALOGUE MUST

Read your dialogue aloud. Not just fight dialogue: all of it. You will be amazed how much bad wording and tortured language you can weed out if you put yourself in the characters' places and speak the dialogue you're handing them. Harrison Ford, sick of the poorly crafted speeches he was given to say as Han Solo, once threatened to tie George Lucas to a chair and make him recite his own dialogue. You're not going to have Alec Guinness at your beck and call to sell ghastly lines such as, "You'll never find a more wretched hive of scum and villainy." So you might as well make it as easy on your readers as possible, lest they threaten to tie you to a chair.

thing out of an old crime drama). That being the case, you'd be well advised to master it thoroughly.

Dialogue should flow naturally from the characters you have either created or that have been given you. As the writer, it's your job to get into the characters' heads, to understand their personalities and then express those personalities through dialogue. If you're hazy on their personalities, find ways to get into their heads. Make lists of their key character traits.

Dialogue should not be interchangeable. If you've written a line of dialogue that could literally have been spoken by one of several characters, it's not a good line of dialogue. It should be informed by their individual personalities. You must determine whether it's an appropriate thing for that particular character to say at that particular time, and the best way for him to say it that reflects who he is.

Listen to people around you. You will find that most people have certain catchphrases or verbal repetitions that they use all the time. Feel free to adapt these little verbal tics into your characters, or even create some of your own. Remember, though, that once you establish it, you have to maintain it if you're going to be consistent. So try not to come up with something that's going to be too annoying through repetition.

Here are some of the verbal tics I hear all the time:

"So I'm like...and then she's like" (a substitute for "So I said...and then she said." See also, "So I go...and then she goes...")

"At the end of the day..."

"Long story short..."

"Y'know..."

"So I axed him..." (Meaning someone was asked something, not actually struck with an axe.)

"You gotta be kidding me!"

"No way!"

"Bub." (Okay, that's actually Wolverine who says that, but you get the idea.)

If you feel these come across as somewhat cliché, that's fine. Keep a notepad with you and jot down repetitive phrases that you hear in dealing with people so you can use them.

USE VERBAL TICS TO DEFINE CHARACTER

Fans will tend to notice these things and it will serve to provide unique voices for the characters, thus making them more "real" to the readership. For instance, in *Fallen Angel*, every supporting cast member addresses the Angel in a different way, underscoring the notion that each one of them has a unique relationship with her. Not only that, but on occasion the Angel will be presented with a situation where someone throws down a challenge. "If you don't like it, why then, you're just going to have to do something about it!" To which the Angel invariably responds with a simple, "'kay," an abbreviation of "Okay." Fans have picked up on the fact that when the Fallen Angel says "'kay," she's about to do something truly brutal.

"It's your job to **get into the characters' heads**, to understand their personalities and then **EXPRESS** those personalities through dialogue."

DIALOGUING IN OTHER ACCENTS

When writing characters from countries other than the United States, many writers tend to seize upon a single word in the character's native tongue that then serves as the identifier for that character's speech. Personally, I tend to go broader than that, endeavoring to match certain cadences and means of expression that are unique to specific cultures. How? Through a combination of research from the Internet and assorted books, and watching movies made in the native countries so I can get a feel for how people in certain places express themselves.

Try to pick up on word order, word choice, sentence structure. It really does vary from culture to culture. For instance, if you want to portray a Jew with a degree of ethnicity, reverse subject/object in sentences. "An order you're giving me?" Or look again for recurring tics. "By me, this is not a real sandwich" rather than "I wouldn't consider this a real sandwich." The British tend almost to throw away their dialogue, so go for short, punchy word balloons. "Everyone here? Oh. Hawkeye's dead and won't be joining us. Well...bad news, that. Right then. Off we go."

With others, such as the Scots, I tend to try and transliterate the Scots burr. "Ye canna be serious! Yuir jokin', surely!"

Avoid the ghastly cliché phrases. I've been to Scotland, to Ireland, to France. I can assure you I have never heard a Scotsman say "Hoot, mon!," an Irishman say "Top of the mornin' to ye," or a Frenchman say, "Zut alors!"

Which isn't to say you can't have fun with the occasional overused phrase. For instance, in *X-Factor* #4, I wanted to accentuate that the Irish Siryn, who was using her rather persuasive voice to sweet talk her way past a cop, was playing up her lilt. Since we're dealing with a silent medium, I used an Irish cliché to underscore what she was doing...and then promptly lampooned it, as follows:

SIRYN: Ohhhh, now officer...faith and begorrrrra, surely you wouldn't want to be keeping ussssss

SOME THINGS ARE CONSTANT

Many of my characters tend to sound intelligent, leading some critics to claim that my characters talk alike. It's really not true. Bruce Banner talks nothing like Betty Banner, Betty doesn't talk like Rick Jones, and Rick Jones doesn't talk like Captain Marvel. They all may talk like educated people, but they come at situations from different directions and the dialogue reflects that. Are any of them capable of coming up with a quip on occasion? Yeah. So are most people in real life. Humor is a constant in the real world, and having characters display senses of irony or sarcasm makes them more true to life, not less.

out...weeee can go throuughhh, caaaaan't we...?

POLICEMAN (with a goofy expression on his face): Sh...sure, Miss. I...guess it would be okay...can't imagine why not...

(As they walk past, Jamie Madrox looks at her incredulously.)

JAMIE: "Faith and begorra?"

SIRYN: Don't start.

JAMIE: What, did someone swipe your Lucky Charms?

SIRYN: I was in the moment. I said don't start.

JAMIE: Wanna borrow my Irish Spring? It's manly, yes, but you'd like it, too...

SIRYN: Shut up.

BATTLE DIALOGUE

Scott McCloud has written about matters such as these at far greater length, and with far more expertise, than I could hope to achieve. I would suggest seeking out his *Understanding Comics* if you want an even more rounded education on the mechanics of comic book conventions (conventions of storytelling, not the ones where you go and people want your autograph). Still, I'll present you with my meager understanding so we can at least discuss some stuff.

Comics are different from movies, television or stage—in short, from every other visual presentation of stories—because the panels as presented aren't intended to be actual, literal "frames" of film. One frame of a film is $\frac{1}{24}$th of a second. And even if it's a frame from a scene in which someone is speaking, it's unlikely that the dialogue will sound like much more than someone saying "Meh," if that.

But one frame of a comic book can occupy far more than a second. It can take as long, or as short, a period of time as the writer wants it to. Dialogue sequences staged as individual frames of film simply wouldn't work. The reader realizes that when he's reading conversation in a comic book, he's looking at a moment frozen in time while simultaneously imparting passing time within his own head.

However, while this is fairly easy to convey, and even standardized, in simple walk-and-talk sequences, it becomes challenging for the reader's suspension of disbelief when you're in the midst of an action sequence. If Peter Parker and Mary Jane Watson are strolling down a sidewalk while ten balloons of conversation are floating above their heads, the reader can fill in for himself that they're just taking a long stroll. But if Spider-Man is doing a somersault while engaging in ten balloons of snappy banter and a robber is firing a gun at him, you're asking the reader to "fill in" a lot of

midair spins in his own mind, plus enough bullets coming from that gun to mow down an entire Panzer division. Although the "fill in" for the fight sequence is no more intrinsically silly than the "fill in" for the walk-and-talk, nevertheless the reality of the fight is going to change in the reader's mind.

Think about it on a practical basis. When did you last hear serious conversational dialogue in a movie during an actual fight? In the old swashbucklers, they developed techniques wherein the heroes and villains could exchange snappy banter during the course of the duel. Invariably they'd lock sword hilts so they could rap out dialogue while practically nose to nose. Or perhaps they'd pause a distance from each other, waving their swords threateningly, while the villain tells the hero that he should never have come back to Nottingham while the hero invites the villain to bite him.

But the only time I can recall actually having heard speeches being made during punches being thrown was *Die Hard*, wherein Bruce Willis' John McClane kept up a steady stream of obscenities and curses while he was pounding on ballet dancer Alexander Godunov. Not exactly Noël Cowardesque in its ambitions, but at least it sounded more realistic than dazzling banter...plus it was particularly satisfying if you just really hated ballet dancers.

In any event, how you choose to play the dialogue in a fight scene says a lot about the overall tone you're looking for.

With the continued drive to try and have comic books emulate "reality" as much as possible, particularly in terms of having single panels represent briefer and briefer segments of time, fight scene dialogue has become the more problematic in terms of conveying it in a convincing manner.

Back in the day, this wasn't a problem. Writers dialogued fight scenes to their heart's content, and no one cared that characters were spouting entire sonnets while frozen in midair. But now comics try to imitate visual medium with moving images…even though the images in the comics are completely static. This can give comics a slightly schizoid sensibility.

Make a decision as to which way you're going to go when writing fight scenes in a particular book. Once you have done so, remain consistent with it. Don't go for ultrarealism in one issue followed by characters yakking away for an entire page in the next.

In this battle sequence, writer Stan Lee makes no attempt whatsoever at realism. Instead he bends, breaks and reknits the conventions of "take that, you rat" battle dialogue.

SUSPENSION OF TIME AND MAKE-BELIEVE

Notice the *suspension of time* required for page 9, panel 3 in *The Amazing Spider-Man #29*, in which Spidey, J. Jonah Jameson and the Scorpion have an extended chat while Spider-Man punches Scorpy in the jaw. It would be utterly impossible for Spider-Man to say everything he does to both Jonah and the Scorpion and vice versa while punching Scorpion precisely one time. Spidey moving with

his normal alacrity, taking a swing at Scorpion. We're talking...what? Two, three seconds at most? Now read the dialogue here aloud and time it. I think you'll see a slight discrepancy.

When I say suspension of time, I mean that the writer is effectively pretending that time is frozen for the duration of the panel. The characters are saying and doing whatever it is they're portrayed as

doing, but the actions they're taking don't match up in terms of timing with the words they're speaking. So we're all going to "pretend" that they do match up, and then marvel (no pun intended) at the spiffy dialogue that Stan has written.

However, even Stan knows that the branches of time and space can only be bent to a certain degree before they mentally "break" for the reader. Rather than push the reader's tolerance too far, on the next page Stan switches purely to thought balloons. Readers will give thought balloons (see page 144) far greater latitude, since a thought can essentially pass through your mind in a second. Then comes the capper of Stan's playfulness as, in the final panel of page 10, Spidey's dialogue balloon is upside down. No one's voice sounds different upside down in real life. But by inverting the balloon, Stan gives the reader a sense of Spidey's disorientation that blends seamlessly with the Steve Ditko visual.

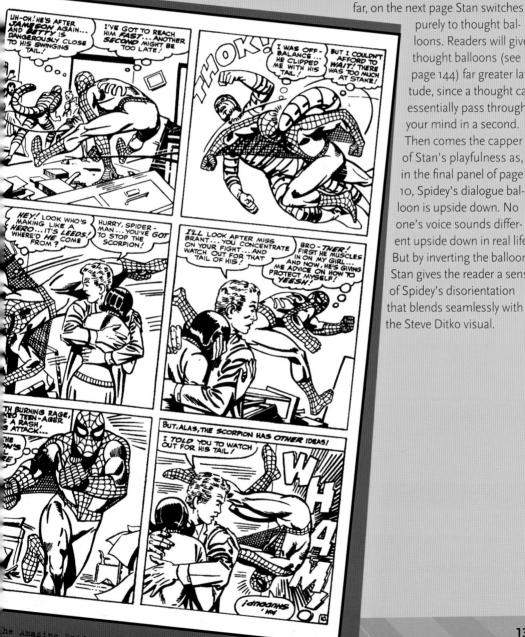

The more modern, "photo-real" approach to comics would have it that each panel of a fight really does represent about a second's worth of time. To that end, it helps to try and keep dialogue in photo-real battles to a bare minimum. None, in fact, to be precise. The intent here is to make a comic feel as much like a movie as possible. So having copious amounts of dialogue during a battle scene simply isn't going to work.

KEEP IT SHORT

By the same token, you don't want to have a fight go on for too long because that's just going to consume page after page with no dialogue to accompany it. The problem with that becomes that readers are going to think you're light on plot, turning page after page with nothing but grunts on them.

It's realistic, though, to keep the fights short. In real life, brawls generally are pretty short. Human beings can't take punch

after punch and keep coming back for more, the way they do in most action films. Usually a couple punches to the face are enough to end a fight fast. See the film *Witness* as an example, wherein an angry Harrison Ford—hiding among the Pennsylvania Amish—punches out a couple of obnoxious teenagers who are unaware that they're mouthing off to, not a peaceful Amish man, but a two-fisted Philadelphia police detective. The fight doesn't take more than ten or twelve seconds, the kids

> "Human beings can't take **PUNCH AFTER PUNCH** and keep coming back for more, the way they do in most action films."

George Pérez and I worked to keep a realistic tone in *Sachs & Violens*. As such, I kept the fight scenes, like the one pictured here, chat-free.

wind up having their faces rearranged into bloody masses courtesy of Ford's fists, and the only dialogue comes from those not getting their clocks cleaned who are begging for Ford to stop whomping on the teens.

If your comic is going to try and match reality, or even reality as presented in movies, that's going to be reflected in a lack of serious fight dialogue. In real life, there's no time for witticisms in fights. You're too busy either being the pounder or the poundee to wax clever. So in such sequences, less is definitely more.

Despite the over-the-top nature of its protagonists, George Pérez and I strove for that more realistic, grim-and-gritty tone in *Sachs & Violens*. Extended banter while punches were being thrown wasn't exactly right for the mood we were trying to convey. Thus, in this two-page sequence, J.J. Sachs finds herself being accosted by a mugger. The extensive word balloons up until the fight are there to convey the hustle and bustle of downtown New York City, the sense that it's packed with people with lots of things on their minds. The moment the attack begins, however, we're dead silent except for the mugger's gasps and grunts of pain...all perfectly believable since a sudden exhalation of air takes no time at all. In this way we convey a tone that grounds the series more in the street level abilities and sensibilities of its protagonists, rather than the bigger-than-life accomplishments of a Spider-Man.

SCRIPTING ODDS AND ENDS: THE OCCASIONAL EXPERIMENT

Just because Marvel style and full script are the two most accepted ways of script presentation doesn't mean they're the only ones. Don't be afraid to experiment. Try new approaches and angles you might not have considered before. Push your limits. If a writer doesn't risk failure at least once a month, he's not trying hard enough.

EXPERIMENT 1: TELL YOUR STORY ENTIRELY IN DIALOGUE, HULK #467

When I wrote the script for *The Incredible Hulk* #467, the last issue of my initial run, I went for a completely different style. After setting the scene visually, I told the rest of the story almost entirely via dialogue, with only minimal stage directions. I gave artist Adam Kubert no instructions whatso-

ever other than to tell the story visually the way the narrative suggested to him. It's the sort of experiment you can only embark upon if you have full confidence in the artist, as I did with Adam.

I present to you here the last couple of pages of my story, followed by the artwork to see what he did with it. The sentences in quotes are being spoken by either Rick or his six-year-old, redheaded daughter who's just run in; the dialogue without quotes is his unseen questioner.

The reason this worked as well as it did—aside from the fact that I knew a brilliant artist had my back—was that I basically told the story in pure screenplay form. Since, as noted earlier, comic book narrative has become more and more "moviefied," this story was sort of the ultimate test

---

THE INCREDIBLE HULK #467 SCRIPT PAGES

PAGE 19

"Daddy? Are you going to be much longer? You said you were gonna play with me. Who's this?"

"This is a writer, honey. He and daddy were talking. Peter...this is my daughter...Betty."

She's lovely.

"Daddy...are you okay? You look like you're gonna cry."

"Daddy's going to be just fine, honey. See? No tears. Look...why don't you escort the nice man out. And then... we'll play."

Look...I hate to keep you...but there's so many other things I'd like to hear...

"Well...I guess you're going to have to hear them from someone else. You

see...I could keep on telling stories about the Hulk...keep on going and going...but there's other things in life, you know? It's like what Bruce told me. Realize what's important... family, loved ones...that's the important things. You're not the first writer to come to me and ask about the Hulk. And yeah, I could keep on talking about him...for ages... but sometimes you just reach a point where it's enough. Where you say, that's it, no more stories. I've said all I want to say right now. Talk to somebody else, okay? I've said enough about the Hulk. And about her, I... I kissed her once...just once, but I can still taste the sweetness of her lips...I...God, don't print that. Just...write that I loved him and her, more than I can say...and that's all. Like I told you...I've said enough...talk to somebody else, okay? I've said enough about the Hulk. I've said enough."

Artist Adam Kubert completed this issue
with almost no direction at all—only dialogue.

to see if it was possible to tell a comic story using movie screenplay format.

Look at the script. Yes, it's broken down page by page. And no, the character names aren't centered above the dialogue. But otherwise it's purely a movie script, with all of the dialogue and only the most minimal of stage direction. You will find that's consistent with screenplays. Although screenwriters will, from time to time, indicate a desire for specific angles, such instructions are pretty minimal. Why? Because it is expected that the director will have his own way of doing things, so why take the time and effort to put them in there when the director is just going to ignore them?

In the case of the typical comic book script, I more or less serve as the director, picking my shots, my angles, my instructions, which the artist then follows. In this instance, I turned the director's reins over to the artist (not to mention those of the director of photography, the cinematographer and the film editor) and said, "Here's my screenplay. Do with it as you will."

Should you do the same thing? If you're working with an artist you trust, sure. Why not? I would recommend, though, that you read some actual screenplays. There are hundreds out there to choose from. I would recommend any of the books of William Goldman's screenplays, not to mention Harlan Ellison's screenplay for *I, Robot* that bears no resemblance to the one that was actually produced and is so far superior to it that it hurts knowing it will never be filmed.

THE INCREDIBLE HULK #467 SCRIPT PAGES

PAGE 20

TIGHT ANGLE on an urn that reads "Betty Banner."

Rick, seated, is looking at it. He is holding it in his hands. Then he places it on a shelf as he says, "I've said enough."

And we pull back, leaving Rick sitting there, Betty's urn to the side, and a few other possible "props" scattered around. The beginnings of his trophy room.

And we pull farther and farther back until we fade to black.

You can only resort to this sort of "moviefied" script style if you *really* trust your artist, as I did Adam Kubert.

"THE LONE AND LEVEL SANDS"
I'VE SAID ENOUGH.
PETER DAVID EX-WRITER
ADAM KUBERT X-ARTIST
STEVE BUCCELLATO COLORIST
JOHN E. WORKMAN, JR. LETTERER
BOBBIE CHASE MOURNING
BOB HARRAS EDITOR IN CHIEF
FINI.

EXPERIMENT 2: TELL YOUR STORY ENTIRELY WITHOUT DIALOGUE

I have done this twice in my life. Since so many people seem to feel that my strength is dialogue, I decided to push myself into unknown territory by producing a story with no dialogue whatsoever. That issue was *Young Justice* #31, in which a typically hyper Impulse wants to hang out with Superboy, and Superboy is only interested in watching a cheerleader competition on TV. The splash page kicks off with Superboy shouting a single word at Impulse: "Quiet!" From that point until the very end of the issue, Impulse speaks not a single word, nor do we hear from anyone else in the issue (although, conveniently, Impulse is long-established as thinking in pictograms, providing me some dialogue-free leeway).

Not long after I finished the issue, much to my shock, Marvel announced that they were going to do an entire month of silent issues, eventually dubbed "'Nuff Said" month. That's the advantage of performing storytelling experiments on your own initiative; you never know when someone is going to ask you to do it as part of your job.

I was writing *Captain Marvel* at the time, and as it turned out, the timing of the story couldn't have been better. The story line at that point involved

Rick Jones having aged virtually overnight into an old man. It had been going on for a bit and I had pushed it as far as I could. So it was time to restore Rick to his more youthful appearance.

Furthermore, the issue would be coming out around Christmas. Christmas, a time of quiet reflection (perfect for a silent issue). Christmas, the time of miracles (perfect for transforming Rick back to normal).

What better time to go for something totally schmaltzy?

So I developed a story in which Rick Jones has reached the end of his rope. He is so buried in despondency that there's no need for words; he's got nothing left. And yet, from the depths of his despair, he pulls himself together and aids a homeless woman who is in the process of giving birth. Not only does he deliver the child, but when the baby is apparently lifeless, Rick administers CPR and saves the newborn's life (resulting in the single "spoken" moment in the issue, a thin "Waaaaaa" wafting through the air).

He then transforms to Captain Marvel, the blast of light from an alleyway attracting a couple of police officers to the scene. The following is my script for the remainder of the issue, followed by the accompanying artwork.

CAPTAIN MARVEL VOL. 3 #26 SCRIPT PAGES

PAGE 20

PANEL A: Angle on the cops discovering Captain Marvel, who is looking off panel...and one of the cops is looking up, because snowflakes are starting to fall.

PANEL B: Now all three are looking up in surprise, because snow is really starting to come down. Snow...in Los Angeles.

PANEL C: The cops look at Captain Marvel, who in turn is shrugging while putting a finger to his lips to indicate they should be quiet.

PANEL D: In a scene somewhat evocative of the nativity, there are Harry and Deb, crouched, with the baby lying in a makeshift crib, while Captain Marvel and the two cops are looking on. The star, identical to the one on Marvel's uniform, remains in the sky.

PANEL E: The police car is in front of a building with the sign "BEVERLY HOMELESS SHELTER." Captain Marvel is flying overhead, waving to Harry and Deb who are being helped in by the cops, their baby in her arms.

My contribution to Marvel's "'Nuff Said" month,
proving that lack of dialogue or captions doesn't have to hinder a story.

PAGE 21

PANEL A: The balcony of Marlo's (Rick Jones' wife) apartment. She is looking upward into the snow AND SEES Captain Marvel descending toward her.

PANEL B: He alights on the balcony. She smiles.

PANEL C: He slams the bands together.

PANEL D: And the transformation doesn't work as it usually does. Marlo is taken aback as energy coruscates around Captain Marvel. The image of Rick's aged, floating head is nearby, and it's tilted back, screaming.

PANEL E: And there's a sudden release of energy that is in the shape of the star burst, so intense that it knocks Marlo backwards into her apartment, over a chair.

PAGE 22

PANEL A: Tight on Marlo as she clambers up, looking goggle-eyed.

PANEL B: Rick is on his knees on the balcony...and he is young. His arm is back. His youth is restored. He is looking at his hands in astonishment, and he has one hand to his face, touching the now smooth cheek.

PANEL C: And Marlo and Rick embrace passionately on the balcony as the rather singular star, framed against a ghostly silhouette of Captain Marvel in the sky, so that it is placed against his chest...but could also be independent of him...glitters in the Christmas night sky, while snow comes down.

In a comic without dialogue, the other elements of your script become extremely important. You have to describe everything you picture to your artist—expressions, specific settings, gestures and so on.

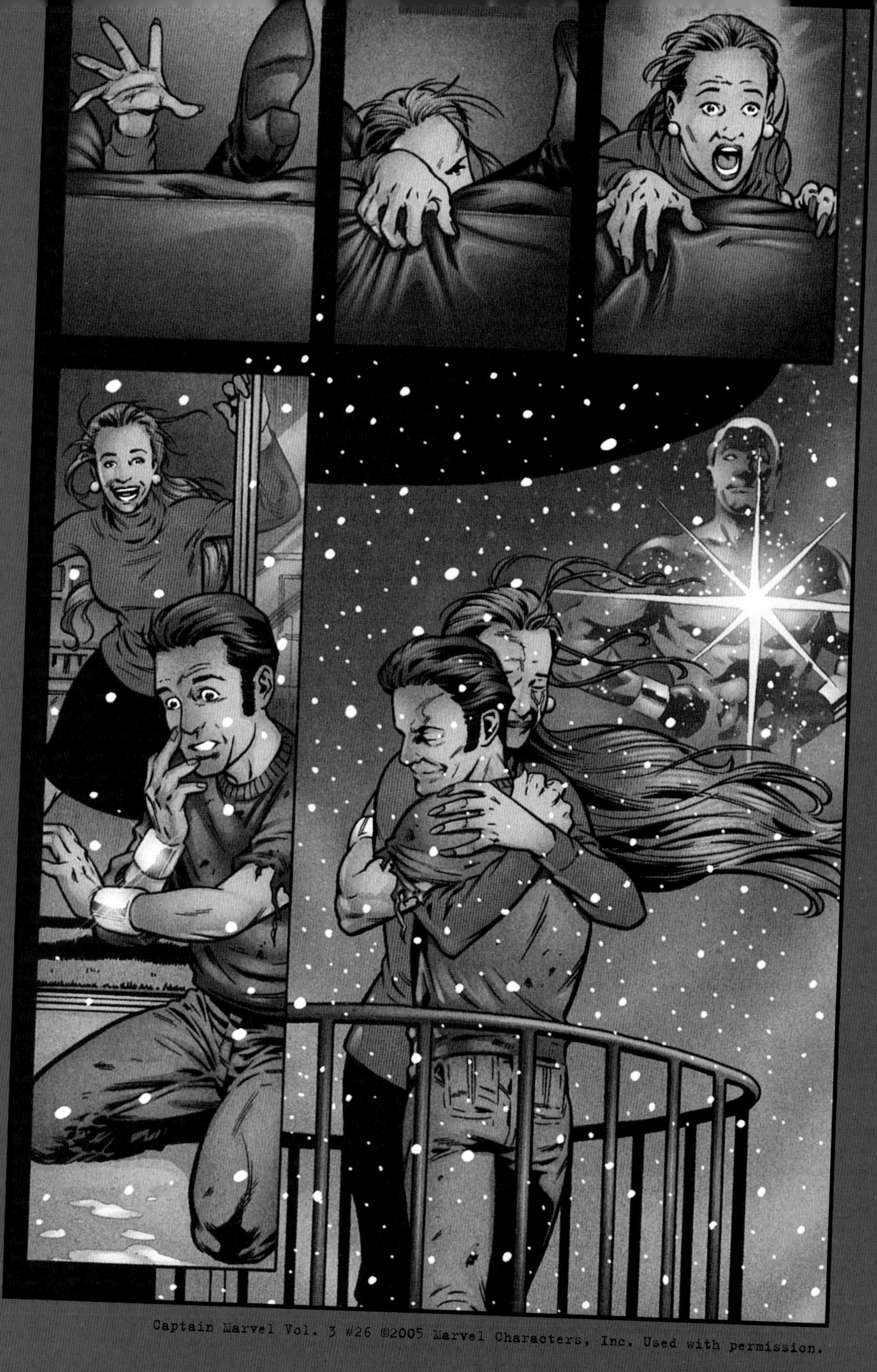

There is a sizable array of options open to writers when it comes to word balloons. As the writer, you are in charge of indicating who is going to say what and how it's going to be said. Over the next pages (courtesy of the lettering genius of Glenn Hauman, thanks Glenn) you'll see the ways in which both the balloon itself, and how you design the words within them, can affect the way your dialogue is read.

If you're working for a major company, someone else will probably do the actual lettering. If you're self-publishing and doing your own lettering, these are some possibilities you might not have considered. Either way, deciding how the lettering is going to appear within the balloons is your responsibility. Yes, most companies have standard policies over how dialogue is depicted (all capital letters as opposed to upper- and lowercase, that sort of thing), but even within those boundaries, you can still call for "special effects" in your word balloons. You indicate which words should be emphasized, either through <u>underlining</u> or *italics*. You indicate varying **typeface** or TYPESIZE. If you want certain words to be bigger than others because a character is upset, you'll want to indicate that as well!

Basically, just as you're sending instructions to the artist when you're writing scripts, you're also sending instructions to the letterer by indicating what sorts of tricks or special effects you want in your word balloons and where they should go. You can either use whatever format indications are available in your word processing program, or—if you still type on paper—just indicate in handwritten notes what sort of effects you want in your balloons.

The reason this is important is that you're writing for a silent medium. You don't have actors' voices to convey mood. So it's up to you to get it done by telling the letterer what you want. Let's say you wanted to put across a girl greeting a guy that she's enamored of, but he can't stand her. (FYI: I write my scripted dialogue in standard upper/lowercase. But typically the comic book company runs it in all caps, as is comic book standard. Which is fine; but if I'm going for a particular effect and am seeking out upper/lowercase, I make certain to let the artist know that.)

Thus an exchange might read:
GIRL: (balloon in shape of a heart) *Hiiiii*, Harold. Good to see you.
HAROLD: (balloon dripping frost) Yeah. Right. Good to, y'know...what*ever*.

IS THAT SUPPOSED TO BE *FUNNY?!?*

USE ITALICS FOR PUNCH
By "punching" or emphasizing certain words via italics, even messing with punctuation a bit, you're conveying that your speaker is irritated.

> IS THAT SUPPOSED
> TO BE FUNNY?

SIMPLE, STRAIGHTFORWARD, NOTHING FANCY

Although some people make a case for the typeface being set in upper- and lowercase, decades of comic book reading and writing have anchored me squarely in the "all capital letters" school. The effect here is toneless. It's hard to discern any particular meaning or intonation from the balloon alone. It could be mild sarcasm. It could be someone who's been told a joke and honestly doesn't get it. The pointer or tail of the balloon points directly at the person who is speaking.

> IS THAT *SUPPOSED*
> TO BE *FUNNY??!?*

BOLD
ITALICS SHOW ANGER

Your speaker is more than irritated: He's angry. The combination of boldface and italics, plus enlarging a couple of words, lets your reader know your guy is shouting but still has enough variation to his voice to indicate a sense of sarcasm.

> *IS THAT SUPPOSED*
> *TO BE FUNNY?*

DARK TYPE TO EXPRESS YELLING

Your speaker is really furious. There's no shading or emphasizing of one word over the other. It's a flat-out shout, and he's yelling at someone.

> IS THAT SUPPOSED
>
> TO BE FUNNY?

USE WHITE AREA

White area can be your friend. By dropping the point size significantly, but keeping the balloon size normal, the vast area of white space conveys the idea that your speaker is speaking in a sort of strangled voice, barely able to get the words out. The smaller you can get the letters and still have them be legible, the more effective this technique is.

THOUGHT BALLOONS

If your character doesn't want to say the words aloud, your balloon takes on the look of a puffy cloud. This is a thought balloon. The only balloon that doesn't include a standard pointer, the thought balloon instead has little floating dots that lead from the speaker to the balloon.

IS THAT SUPPOSED TO BE FUNNY?

IS THAT SUPPOSED TO BE FUNNY?

BECAUSE I DON THINK IT WAS.

THE DECLINE OF THE THOUGHT BALLOON

Once a standard narrative device, thought balloons are becoming less and less popular for many writers. Why? Probably because most writers watch more television and films than they read books, with the result being that comics are imitating movies (yet another reason for the so-called "decompressed" method of storytelling mentioned earlier). In books, authors routinely convey their characters' thought processes without the characters actually saying what's on their minds. But since it's atypical to "hear" what a character is thinking on screen, you see it happening with less frequency in comics.

ATTACH BALLOONS FOR CONVERSATION

You can have several balloons in a panel, attaching one to the next through a bridge or connector or—as I like to call it—that little attachment thing. Usually this is stylistically preferable to having multiple pointers to the same speaker. You'll want to break up sentences for several reasons: 1) to convey individual thoughts; 2) to emphasize certain beats; 3) to indicate a measured way of speaking because your speaker is deliberate, or perhaps a Vulcan; 4) just to avoid too many words in a balloon and a massive block of type.

ILLEGAL IMMIGRANT EFFECT

I call this the illegal immigrant effect because it requires cutting across the border. By having the words emerge from the balloon border and progressively dwindling the typeface, you're indicating that the speaker is being dragged away and we're hearing his voice tailing off. More fun can be had by taking those same extended letters and dropping them progressively down toward the bottom of the panel border. That shows your poor speaker has just been pushed off a cliff or out a window.

IS THAT SUPPOSED TO BE FUNNN$_N$

N
N
N
N
Y

144

STACKING BALLOONS

Stacking balloons work when you have two (or more) characters speaking to each other. One balloon is inserted between two others to indicate an exchange of dialogue. You can either have the balloons run horizontally or vertically, depending on where your characters are positioned on the page by the artist.

IS THAT SUPPOSED TO BE FUNNY?

THAT HAD BEEN MY HOPE, YES.

WELL, I DON'T THINK IT WAS.

Is that supposed to be funny?

WAVERY BALLOON

By going upper/lowercase and giving the balloon a sort of "wavery" look to it, your speaker is clearly speaking with much effort. Particularly effective if the speaker is supposed to be hammered.

IS THAT SUPPOSED TO BE FUNNY?

USE THE BURST WITH CARE

This is called a burst (yes, you're bursting your balloon). The zigzag pattern indicates an explosive shouting of the words within the balloon. If your character gets much angrier, he's going to have a cerebral hemorrhage. The burst serves a double purpose:

- Conveying volume and extreme anger
- If your words are in normal type (eliminating the indication of shouting) and the pointer of the balloon is to a telephone or radio, this becomes a "static burst," which indicates that a voice is being transmitted in some way.

145

IS THAT SUPPOSED
TO BE FUNNY?

IS THAT SUPPOSED
TO BE FUNNY?

IS THAT SUPPOSED
TO BE FUNNY?

NARRATIVE CAPTION

Thought balloons are becoming replaced by narrative captions. Voiceover narrative is standard issue in, say, hard-boiled detective films. So, if you want to give your comic and character that sort of feel, narrative captions can get the job done for you.

Now, some writers use multiple narrative captions to indicate multiple points of view. Personally, I'm not a big fan of this. When was the last time you saw a detective film with half a dozen people doing the narration? It can be done, sure, especially if you're interested in giving screenwriting teacher Robert McKee fits. (He despises voiceover narration of any sort.) But my feeling is, if you're essentially deciding to provide a point of view for your story, have it be a single point of view. Otherwise it sounds cluttered.

USE THE FROSTED BALLOON FOR SARCASM

For no reason that I can explain, I find frost balloons—balloons literally dripping icicles off the bottom to indicate extreme sarcasm or a chilly tone from the speaker—work best with female characters. Perhaps I've just annoyed more females in my life than males, and thus am used to women talking that way to me.

IS THAT SUPPOSED
TO BE FUNNY?

IS THAT SUPPOSED
TO BE FUNNY?

CHARACTER BALLOONS

Just as an aside: If you're writing Wolverine, by this point first-person narrative caption is practically expected since he's been doing it for so long.

THE WHISPER

A whisper balloon works with pure uppercase. Basically a broken line around your balloon informs your reader that the speaker is whispering. I have to say that I didn't understand that as a kid. Whenever I saw a whisper balloon, I'd crack out a pencil and join the broken lines, thinking it was some sort of participatory thing.

IS THAT SUPPOSED TO BE FUNNY?

THE "HMMM" BALLOON

I picked this up from manga, or Japanese comics. In essence, it serves as a sort of place marker where your character has just received some piece of information, doesn't quite know how to react and is pondering what to say for a moment before speaking. In screenplay writing, it would be called taking a "beat," and it's convenient if you don't have room for a panel that consists of nothing but your character sitting there silently and thoughtfully staring off into space...as if pondering whether something was supposed to be funny or not.

IS THAT SUPPOSED TO BE FUNNY?

THE HEART BALLOON

Not to be overused (it shows in a story of mine maybe once every six months or so), by having your balloon shaped as a heart, you're indicating that the character is speaking with love and affection. In this case, the speaker clearly thinks it's adorable that whoever he's talking to believes what he said was amusing. Isn't love grand? For additional fun, you can add musical notes to indicate a singsong voice.

BALLOON TIPS

Always endeavor to have the tail pointing at the speaker's mouth or at least the general area of his head. It's bad form to wind up having your character speaking out his behind if there's any alternative.

Balloon placement is another one of those aspects of comics where there's no one right way or wrong way to do it. There are just various theories and techniques. Again, all I can do is indicate to you the way I do it.

BALLOON PLACEMENT "GUIDELINES"

* **Keep your balloons "anchored."** Rather than having balloons just floating around aimlessly on a panel, unattached like a bachelor with commitment problems, place balloons so that some part of them is adjoining the panel border. Why? Oldest reason in the world: That's what I was taught when I first started doing balloon placement.

* **Minimize the amount of the characters being covered.** This isn't always possible. One of the more notorious

balloons in comic history was in the original *X-Men* #1, wherein Magneto had so much to say and so little space within which to say it that the villain's entire head and torso got annihilated by the word balloon (see below).

Notwithstanding that, artists will usually leave you background space with nothing much of importance there that you can drop balloons over with impunity.

Keep in mind that the more of a close-up you have, the fewer words you'll want in your balloons. As a general rule, cover as little of your character's face as possible.

BALLOON RULES IN ACTION

I've reproduced here two pages from *The Incredible Hulk* #424, written in Marvel style. I received the pencil pages from artist Darick Robertson and then wrote the dialogue to accompany it. Each page of dialogue was on a separate sheet for easy reference, and as I wrote each dialogue line, I used a marker to indicate where the balloons should be placed.

I specifically chose these two pages because they are at odds with some of the guidelines.

◄ How not to place a word balloon. This is a rare lettering gaffe from *X-Men* #1, the Stan and Jack days.

Consider it a practical application of theory vs. practice. Note the following:

- **Page 9, panel 1.** The character of Achilles is essentially talking out his legs. No choice. The artist framed the shot so that only Achilles' legs are visible.
- **Page 9, panel 2.** Achilles has two balloons with pointers rather than a connector. In this instance, I was going for a specific verbal effect. Note the dialogue of the individual balloons: "Alone, if you don't mind." "Or even if you do mind." I was trying to put across terseness: Achilles looking from one guy to the other and barking orders to each of them.
- **Page 9, panel 4.** Again, individual balloons rather than connectors. This time it's personal preference. I didn't want to have a bridge running straight across Achilles' forehead.
- **Page 9, panel 6.** Talk to the hand. Again, that's the only part of Achilles available.

vid/HULK #424/GIVE TO BOBBIE CHASE

PAGE 9

ARD 1: Hello, Mr. Achilles.

HILLES 2: Hello, Meyer. Boyajian.

HILLES 3: I'd like to talk to the prisoner.

ILLES 4: Alone, if you don't mind.

ILLES 5: Or even if you do mind.

RD 6: Well, sir, we're not supposed t--

ILLES 7: On my authority.

ILLES 8: Now amscray.

ILLES 9: So. It's come to this.

ILLES 10: I told you Banner would be nothing but trouble.

LLES 11: If you wanted to go walkabout, you should have lef
n charge.

10

ERTAINMENT ID:576-9289
JUL 28'94 15:57 No.032 P.04
Book Hulk
Issue 424
Story Page # 9

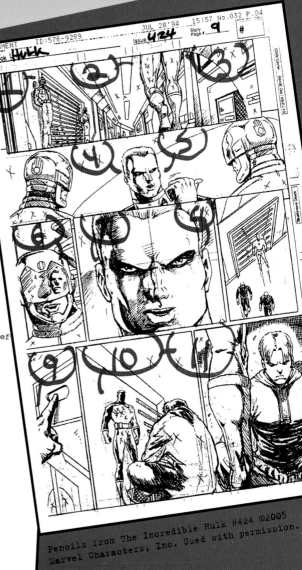

Pencils from The Incredible Hulk #424 ©2005 Marvel Characters, Inc. Used with permission.

Page 10, Panel 4. Balloon 6 isn't attached to a panel border. That's because I wanted to connect it to balloon 7, which I placed in panel 5 so Achilles' cry of "Speak to me!" would specifically be shown as eliciting no response. Notice that balloon 7 is attached to a panel border, so balloon 6 is border-anchored by extension, like an unwanted relative.

ARE YOU MAKING YOUR INKER'S JOB EASIER?

The more you cover up with balloons, the easier you're making the inker's job since he doesn't have to ink the stuff that's covered with word balloons.

David/HULK #424/GIVE TO BOBBIE CHASE

PAGE 10

ACHILLES 1:   I'm your son!   I was always good enough to do whatever you needed before.

ACHILLES 2:   Why didn't you trust me?

ACHILLES 3:   ...

ACHILLES 4:   Now I'm not even good enough to be spoken to?

ACHILLES 5:   Blast you, Agamemnon!   I sold my soul to you!   I'm entitled to something back!

ACHILLES 6:   I could crack your skull like an egg!

ACHILLES 7:   Speak to me!!

ACHILLES 8:   You just lost the best friend

11

THE FINISHED PAGES.

OFFSCREEN DIALOGUE

Characters don't necessarily have to be on panel to speak. A balloon pointer that points off panel is routinely used to indicate that someone is speaking from "offscreen."

I HEARD THAT: SOUND EFFECTS

As a writer, you're also responsible for indicating sound effects where needed. If you're writing full script, you indicate them in the appropriate panel with the abbreviation "SFX" instead of a character name. It's not necessary to number them. If you're writing Marvel style, just hand-letter them on the photocopies when doing your balloon placement.

Like thought balloons, sound effects are another of those comic book tools that are falling out of favor with some writers. This is likely a consequence of the 1960s *Batman* TV series, in which huge sound effects such as "POW!" "BAM!" "ZOK!" would spiral onto the screen every time Batman and Robin got into a slugout with the bad guys. This kitschy view of comics storytelling subsequently took root with the media. As a result, just about every newspaper or magazine article from then to now would carry comic book sound effects in the headline...usually in a derogatory or snide manner. ("Pow! Wham! Comic Book Geeks Hold Convention." That sort of thing.) So when the entire mainstream media is singling out one particular aspect of comics storytelling to symbolize silliness and camp, it's natural that some writers would develop an aversion to it.

WHEN ARE SOUND EFFECTS NECESSARY?

To some degree, sound effects aren't necessary. If the artist successfully conveys the action of, say, a villain firing a gun, do you really need to write "BLAM!" under it? Well, it depends. If that's all you want to depict, perhaps not. On the other hand, if you want to add a layer of emphasis to it, "BLAM" can help make up for the silent medium that comics represents. Also if the shot comes from off panel, you may well need it for clarity's sake so the reader knows a gun has gone off. Plus, if you write "BLAM BLAM BLAM," you can convey that multiple shots are being, or have been, fired.

Sound effects can also provide some amusement value, for yourself and attentive readers. I don't know who first coined the sound effect of BA-THROOM for an explosion, but that gave me a few giggles the first time I saw it. I came up with my own huge explosion noise that's slightly more subtle: RAK-O-VLAAAAM.

Plus there are some sound effects that have been around so long, and been used so consistently, that they've taken on lives of their own. If there are some bad guys skulking around in the shadows, thinking they're unseen, and the

sound effect "snikt" appears in the darkness, you know that Wolverine has just popped his claws and is about to carve them into Chiclets. "Thwip" tells you that Spider-Man's just fired his webbing. And "bamf" informs you that Nightcrawler has just joined the party.

Love them or hate them, sound effects are another tool in your kit to be utilized as you see fit.

For every story (or even series), you have to decide whether you're going to go with sound effects or not. Sound effects automatically make the page look more "comic book-y," for lack of a better phrase. Lack of sound effects avoids the kitsch factor and adds a more "mature" feel.

Make a decision and stick to it. This should be determined by (a) your own preference for the mood you're going for, and (b) the quality of your artist.

For instance, you may decide that you want to eliminate sound effects but, as you go along, you discover that the artwork needs them because it's unclear what's happening on the page. The simple truth is that much of what we do as writers is trial and error. You see what works, what doesn't work, and then obviously go with the former as much as possible.

WATCH WHAT YOU SAY

The sad fact is that language is an imperfect means of conveying thoughts. No matter how meticulous you are in describing to your artist exactly what you want, sooner or later you're going to suddenly find yourself—like Strother Martin and Paul Newman in *Cool Hand Luke*—with failure to communicate.

If you can provide your artist with a frame of reference, do so. ("Remember when the skeleton pirates walked across the ocean bottom in *Pirates of the Caribbean*? That's the feel and angle I'm going for here.") If you can provide handy sources, go for it. ("Tight shot of Bela Lugosi's tombstone. Reference can be found at the following site: www. seeing-stars.com/ImagePages/BelaLugosiGrave Photo.shtml.") There's simply no such thing as giving your artist too much information.

SCRIPTING CAN LEAD TO ILLUSTRATION MISTAKES

Even with all that, crossed wires can occur. One time I wrote as an instruction, "Gradually descending helicopter shot, the surface of an alien planet depicted over several panels," meaning that I wanted a steady progressive aerial view. Instead, the artist drew an Apache helicopter shooting at the planet, because he didn't know a "helicopter shot" is a movie sequence filmed from the point of view of a helicopter, such as in the opening of *The Birdcage* or *Lethal Weapon*. So that had to be fixed.

Occasionally, though, screwups can work to your benefit. For instance, when scripting *The Atlantis Chronicles* #1, I described how a giant asteroid was slowly approaching the at-the-time surface continent of Atlantis; the asteroid's landing being the

A mistranslation between artist Esteban Maroto and myself resulted in the "face" of the asteroid becoming an actual face, heightening the feeling of approaching jeopardy in Atlantis.

reason for Atlantis becoming submerged. At first the asteroid was little more than a speck, but as it drew nearer, I wrote at one point, "The asteroid has gotten closer. We can now see the face of the asteroid: its craggy surface and rocky exterior."

Now when I said "face," I meant "front surface." Instead, artist Esteban Maroto took "face" to mean "visage" and rendered a death's head skull right onto the asteroid. On the one hand it was ridiculous; on the other hand, it was amazingly creepy. When editor Bob Greenberger asked me if I wanted art corrections done, I stared at the art for a long time and then said, "You know what? Leave it. I like an asteroid with attitude." My reasoning was that, if an asteroid is heading your way and it's just a ball of rock, well...you figure maybe it might miss. Maybe everything will be okay. But if you see an asteroid coming and it's got a death's head skull glaring down, forget it. You're getting your ticket punched, baby, so don't start reading any continued stories.

EXERCISE

THE AARON SORKIN SCHOOL OF DIALOGUE

You will slowly find yourself noticing what other writers do, both in terms of their plotting and—most conspicuously—their dialogue. You will notice patterns and quirks that can be instructive. If you like what they do, you can allow yourself to be influenced by it. If you don't like it, avoid it.

To start out, I suggest studying the dialogue stylings of Aaron Sorkin, creator of *The West Wing*. Not only is there a lot of it, but it's a fascinating means of watching both the best and worst of scripting simultaneously.

For instance, Sorkin has completely nailed the concept that people often don't speak in perfect, linear sentences or complete thoughts. Anyone who has ever done a transcript of an interview knows full well that in normal, extended conversation, people stop, start over, rephrase, interrupt themselves, leave thoughts dangling, reiterate and go off on complete tangents, occasionally never to return to the original subject.

Sorkin's dialoguing style captures that perfectly. (For that matter, so does the comic book scripting of Brian Michael Bendis.)

On the other hand, remember when I told you that people have certain verbal tics or phrases they tend to repeat? Well, last time I checked, writers are people and are no less creatures of habit than anyone else. The result is that there are certain recurring phrases that have crept into Sorkin's dialogue that undercut the notion of giving each character a different voice, because they all use the same phrases.

So: Sit down with a Sorkin-written episode of *The West Wing*. (The complete series is on DVD, and are also run on Bravo. Also a number of scripts have been collected in trade paperback.) Analyze Sorkin's style by checking off on a notepad:

1. Every time a character stops in the middle of a sentence.

2. Every time a character repeats a line that someone else just said.

3. Every time a character repeats himself.

4. Every time a character says, "I'm just sayin'."

5. Every time a character says, "Yeah." (Not as part of a long sentence. Just "Yeah.")

6. Every time a character refers to an event or an appointment as a "Thing." ("We've got this thing we gotta do"; "I thought it was minor, but now it's a thing.")

You might try several episodes. See how prevalent it is.

Now you may find yourself wondering what the best direction for your talents may be.

Do you want to focus on developing your own characters, carve out your own path in the comic book publishing world, either by producing a creator-owned title through an existing publisher or by self-publishing? Or do you want to work within existing comic book universes and produce the adventures of characters you grew up adoring?

When it's your own characters, you have total freedom to do whatever you want. Freedom is a natural state of being, and that applies to writing as much as anything else.

On the other hand, being part of a shared universe allows you to contribute to a vast tapestry, making you part of something that is bigger than yourself. Plus, there's simply the kick of putting words into the mouth of characters you've long enjoyed reading.

Now...I'm not going to advise you on self-publishing. For starters, that's a whole book in and of itself. But as for your own characters vs. company owned? Well, some of that decision stems from your personal muse. There are writers who simply can't wait to get their hands on Spider-Man or Batman. There are others who wouldn't touch long-standing superheroes with a ten-meter cattle prod, feeling they have nothing to say in such venues.

Personally, I think from a career and creativity point of view, it's smart to do both.

This is a broad generalization, I know, and as such you can always find exceptions, but go with me on this. Think of fandom as Hollywood. Think of company titles as movies. Think of creator-owned books as the stage.

Think of yourself as an actor.

As long as you're acting in movies, there is an awareness of your name and your activities. For good or ill, everyone knows what you're up to. You're on the radar.

Now, some actors believe (and I tend to agree) that the most fulfilling, exciting, challenging form of acting is live theater. Getting up on stage and working without a net. It's low paying. It's low profile. But as a creative individual, you just can't beat it.

So, you leave movies and go back in a play. In a touring company, on Broadway...doesn't matter. You do a play for a year.

You return to Hollywood.

Hollywood stares at you blankly. "Oh? Where have YOU been? You haven't been working, huh?"

If you're not doing movies, you drop off the radar.

Same with comics. Work exclusively for indies, or self-publish, and either you'll drop off the radar of fandom or you may never get there in the first place. Your books won't sell to as many people; many comic book stores won't even carry them.

That might not matter to you. Perfectly fine. But if you want to build a career, and you measure the success of that career by (a) the size of your audience, and (b) your ability to earn a living writing, you might want to consider the following course of action: Write a mainline comic or two while at the same time producing comics featuring characters entirely of your own invention. Writing the mainline comic keeps your name out there in front of far more fans than are going to read your creator-owned book published by a smaller company. The name recognition gives you a fighting chance to get the kind of publicity and retailer support your book is going to need if it's to survive in today's toxic marketplace.

Furthermore, it's not always easy to get word out about those projects that can be near and dear to your heart. For instance, a couple years ago at San Diego Comic-Con, fan after fan came up to me and told me how excited they were about my (then) impending return to *The Incredible Hulk* and the just announced *Madrox* series. They said they loved my work, and they also said—most significantly—that they read everything I wrote.

So I asked every single one, "Do you read *Fallen Angel*?"

Nine out of ten looked at me blankly. They'd never heard of it. *Hulk*, *Madrox*, news of these hadn't been out for that long, but they knew about them. *Fallen Angel* had been on the stands for a year, and they'd never heard of it. That's my target audience, plus it was then published not by a smaller company, but DC Comics, one of the top two. And they'd never heard of it.

Don't get me wrong: I'm not saying you should take on high-profile books just to have your name on them. You shouldn't be writing *Spider-Man* if you feel you have no Spider-Man stories to tell, because your lack of interest in the character will show through in the work.

THE BOTTOM LINE

So I hear you say, "Peter! Now that I know all these basics, how do I go about getting myself published, so I can be Mr. Big Shot Fancy Shmancy Thinks He Knows Everything Writer Guy like you?"

Short answer: It's tough. Really tough.

An editor can tell just from looking at art samples whether a potential artist is worth pursuing. It's a judgment that takes mere minutes. Writing is far more problematic. It takes longer to read a proposal than to look at a sketch, and longer still to read a script than a proposal.

You can certainly try hooking up with an artist. The upside is that it provides editors with something to look at other than just words on a page. The downside is that, if the art stinks, it's going to drag your story down.

To give you some more specifics as to how to break in, editor Andy Schmidt has provided material and specific advice as to what they're looking for, and how best to provide it.

BREAKING IN DON'TS

- **Don't be an idiot.** This sounds reasonable, but some people don't get it. There was an unpublished writer whom I met at a convention who approached Marvel with a twelve-issue maxi-series that would wipe out the entire Marvel Universe and repopulate it with heroes of his own invention. Why? Because, according to him, "Your characters suck and mine are much better." Yeah, that's the way to make friends.

- **Don't go to established writers and say you want to work with them.** Many writers (including myself) and even publishers don't read unsolicited material in order to avoid lawsuits. I'll never forget one fan who claimed that a well-known comic book writer had ripped the fan off because the fan had sent a letter to the comic title suggesting a story line that was vaguely similar to one the writer later did. Comics publishers get hundreds of letters a day, and the writers typically see none of them.

- **Don't send comic book publishers your 700-page fantasy manuscript or your unproduced screenplay.** Just as looking at pinup posters doesn't tell an editor if you can draw, a novel or screenplay doesn't tell an editor if you have the storytelling technique required for producing comic books. That ability to think visually and pace your story in a series of shots that represent frozen moments in time that also move.

BREAKING IN—
AN EDITOR'S PERSPECTIVE

You're reading this because you want to break into the comics industry. As the founder of Comics Experience, an organization determined to educate and help would-be comic writers and artists achieve their dreams, I'm going to speak plainly about the realities of the industry. First, let's lay a few ground rules.

Number one, this section can only serve as a guide. There are no hard-and-fast rules on this subject; what works for one person will not necessarily work for another.

Two, I'm working on the assumption that you are talented. I can give you advice and a few tools and hints to getting better, but no matter what, YOU will have to do the work.

Finally, following my every step won't guarantee you success. I'll give you notes on form and networking, but it's up to the working professional to actually pull this off with a great story.

I'll focus quite a bit on communication, because communicating with your editor, your artist, your colorist, etc., is the single most important thing you can learn from this section.

Good luck, and I hope this helps.

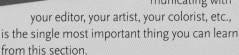

ANDY SCHMIDT

THE ROAD AHEAD OF YOU: THE THREE TOOLS YOU NEED

The comic book business landscape is a harsh one. There are many talented writers out there who want to do the same thing as you. Few things will separate prospective writers from one another—talent, persistence and luck.

You have to hone these three fundamental attributes in order to get your shot at the big time.

I'll talk about these attributes first, then I'll roll into how to network and pitch, and lastly, I'll deal with how to stay around once you're in the biz.

TALENT

You've got to have skills and prove it. Here's the thing: You may have a great story idea, but that doesn't mean you're a great storyteller. You have talent—maybe a little, maybe a lot, but you've got some. All of us do. You want to present yourself in a manner that shows off your strengths and downplays your weaknesses. But before you get to that, you need to know what your strengths and weaknesses are and how to build them up. As a writer, you cannot accept that you are poor with dialogue or that your action sequences are rocky. Once you've spotted a shortcoming, you have to work on it until you're confident you write the sharpest dialogue and most intense action sequences the world has ever seen.

So how do you do that? First, like all good writers, you research. You've already bought and read this book, so that's an excellent start. Furthermore, if you haven't read *Story* by Robert McKee, go buy it right now. Put down this book and go get it. No, seriously. Go. You're back? You got the book? Great. Now read it. All done? Awesome—then let's move on.

In McKee's book, you'll find out how a story works, what parts make up a story and, hopefully, what skills you possess. Personally, I've found that in person, I'm good for a funny story, but on the written page, my dry sarcasm loses something—namely, all cleverness (check out my text page in the back of *Defenders* #1 if you don't believe me)—it doesn't work because you can't "read" the tone of my voice. You'll figure out where your talents are (there are books that can help you do this as well), and from there, you'll need to work on your weaknesses. For my own writing, I have trouble giving my characters different voices.

Look honestly at what you do well and what you need to work on. Then build your skills. As you get frustrated with yourself, always remember that you do have skills and can learn new ones. Don't listen to someone who says you "just don't have what it takes." That may be true for the moment, but you can learn the skills and how to apply them successfully to writing comics.

PERSISTENCE

Keep trying; keep refining your skills. Don't pester editors, but be persistent. Part of persistence is refining your skills. The moment you say, "I'm finally good enough, I don't need to improve anymore," is the moment you've stopped being good enough. As an artist, you must always strive for better. A writer never learns enough. You may know everything there is about turning points, rising action, character interplay and so on, but you would still need all the accumulated knowledge of human history to know "enough." Writing doesn't end with mastering the craft—that's where it begins. Be persistent in your pursuit of knowledge and skill. Be persistent in your pursuit for a job. There's a great essay in the back of my book, *The Insider's Guide to Creating Comics and Graphic Novels*, that tackles this subject very well and from a different perspective. Check it out.

When applying for writing work at comic companies, remember a few key things. Before you write your cover letter, ask yourself who your audience is and research that audience (told you research was going to come in handy). If it's Marvel or DC you're writing to, don't ask for work outright. I recommend asking for an informational interview. If you have already published something, send it along. At the very least, published material shows editors you can carry the ball down the field. If the editor likes what you've published, you've got a shot. Until you know an editor has read your work, your attempts at getting freelance gigs are futile.

When you get a response from an editor at Marvel or DC, don't let it end there. Try to continue the dialogue. Wait a day or two (if by e-mail) to reply. That's not to make you look less desperate, but rather to give the editor time to get some work done before dealing with you again. If you start demanding too much time too fast, you'll irritate an editor, and that's not good.

While networking, which I'll talk about a little later, be persistent enough to follow up with people. Ask the people you meet to introduce you to others who could give you advice. Don't leave a meeting empty-handed. You may not get work, but ask for that person's e-mail address, or the e-mail address of someone else who may have ideas more like yours. I'm usually happy to do that. There are good writers who simply tell the kinds of stories that I'm not suited to edit. I've told writers this before and they think I'm criticizing them, but that's not the case. Like the writer, the editor must also be honest with himself.

As a writer, you will most likely take criticism personally. I do. I'm always trying to improve, but it gets under my skin when someone calls me out personally in a public forum. For one thing, it's not about you, but your work; try to divorce yourself emotionally from your work once it's done. That will make taking criticism easier and you'll probably learn more from it. Believe it or not, how you take criticism from an editor is just as important as writing. I'll talk later about professionalism when we get to how to stay in the comics business (see page 164).

LUCK

This looks as if it's out of your hands. But truth to tell, you do have control. Boiled down, luck is about being in the right place at the right time. Which, again, sounds as if it's out of your control, and to a certain degree it is, but you can improve your luck in a number of ways.

To increase your chances of being in the right place, go to places where comics professionals gather and start meeting them. Networking is your friend. The more professionals you befriend, the more minds you'll be in when discussions occur about who should write what, or who has a good take on such-and-such a character. Just the other week I was out to dinner with two other editors and one freelance writer. We were discussing good writers on different characters. Will that lead directly to those writers working on the respective titles? I don't know. But if the editors were looking for writers, wouldn't it have been cool if that freelance writer had named you as his choice to write *New Avengers* after Brian Michael Bendis? Networking allows you to be in more than one place at one time. The more minds you're in (and have made a good impression on), the better your chances for getting recommended to a writing gig.

Networking doesn't end with getting to know other freelancers. It's about meeting editors, colorists, pencilers, anyone whom you may want to work with or who may want to work with you or who can introduce you to people you want to know. Additionally, the more writing credits you get (writing a video game for example), the better off you'll be. That's about building your résumé.

Networking is also about professionals learning from each other. One of the best things about the comics community is how open most people are.

THE GOOD NEWS
Any two of the three attributes (talent, persistence and luck) should get you your shot eventually. The "if" clause implied here is: "If you've been persistent enough, you've got talent enough and/or you've got enough luck, you will get your shot at a writing gig." But, I'm talking about ways to increase your "enough" factor in all three categories.

NETWORKING
Assuming you've got the portfolio or the springboards and are armed with enthusiasm and a healthy attitude about life in general, where do you go to get a chance to be noticed? There are typically ten places or methods to get your work looked at—some are more likely to turn up work than others, but here we go...

THE CONVENTION CIRCUIT
It used to be that conventions took place only during the summer, but now they occur throughout the year. *Wizard Magazine* holds several. The largest is the San Diego Comic-Con. Publishers there often hold portfolio review sessions for artists. This won't do you as a writer much good, but most publisher booths are staffed with editors. It's worth your time to familiarize yourself with all the editors' names you can and what books and projects they're working on. This way, you can introduce yourself to them and hopefully comment on their work. If you're interested in their books, editors are probably (unless busy or just plain tired) interested in talking with you.

If you get a conversation started with an editor, don't just start pitching your ideas. Let the conversation go naturally; you're not wasting the editor's time. As you size up the editor, she will be sizing you up as well. How you discuss the editor's work informs the editor of how you relate to your own. The criticisms and comments you offer inform the editor of how much you know about storytelling and structure. The discussion is valuable—jump into your pitch too soon, and you're written off because the editor doesn't have a real gauge of who you are and what you can do. Let the editor know by the end of the conversation that you'd like to communicate further and bounce some ideas off of her. As a writer at a convention, this is probably as far as you want to go unless you've already got a relationship with an editor, in which case, hey, you're ahead of the pack.

COLD SUBMISSIONS TO PUBLISHERS
This is less likely to yield results with the larger publishers like Marvel and DC, but with smaller press publishers looking to expand their talent pool, it may work (see facing page for how to pitch your project). If you're going to submit ideas to Marvel or DC, be prepared to sign some legal jargon papers first. It usually says something to the effect that "so-and-so company may be developing similar ideas independently of you, and you recognize that, so if we publish a comic similar or even identical to your idea, you can't sue us." It's pretty standard, and don't be afraid to sign it. Most of us are good people, and no one wants to be accused of stealing your idea. That's not good for anyone.

ONLINE RESOURCES
Several websites can connect you with an artist or other writers. This includes working professionals. Go to publishers' websites. Go to individual writers and artists' websites. Make the rounds. Many publishers post rules for how to submit to them right on their websites.

WORKING WRITERS AND ARTISTS

Most writers and artists are pretty cool people. Don't be afraid to talk with them online or at a convention. If you happen to be at a convention, don't pass up artist alley. Take a good long walk through it and meet other people who are breaking in. You may hit upon the perfect artist for the book you want to write. If nothing else, you'll probably meet people with similar interests (I can almost guarantee that) and you can start networking with them. After meeting a good contact, make a note of what you talked about or what the contact's work was like so you can clearly remember later.

SCHOOLS

The only comics writing school I'm aware of is my own: Comics Experience. We hold classes in both New York and California as well as do one-on-one consulting. See what's new at www.comicsexperience.com. In addition, you can always take courses on writing. Most major universities offer screenwriting courses and there are workshops that travel across the country. I can't stress enough how much continuing your education can help you.

CREATE A WEBSITE

You can develop your own website. Typically, this is more useful for an artist than a writer, but having a place to self-promote sure doesn't hurt. Check out Marc Sumerak's website (www.sumerak.com) to see what I mean.

SELF PUBLISHING

If you can afford it, I recommend self-publishing. There are two reasons for this: first, you'll have something published, which puts you above those who don't; second, you will learn so much about how the industry works and how difficult it is to put together a working project that you'll become more tolerant of people who make mistakes and you'll hone your craft that much further. Nothing teaches you the lessons you need more than jumping in and doing it.

TRADE MAGAZINES, JOURNALS AND PAPERS

Trade magazines and journals can connect you with other creators and provide insight into the industry as a whole. Primary research is always more valuable. That is, research you've collected, meaning you didn't read the interview—you conducted it. You didn't hear from a friend about a conversation with Joe Quesada—you talked with him yourself. Primary research is great. If you can, try to interview working professionals. You'll gain valuable information and make another contact. It was performing interviews that most directly led me to my original position at Marvel.

PITCHING

When pitching a project to an editor, there are two ways to do it: verbally and in writing. The following pages are a quick guide on how to format your pitch each way. But know one thing going in: An editor has the right to terminate a project at any time. That said, I know of no working editor today who enjoys asking a writer to do a lot of work just to pull the plug later on. Every step you move to a new level with an editor, it's an indication, though not a promise, that the editor has confidence in you and your project.

QUESTIONS YOUR EDITOR WILL ASK

Before you commit to paper, flesh out the story and characters in your mind. Try to think like an editor in deciding how to format your pitch. What information will the editor need to know? I judge a work on its merits only—no freebies due to past credits.

Here are a few questions I ask before I even start reading a pitch:

* Do I know the writer? If so, what has he done previously?

* Do the major characters interest me?

* Is there any buzz or fan interest I can tie to this pitch?

If I'm satisfied with the answers to those questions, I read the pitch and ask:

* Does it have a compelling title?

* Does it have a hook that I can understand and communicate to fans?

* Can I swap out a major player for another character? If so, the story probably isn't about the characters, but about the plot only. That's not good.

If all that stacks up well, I ask around the office to determine:

* Are these characters free or will they soon be free? If not, is that a problem?

* Are you altering the status quo of any important characters? If so, is that okay?

* Am I currently working on something similar? If so, do I want to pursue this?

Only at this point will I read the body of a pitch. I'll read the story or the outline if broken down into chapters or comic book issues. What I ask is:

* What makes this story worth telling?

* What do you say about the characters?

* How do the characters change?

* Do I buy into the decisions that the characters make?

* Does the story have a clear and concrete ending?

* Is it a story that should and can be told visually?

* Does it feel formulaic? If so, is that a problem? Is it a cliché story?

Assuming I'm still with you after answering all these questions, I'll still have to put your pitch through one last round of questions.

* On a gut level, do I like the story?

* On a gut level, do I have confidence in the writer? If not, is it worth a conversation with him to gauge my confidence level better?

* Can I see the story in my mind's eye? Can I find a proper artist for the project?

If you've gotten this far, you've already accomplished more than 95 percent of the pitches I read. Yes, I'd say not more than one in twenty makes it this far. But I've never read a pitch that hit all of these questions perfectly. If enough of these questions are answered positively for me, I go back to the writer and work with him to see whether we can shape it up and strengthen it. If you have gotten this far and the project derails, you've done extremely well. Be proud of that. Unless you had a personality conflict with the editor, you've made it far enough that I imagine she would be willing to accept another proposal from you. That means you've made real progress.

FORMATTING YOUR PITCH

Now that you know what goes through my head when reading a pitch, you're ready to begin formatting yours.

You don't have to adhere to what I've just said as if it were a binding law. Every writer has different strengths; make sure your pitch shows yours off. If you're great with dialogue, put snippets of conversation in the pitch. If you don't want to do chapter outlines, don't. If you're good at talking about themes or concepts or character interplay but not a great plotter, don't give me a plot synopsis. Give me a character study instead of the synopsis.

I can't tell you how best to formulate your pitch. I can only try to guide you to the best way to present your ideas. On a side note, if you're pitching on several different projects, not all your pitches need to follow the same format. Yes, you want to play to your strengths, but different stories have different needs. For example, a straightforward story synopsis might be great for a Superman pitch but not so great for a Batman mystery pitch.

Let's say you've got all your ideas in order, figured out your characters and know the perfect structure of your story. Now we're ready to talk about the actual pitching process.

VERBAL PITCHING

There are two keys to verbal pitching. The first is finding the right time and place to do it. The second is the pitch itself. It's easy to know the appropriate time to pitch. The simplest way to find out is to ask. Just say something like, "Hey, are you open to hearing a story idea right now?" Most editors will tell you whether it's a good time. In general, if you're at a social function or the editor is off duty, it's not the right time.

So, when is a good time? If you're at a convention and the editor is on booth duty, you've got a good shot. If you've made an appointment, you're golden. Conventions are the best places to meet editors to set up an appointment.

Pitch the characters you like. If I'm interested in pursuing a particular character, I go to guys with whom I already have a good working relationship. You'll get nowhere asking me if I'm interested in hearing a pitch on a particular character. The only pitch I want to hear from you is one you love. If you're passionate about it, it'll come through in your pitch. If you're not into the character, I'll know it and you're done.

If the editor isn't interested in your pitch and says so, think of another pitch. Don't take stabs in the dark. Ask for advice or for names of other people with whom you might talk. Always want to put your most passionate and best work forward.

When pitching, be brief and excited. Don't go overboard with the excitement or bring props. But do show that you're involved in what you're pitching. Be able to tell the story in three minutes or less. Make sure that besides giving the editor the story, you also give the editor enough of the flavor of your story that she understands how you intend to execute it. In other words, what other things might your story resemble in style, structure or tone? Boiled down to its simplest form, no one knows for sure which story will be great and which one won't. Ninety-five percent of a great story is in the execution. Unfortunately, I can't know how well you can execute a story from your verbal pitch—but you're not looking for an approved project in your verbal pitch, just for enough interest to lead to a follow-up conversation.

The reason editors rarely give new writers work is because we don't know how well they can execute their stories. This unease on the editors' part can lead to a couple of different next courses of action. You may be asked for a first script on speculation (spec, for short). If the script is good, you might be asked for a detailed outline. Again, if that's good, you may be asked for a published writing sample. If you've got one, hand it over or mail it in. If it's well received by the editor, she will take you and the project on to the next steps.

When talking with an editor, always be polite, respectful and relaxed enough to put the editor at ease. Take any questions or suggestions seriously and try to address any concern the editor has. If the editor's concern makes sense, you may have a problem, but don't let that stop you. Think before

you speak—don't just fill the silence with your voice. Take your time, and articulate your point or story clearly and succinctly.

WRITTEN PITCHING
Look for one of two things: a major character for whom you propose a one-shot or limited series, or a smaller, out-of-use character on whom you've got a new take and whom you can make really cool. (It's important to note that I'm just talking about what works best with me. Other editors may tell you something different and they're not wrong to do so.)

Why pitch a major character? While I'm not going to hand you the reins on *G.I. Joe*, I might try to set you up with a one-shot about one member of the team. Why would I give you a chance with *G.I. Joe*? That's simple—*G.I. Joe* sells regardless of who the creator is. What sells a project is a combination of creator, concept and character. It's a simple thing. If you're not a popular creator, that only leaves a great concept (which you'd better have) and a popular character to sell your series. For example, you and Spider-Man and a great concept will probably work. If you come in with a great concept for a limited series based on Spider-Man, it's easier to get it off the ground than, say, a great idea for a limited series about the Shroud.

The second kind of story to pitch is the kind I just said won't work (yeah, I know). Pitch a project on the Shroud, Sidewinder or Blue Devil, and your pitch usually won't see print. But a pitch on one of those characters that raises my eyebrow will cause me to write back to you and start a dialogue. A dialogue with an editor is your first goal.

However you decide to pitch, be passionate about what you're pitching, courteous, relaxed and open to suggestions and changes. Any correspondence back from an editor—even a rejection—could be the passage to a different, and better, writing gig.

I GOT MY FIRST GIG. WHAT'S NEXT?
For the sake of argument, you've got your first gig offered to you. What do you do then?

I know this sounds obvious, but the first thing you do is commit to actually doing it. I once offered a gig at writing a Marvel story to a writer whose work I like. I knew he wanted a chance, but for whatever reason, he never got back to me with an idea. He did respond to the e-mail so I know he got the offer. After his initial response, I waited about three weeks before moving on to the next guy. Did he burn a bridge with me? Honestly, no. If he wants, I'll try to give him another shot—but many editors wouldn't.

Once you've accepted the gig, you've got three categories upon which you'll be judged. As an editor with several books to edit in a month, I'm looking for talented people who can sell my books with great stories. I'm looking for people who deliver when I need it and are fun to work with. In short, I'm looking for people who make my life easier. I work with people like Brian Michael Bendis, Peter David and Keith Giffen because they're all talented (in very different kinds of writing), because they're easy to work with and because I like them. If I have my own way, I'll be working with these three writers for a long time to come.

STAYING EMPLOYED

There are three fundamentals you should possess to help you stay employed in the comics business: talent, courtesy and professionalism.

TALENT

Sorry to say this, but you will actually need at least a little talent to stay around. But even if you're not the most talented writer, there are other factors that are important. If you turn in decent scripts and on time and are a cool person, I'm likely to work with you again. Not every comic is going to be *Watchmen*. Remember, I'm on a schedule; I need a comic to be there each and every month.

Again, if you don't get another shot right after your first one, go back to your weaknesses. Build them up. Make them your strengths and then come back and impress me. Ultimately, you and I want the same thing—we want to tell some great comic book stories. As long as we're on the same page and you're getting better with each assignment (these can be from different editors), you're on the right track.

COURTESY

I've tried to think of some other way to put this, maybe "fun" or "cool," but "courtesy," or specifically "being courteous," seems the best word choice. If you're gracious and editors like you, and have fun

working with you, that'll go a long way. Sometimes, I read a comic that a friend of mine edits and I think it stinks. I'll ask the editor, why did you hire so-and-so back after that awful issue he wrote? The answer often is, "I have a lot going on, and so-and-so turns in decent scripts on time. They don't blow me away either, but he's really good to work with and he takes notes well and takes them to heart." There it is, folks. Be easy to work with. Which leads me to…

PROFESSIONALISM

How is this different from being gracious? You can be a jerk but still be professional. Here are the things that professionals do and don't do:

1. **Professionals don't complain when they get edited.** They may argue, but they'll do so rationally. If I tell you I think a scene should be cut because nothing important happens, a professional may argue with me on the point, but he will do so by telling me what does happen and where he is going with it. A professional doesn't take it as a personal affront when an editor does his job. And there is the gracious guy who is not a professional—he would just cut the scene, but that is risky, too. What if that scene was building to a great dramatic climax and I just lost it? Perhaps the scene simply needed to be reworked but not cut altogether.

2. **Professionals format their work properly.** There is no template for this in comics. Correctly really means logically. The most common method is to describe the panel first, then add dialogue. You can do this in Microsoft Word. You can use Final Draft, but it's got to look and be consistent. Once you set up your system and your writing works on the page, don't stray from it.

3. **Professionals check their spelling and grammar.** Just do it. But remember that spelling and grammar checks don't catch every misspelled and misused word.

4. **Professionals know they're not the boss.** As your editor, if I disagree with you and it's my final decision, it's your job to do as I say because I'm your boss.

5. Professionals do rewrites. I've gone as many as eight rounds with a writer on a script before I've approved it. If you seek to be a professional writer, you're going to have to do rewrites. You're more than welcome to discuss the rewrite notes.

6. Professionals hit deadlines. When you agree on a deadline, make sure you hit it. I don't need excuses. I need people I can depend on.

7. Professionals stay in constant communication with their editors. They also talk with the penciler and the rest of the creative team. This shows that you care about the final product. One minor note on this: Don't try and overrule your editor if she has told the colorist or penciler one thing and you want another. That discussion is between you and the editor, not you and another member of the creative team.

8. Professionals know they're a part of the team. One of my angriest moments as an editor was when I had three members of a creative team arguing with each other publicly. Being a part of a team is like parenting—you put up a united front.

Once you've been offered your first gig and accepted it as a writer, you should only need two of these attributes (talent, courtesy and professionalism) to stick around. Ideally, you'll have all three attributes, like the gentlemen I mentioned earlier—Peter, Keith and Brian are all easy to get along with,

talented and very professional. Hence, I continue working with them. Try to get hired back by the same editor over and over again until you've built a trusting and mutually beneficial relationship.

Your first step is to hone your skills and craft. Then you need to meet the right people. You've got to be a social animal to some degree. You can be shy, but you'll have to come out of your shell enough and understand how conversation works. Most people like talking about themselves. Ask editors questions about what they're working on. That'll get them talking and you'll learn what interests them. Once you've got contacts willing to talk with you, structure your pitch properly, as I discussed earlier (see page 162). When pitching, always be polite and courteous. Make sure you follow up on your correspondence with editors. Take criticism and notes well. And always, always, always be practicing and learning your craft. If you skillfully do all of this, you'll become a comic book writer.

Andy Schmidt is the senior editor at IDW Publishing and is the founder of the comics professional school Comics Experience (www.comicsexperience.com). He has edited smash hits for Marvel and small critical successes, and has written a handful of comics of his own. He is committed to furthering the comics industry by helping the next generation of talent rise above the industry obstacles. His comprehensive book, The Insider's Guide to Creating Comics and Graphic Novels, *was published by IMPACT in January 2009.*

The problem with an endeavor like this is that, since I'm trying to cover everything I can think of that you might need to know, it's hard to put an emphasis on any single aspect. To say, "Watch out for this above all."

So I decided to get some help on the subject. I asked Wendy and Richard Pini of Elfquest renown, and Marv Wolfman of Teen Titans and Blade, what they think is the single most important aspect when it comes to writing a comic book story.

Elfquest: The Grand Quest, Volume Two ©2004 WARP GRAPHICS, INC.

From *Elfquest: The Grand Quest, Volume Two*, some of the most memorable sequences from the coming together of *Elfquest*'s leads, Cutter and Leetah. She utters his "soul name" for the first time, and the effect it has on him requires no words whatsoever.

THE WORD SERVES THE PICTURE

BY WENDY AND RICHARD PINI

In a scene from a movie called *The Bad and the Beautiful,* Dick Powell and Kirk Douglas—playing, respectively, the writer and producer of an upcoming film—are arguing about the treatment. Their dialogue, paraphrased, goes something like this:

Powell: But that's my best scene you just threw out! The boy's going off to war. The mother knows she may never see him again. It's her last chance to say...

Douglas: ...that's why she says nothing. The camera will move in on her face. The audience will supply the feelings and, believe me, what they'll imagine is better than any words you or I could come up with!

There have been many learned articles about the close and obvious relationship between the cinema and the graphic novel. Comics, we agree, are essentially movies on paper; and whether one is the sole artist/writer or a writer who teams up with artists, we agree with Mr. Douglas's character that the single most important thing to know in the scripting process is when to shut up!

CHOOSE BETWEEN VIRTUOSITY AND IMPACT

Some comics creators are able to both write and draw. If you're one of these lucky ones, and if you have honed your ability, this knowledge becomes practically second nature. Your script may be fairly polished, but when you get to the layout stage, you realize automatically where less is more. If a character's facial expression or body language can convey all the information needed, why use words? Because they're pretty? Well, yes, a nicely turned phrase can be full of music and fire, but to get the most out of a moment the writer/artist must make the difficult choice between virtuosity and impact. Telling the story as effectively as possible is the ultimate goal, and often that means letting the art carry the scene.

> "The single most **important thing** to know in the scripting process is when to SHUT UP!"

MOST COMICS ARE ART DRIVEN

Making that choice can be a real poser for the writer who collaborates with an artist to realize his vision. A comics writer whose work is both his craft and his passion can't help but think of the art as secondary (which in some cases it is, producing more of an illustrated narrative than a panel-to-panel progression). But "meat and potatoes" comics are art driven, and the working writer must acknowledge that the word serves the picture as much as the picture serves the word. At best it's a crapshoot, especially when the artist and writer live in different locales. But the more visually oriented you, the writer, are, the more able to give explicit art directions, the better chance you will ensure your vision ends up intact on paper. And the less likely will be your need for overdone dialogue to compensate for unclear staging.

In other words, you have to know when to speak, and more importantly, when to shut up.

Also from *Elfquest: The Grand Quest, Volume Two*, the consummation of Cutter and Leetah's romance requires no words at all. Proving that Wendy and Richard follow their own advice, what words could possibly have been added that would have improved upon it?

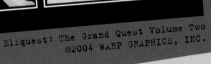

ABOUT WENDY AND RICHARD PINI

Wendy and Richard Pini have been co-creators extraordinaire since 1977, when a deeply personal project called *Elfquest* was born. The first continuing fantasy/adventure graphic novel series in America to be co-created, written and illustrated by a woman, *Elfquest* became a phenomenon in the comics industry. Appealing to comics and SF/fantasy fans alike, it attracted a unique and unprecedented audience, an equal mix of male and female readers. Over three million copies of the collected graphic novel volumes have been sold to date.

Largely self-educated, Wendy first began exhibiting her artwork in fanzines and at

science-fiction conventions in the mid-1960s, garnering awards and recognition. In 1972 she married Richard Pini and in 1974 began her professional career as an illustrator for magazines such as *Galaxy*, *Galileo* and *Worlds of If*.

Most recently, Wendy provided the control art and worked closely with the sculptors on the first three series of Evil Genius Toys' line of action figures based on classic *Elfquest* comics. Following her bliss, she continues, with the ever-present support of Richard and assistants, to produce new *Elfquest* stories and art, from graphic novels to coloring books to fine art prints.

Richard's educational background is in astronomy (a love of heavenly bodies and all that), which prepared him ideally for his careers in planetarium entertainment, teaching high school, programming big computers for IBM and, presently, publishing comic books and graphic novels.

In the span of over two decades Richard has done nearly everything possible for someone in this line of work to do: write, edit, publish, market, manage, succeed, fail and administrate. One of his favorite sayings has been, "Everything's negotiable." In the course of business, it works well. In the course of learning about and from life, that phrase is tied for first place with, "Everything's learnable." As vast and mysterious as is the external universe, uncovering what goes on inside the head, heart and soul is the truest quest of all.

You can subscribe to the free *Elfquest* e-mail newsletter at www.elfquest.com.

CHARACTER COUNTS!

BY MARV WOLFMAN

To me, writing the characters is, hands down, the most important aspect of writing comics. Fight scenes are a dime a dozen. Plots are important, sure, but let's face it, when you're writing super-hero comics, or detective comics, or westerns, or most adventure-oriented comics, the stories ultimately revolve around: Who is the bad guy, what is he doing and how does the hero stop him? This is repeated time and time again with only minor variations.

Whether a hero has to stop a small-time hood from stealing a purse or a fifty-foot (15m) planet-eating giant from devouring the Earth, the underpinnings of the story actually aren't very different. Sure, you need to make the plots interesting, different and exciting, but the root of the stories aren't that dissimilar.

The characters are what make you care about whether the hero finds the bad guy, be he purse snatcher or world gobbler. If we care why the purse snatcher is stealing that purse, we immediately become involved with the story. If we feel bad when he's arrested, we create a sense of pathos that rings with us emotionally. If we care about the purse snatcher's victim, we add another emotional dimension to the story. If we truly care about the hero, we want to see him succeed or make a brave decision or even screw up totally. We care about the story not because someone robs a purse, which we've seen a hundred million times before, but because of the characters involved and how they pull you in different, and one hopes, surprising directions.

By the time you've read comics for a year or two, you've seen almost every possible variation of a fight scene. You've seen most of the basic plots, too. What keeps you coming back are the characters: the heroes, the villains and especially the incidental bystanders. Where there may be, as we've been endlessly told in writing classes, only eleven (or pick a number) plots, there are over six billion people in this world and each one can have a different and fascinating story to tell.

Our job as writers is to find the characters and to tell their stories in the most interesting way possible. If you succeed in that it won't matter if the plot is only about someone stealing a purse or rescuing a cat from a tree. You'll be composing a story about a person that the reader will want to read.

MARV WOLFMAN

ABOUT MARV WOLFMAN

Marv Wolfman has been told that he's created more characters that have been adapted into movies, TV and animation than any writer with the exception of Stan Lee. He is the writer of comic books, movies, television, animation, children's books, theme park shows and rides, novels and Internet animation. You can find out more at www.marvwolfman.com, from where I ripped off most of this bio.

"By the time you've read comics **for a year or two,** you've seen almost **every possible** variation of a fight scene."

Marv Wolfman created the character Blade in 1973.

Blade ©2005 Marvel Characters, Inc. Used with permission.

"HEY! I KNOW WHERE YOU GOT THAT IDEA!"

In trying to prepare you for all the aspects of writing for comics, be aware of one of the downsides: Whatever you come up with, the chances are sensational someone else came up with something similar at some point before.

"What a rip-off" is one of the favorite mantras of fans with an eye toward being critical: The declaration that something is a rip-off of an earlier work because it shares some common factors (you remember: like Superman and Batman did with their inspirations). So, if you have any interest whatsoever in being a writer, be aware that sooner or later—if you're successful enough—people will accuse you of achieving that success by standing on the shoulders of others and swiping their ideas.

RIP-OFF POLICE

Such a mindset is hardly restricted to fans. Back in 1977, some film critics who were oblivious to the fact that they were witnessing the launch of the most successful film franchise of all time dismissed *Star Wars* as a rip-off of *The Wizard of Oz*. They did so by making comparisons hinging on the flimsiest of surface similarities, ranging from the barely palatable (the metallic sheen of both C-3PO and the Tin Woodsman or the hirsute nature of the Cowardly Lion and Chewbacca) to the staggeringly ridiculous (Luke being a Dorothy clone because they both come from arid regions, or Darth Vader being similar to the Wicked Witch because they're both outfitted in black).

Several years later, *Star Wars* was well on its way to achieving iconic status, and critics were no longer drawing lame comparisons to *The Wizard of Oz*. (Indeed, on *Saturday Night Live*'s *Weekend Update*, then-cast member Julia Louis-Dreyfus portrayed a dippy teenage movie reviewer who had just seen *The Wizard of Oz* and was dissing it as a cheapjack *Star Wars* knockoff.) Nevertheless, unable to win for losing, George Lucas produced *Willow*, a fantasy involving an adventurous little person on a quest, teamed with a wizard and a swordsman, and was promptly accused of ripping off Tolkien and, of course, his own previous movies, even though the film bore no resemblance either to *The Lord of the Rings* or *Star Wars*.

PETER DAVID THE PLAGIARIST?

Have I been accused of plagiarism? Only all the time. The most frequent occurrence was when I was writing *Supergirl*. Fans charged me time and again with riffing Joss Whedon's *Buffy the Vampire Slayer*. The demonic character of Buzz was initially dismissed as a John Constantine rip-off, but later revised to be a rip-off of Whedon's Spike, especially when it became clear he was in love with the titular hero. This, even though Buzz's creation predated Spike's by a year, and his being enamored of the book's blonde heroine predated Spike's similar crush on Buffy by three years. Curiously, despite my consistently beating Whedon to the punch, no one ever accused him of ripping me off.

The best was when one fan claimed that that week's issue of *Supergirl* was a direct rip-off of the preceding week's episode of *Buffy*...even though that episode was first-run and I couldn't possibly have known its contents. Think about that: The fan was essentially claiming that we'd had an issue of *Supergirl* written, penciled, inked, lettered, colored and printed in seven days in order to steal from Whedon...and a good thing, too, if I hadn't been inspired to rip off Whedon, we'd have had absolutely nothing to print in that issue.

And when *Supergirl* ended and I was busy describing the then-forthcoming *Fallen Angel* in

"Ain't nothing new under the sun— INCLUDING THIS SENTENCE."

an interview, it prompted one well-known writer/artist to seize upon the surface elements and pronounce it merely a rip-off of *Buffy*, even though anyone who went on to read the book would be hard-pressed to find any serious parallels between the two.

IT'S WHAT YOU DO THAT MATTERS

Ain't nothing new under the sun—including this sentence. Consider the core heroes of DC Comics besides Superman and Batman:

* **The Atom** (inspired by *The Incredible Shrinking Man*)

* **Green Arrow** (Robin Hood meets Batman, with trick arrows instead of a utility belt)

* **Wonder Woman** (Greek myths combined with flag-waving patriotism and some less-than-subtle bondage weirdness)

* **Aquaman** (a Sub-Mariner redux)

* **Green Lantern** (a recycled Golden Age character melded with concepts from Doc Smith's *Lensman* series)

* **The Flash** (lifted from a Golden Age character who, in turn, owed his visual to the Roman god Mercury, and by the way, Mercury was a rip-off of the Greek god Hermes)

But are the likes of Julie Schwartz, John Broome and many other greats in the industry mere plagiarists? Of course not. As noted, it's not who you come up with, but rather what you do with them that matters.

Two of the most popular new comic books to come along in recent years are Bill Willingham's *Fables* and Brian K. Vaughan's *Y: The Last Man*. But *Fables* simply recycles standard fairy-tale folk (remember our earlier discussion about literary characters). And *Y: The Last Man* uses the concept of a single existing man in a hostile environment, which has been explored in everything from Daniel Defoe's *Robinson Crusoe* to Richard Matheson's *I Am Legend* to a cheapjack soft-core porn flick

called *Petticoat Planet* (which recycled costumes and scenery from the Full Moon film *Oblivion*, written by yours truly).

Of even more recent vintage is *The Incredibles*. Any number of fans have noted, not without condemnation, the central family's resemblance to the Fantastic Four. On the surface, there are unmistakable parallels. However, it's hard to argue with the thematic logic of why the Parr family is the way they are.

* Bob Parr is expected to be the big, strong, tough foundation of the family, and thus his Mr. Incredible is mainly big and strong.

* His beleaguered wife, Helen, is feeling pulled and stretched in several directions at once, so she becomes the stretchable Elastigirl.

* Young Violet, a teenage girl, fades into the background at school and produces emotional shields to keep others out. Naturally, invisibility and force shields are her powers.

* And Dash is unfettered id, a hyperkinetic ten-year-old whose greatest joy in the world is the simple act of movement. Thus he is a speedster.

So the characters make sense within the context of their own story, and their abilities don't stem from hurtling into space and being bombarded with gamma rays (at least, we don't think so; we don't actually learn their origin). But that doesn't stop all manner of speculation as to how the film's originator, Brad Bird, decided to lift the Fantastic Four bodily from the comics and deposit them into his CGI masterpiece.

What do readers want? Particularly readers of ongoing comics. How do you keep old characters fresh? Provide new characters that seize the imagination? What sorts of story lines will satisfy them? Are you still not sure, after looking into your creative heart and mind?

The bottom line is that there is no bottom line. There's no one, consistent, surefire way to keep characters fresh and interesting because they are, and always will be, mere shadows. They are a semblance of life, given form and substance by the writers and imparted importance by the audience. The audience, in turn, comes to the work of fiction with their own life experiences that help make the fiction relevant to them.

The thing is, people's lives change. Their priorities change. Even their recollection of their own pasts changes, memory being a tricky and amorphous thing. And what made a particular character's fictional realm important to them once can lose its luster. That's equally true for the audience and for the writer.

As you build up the character's universe, there's always the temptation to use that universe as your prime resource, rather than the real-world elements that fueled it in the first place. As a result, you get a copy of a copy. What's necessary in keeping a character and his world entertaining is finding ways to redefine it in relation to the real world, to keep it grounded.

But hey, if you don't like that answer, I've got plenty of others. As it so happens, I have made a careful study of this very issue. Thousands of people have been surveyed...dozens of websites have been studied...a few guesses are being tossed out and presented as fact...in order to answer the question that bewilders folks who are trying to snag the imagination, attention and purchasing dollars of the buying public. So I'm here to lay it all out for you in bite-sized pieces.

PEOPLE WANT WHAT'S NEW

There's an insatiable appetite for the new, hot thing. Old need not apply. Your father's Oldsmobile can pull right out of the lot. Heck, even referring to your father's Oldsmobile is passé. Bring out what hasn't been seen before. Be new. Be different. Be daring. People want to see innovation (not the publisher Innovation, just real innovation). People want to see comic book creators and comic book companies stretching, using their imaginations to present exciting and novel visions that will absolutely command attention. Different situations. Different characters. They want to see old creators flexing their wings, pushing the envelope. They want to see new creators coming up with fresh, invigorating ideas. They want to see new and different series, like *Fables* and *Y: The Last Man*. Don't be afraid to let your vision run wild.

PEOPLE WANT WHAT'S OLD

When Americans go to foreign countries, where do they like to go to eat? McDonald's. Why? Because it's familiar. They know what to expect. It's comforting. And that's what they want from

> "There's **no one, consistent, SURE-FIRE WAY** to keep characters fresh and interesting because **they are, and always will be, mere shadows.**"

their comics as well. They want the old standards. They want the superheroes who have been around for decades. The ones in which they have an emotional investment. They want to see old creators working their magic on classic characters. They want to see new creators bringing new, modern sensibilities to the heroes who have been doing their hero thing for a good long while. If there are new series to be produced, they should be reinterpretations of time-honored themes that are easy to wrap one's self around, such as classic fairy-tale characters or the hoary "last man on Earth" concept. Be afraid to let your vision run wild, because no one will run with you.

PEOPLE WANT LOW PRICES

Let's face it, the economy is in a slump, and the only way you're going to get money flooding your way is if you're living in a country we happen to be bombing or already have bombed. Money's tight. Everybody knows that. And they're watching their pennies. So publishers should be doing everything they can to keep the prices as low as possible. Raise the cover price from $2.99 to $3.99 and it's pretty much the death knell for the title.

PEOPLE WANT HIGH PRICES

Why in the world should retailers be devoting shelf space to books at incredibly low cover prices such as $0.10 and making minimal-to-nonexistent amounts of money per unit? Marvel put out books priced at $0.99 and people were no more inclined to purchase those than they were anything else. In the meantime, rent and utilities and other store costs are just going up, not down, and low-balled cover prices aren't helping matters.

PEOPLE DON'T CARE ABOUT PRICES

Hey, if they want the book, price is just not going to matter. They'll pay $2.99, $7.99, whatever. It's of no consequence. Just concentrate on producing

> "What's necessary in keeping a character and his world entertaining is **finding ways to redefine** it in relation to the real world, **to keep it GROUNDED.**"

dazzling, brilliantly innovative titles that embrace everything that's gone before, and you'll be fine.

WE NEED BOOKS WITH FEMALE LEADS AND BOOKS THAT CATER TO KIDS

The only way the industry is going to survive is to pull in more female readers and more younger readers. At the moment, it appears we're mainly aiming books at male teens. If we don't produce titles that cater to, or seize the interest of, female readers and younger readers, we are foolishly ignoring an untapped resource.

WOMEN AND KIDS AREN'T COMING INTO STORES

Really, what's the point? Women aren't interested in buying comics and younger kids are far too involved with playing their Game Boys and PlayStations or chatting online to be interested in spending time picking up an overpriced, underpriced comic they have and haven't seen before.

PEOPLE WANT CREATORS TO STICK AROUND

It is so frustrating when writers and artists are on a book for a few issues, or a year or so, and then vanish off the title. Whatever happened to long-term devotion to a character? It's grotesquely unfair to fans that creators don't stick with a job but instead flit from title to title. Where's the consideration for the readers?

PEOPLE DON'T WANT CREATORS STICKING AROUND TOO LONG

Old news. Old hat. So it's the same creative team for five, six, seven years on a title. Who cares? What seizes readers' imaginations is fresh blood, new ideas and new directions. And from the point of view of a comic book creator, staying on one title too long is career suicide. Jumping from one new project to the next to the next, that's what gets people talking about you. It's important to know when to stay around for long enough, but not too long on a character that's new but old and priced very low but not too low and perhaps even over-priced aimed at kids and women who aren't buying the books anyway.

PEOPLE WANT THE BOOKS OUT ON TIME

Nothing kills interest like books failing to ship when they're supposed to ship, unless it's books that require months between issues.

PEOPLE ARE WILLING TO WAIT

Creativity can't be put on a time clock. In the words of Michelangelo to the Pope, it will be finished when it is done! And that's all that matters.

PEOPLE WANT REVAMPS OF CLASSIC CHARACTERS

It's so distressing when no one bothers to do justice to the characters who got comics going in the first place. All that readers really want is to see those great second-string characters elevated to first-class status where they belong. Primo characters like Hawkman, Spectre, Aquaman, the Sub-Mariner...let's see them done and done right!

PEOPLE ARE SICK OF REVAMPS OF CLASSIC CHARACTERS

They're second stringers for a reason: No one gives a damn. Nothing is worse than watching yet another retelling of some low-interest lame character. They're just taking up shelf space. Please, spare the readers yet another soon-to-be-canceled title that can collect dust with all the previous versions in the back issue bin.

PEOPLE WANT TIGHTLY WOVEN CONTINUITY

Nothing destroys suspension of disbelief like stories that don't adhere to established continuity. Furthermore, it's a waste to ignore decades of already existing material that can lay the foundation for more stories to come.

PEOPLE ARE SICK OF STORIES HINGING ON CONTINUITY

It's ridiculous to expect readers to have to be familiar with decades worth of continuity to enjoy a story. Furthermore, stories should be 100 percent accessible to new readers, who shouldn't be made to feel they're coming in late on a long-running saga, because that's just going to be a turnoff.

DON'T WORRY ABOUT THE INTERNET

It's entirely populated by readers whose tastes are so marginalized that they're not remotely representative of the readership as a whole, and are simply not worth your time.

CATER TO THE INTERNET

Set up websites. Talk to fans constantly. Respond to all their questions and get info out on the various news boards. The Internet is the first, best line of offense when it comes to getting word out on your product.

SO, TO SUMMARIZE

What you want to do is create a comic that's daring and innovative while comfortably familiar, priced low enough to be affordable but not so low that the retailers are being screwed and make it salable enough that price doesn't matter, featuring a lead who is a teen girl white male in his thirties—ideally a revamping of a classic character who's brand-spanking new—firmly established in continuity that's never been seen before. At which point the creative team should turn it out intermittently on a monthly basis before quitting in a year or two after a six-year stint. And be sure to spend lots of time doing nothing to interest people on computer boards.

Welcome to comics! Enjoy the ride!

From Fallen Angel #2, art by Dave Lopez. Published by IDW Publishing ©2005. Peter David and J.K. Woodward.

Carl Jefferson, Charlotte, NC:

Q: *I'm wondering about the best way to structure ideas for a long-term story. I come up with new ideas and want to organically put them in place, but something already established ends up moved around. Are there any tips you have for addressing this problem?*

A: Well, the best way to avoid the problem is probably to outline the story within an inch of its life. That is, for instance, what J.K. Rowling reportedly did when crafting the *Harry Potter* series, and it worked out pretty well for her. It is certainly possible, even under those circumstances, to come up with new ideas, but if they don't fit in with your overall arc you're precluded from using them. Then there are some writers who will barrel through a first draft, writing in an almost stream-of-conscious manner, one development contradicting an earlier one in a sort of Big Bang, willy-nilly creative style. In that instance, the first draft might make absolutely no sense. To such a writer, that doesn't matter, because the reasoning is that that's what second drafts are for: to fix the problems with the first draft. Now let's say you're writing an ongoing comic book series and you come up with something in issue #10 that's incredibly clever, but contradicts issue #3. And issue #3 has already been drawn or, worse, been published. Then you really don't have much of a choice; you have to dump the idea. But fear not, for you are a writer and ideas are your stock in trade. File that new idea away and use it to build an entirely new story.

Byron Dunn, Kansas City, MO:

Q: *What is the best way to start writing a serialized comic? If I have the characters created and the concepts all set up, how do I go about this? Should I just start writing or should I plot things out, and if I should plot it out, how?*

A: Again, there's no right or wrong answer to this. Everyone works differently. I've written over fifty issues worth of *Fallen Angel* and in that time I've never outlined the series. I've had ideas kicking around in my head, general thoughts for direction, but nothing concrete. It's always been far more interesting for me simply to create situations, put the characters into those situations and see how things develop. On the other hand, there are writers who compulsively outline every issue for the next year or two. When working in mainstream comics, the latter approach is probably the more viable since it simplifies life for both editors and marketing people. Editors can coordinate more easily with other editorial offices and head off problems ("Yeah, this Captain America guest appearance you had planned for six months from now? Captain America's going to be dead so that's off the table"), and marketing can plan ways to promote something exciting ("You're having two characters get married? Let's do a press release and schedule some interviews"). On occasion I have indeed worked up outlines for ongoing series, but they're really more guidelines than full-blown outlines. Generally these consist of capsule descriptions of the next six or so issues—sometimes more, sometimes less—with each description somewhere between 50 and 100 words. Enough to convey an idea of what the overall story arc is, but loose enough that if I come up with something interesting on the fly, it doesn't become a massive hassle to incorporate it.

Sometimes I combine the concepts. When I first began writing my novel, *Sir Apropos of Nothing*, I had absolutely no idea where the story was going. I wrote between 500 to a 1000 words every morning and after two months I had 50,000 words. At which point I said, "Okay...I have to figure out where the rest of this story goes." And I sat down and outlined the rest of the book.

So again: There's no right or wrong way to do it. Whatever works for you.

Cary Kingdom, Johnstown, NY:

Q: *Vaguest one first: What is the best way for a new writer to get read by editors or publishers?*

A: Staple twenty dollars to your cover letter. Other than that, probably the best way is to bite the bullet and find a way to get to conventions, such as the San Diego Comic-Con, where editors and publishers are going to be set up. In many such instances they actually have times set up to meet with aspiring writers and go over material. That's the short answer. For a far more detailed answer, consult Andy Schmidt's essay on page 158.

Q: *Should comics writers get literary agents, like they would for nongraphic work, or try to go it alone?*

A: Although there are a handful of literary agents who handle comic book writers, typically such sales are simply too low-ball for agents to take an interest in. Remember that agents work on commission, and 15 percent of a comic book script really isn't worth their time.

Q: *If you're only a writer, how important is finding an artist when you're first trying to get your work read?*

A: Depends on the artist. If you can find a talented artist who can do a good job of visually conveying your story, it's a definite plus. On the other hand, a lousy artist can drag your story down and present an impediment to the reader's being able to appreciate your scripting. So it's a judgment call.

Torsten Adair, New York City, NY:
Q: *Are creative writing courses offered at universities and other educational institutions worthwhile? What should a novice or amateur writer (as in one who does not get paid to write) expect from these classes? How should a student approach these courses, and how can he mold the lessons taught to what he wishes to learn?*

A: I've never taken one. My last creative writing course was back in high school, taught by a wise and wonderful teacher named Adria Mednitsky, who was very influential and supportive of my efforts. My father has taken a bunch of them, though, joining local writers' groups, and they have been greatly beneficial to him in his short story writing endeavors. It's my belief that they can't

instill talent that isn't already there. But at least they provide you with an audience that consists of someone other than friends or relatives.

Q: *When considering the basic techniques of writing, how does sequential storytelling differ from prose?*

A: Mostly it differs with the need to emphasize the visual aspects of the story. In a prose book, you can have two people in a room doing nothing but talking for pages at a time, and as long as the dialogue and characters are compelling, you've nothing to worry about (although moving along the plot certainly never hurts). In a comic book, however, you always have to keep in mind how it's going to play visually. That's not to say you can't write compelling comics that consist of nothing more than people talking, but you'd better have an artist who is ready and willing to execute what you want him to. I once wrote a nineteen-page *Batman* story that was almost entirely Commissioner Gordon in a room with the Penguin, trying to get information out of him that would save Gordon's wife (whom the Penguin had imprisoned in a death trap). Quite a few artists were offered the story and passed on it because they were daunted by the prospect of a tale that was mostly talk before we finally found an art team up for the challenge.

Q: *What is your least favorite type of story to write? How do you persevere when assigned a mind-numbing story, or are involved in a company-wide crossover event?*

A: Ideally, I don't take on a story that I would consider "mind-numbing." If it's boring to me, it's going to be boring to the reader, so I have to find some way into it that's going to make it compelling. Find some theme, some narrative that I can identify with personally. As for company-wide crossovers, you have to realize that—as with many things—there are advantages and disadvantages. Granted, traffic management can be a pain when getting involved with crossovers, and the approvals process can be a bear. On the other hand, the harsh reality of today's marketplace makes cross-overs a virtual necessity.

Readership attrition is a serious problem that just about every series faces. Books can lose readers for any number of reasons. And with the price of comic books nowadays, readers are disinclined to sample titles simply because they've heard good things about them. Oftentimes they require further incentive to sample your book, and crossovers are a good way to encourage it.

And, ultimately, crossovers can be fun if you approach them from the point of view of camaraderie. Writing is, by its nature, a solitary pursuit. So a change of pace can be welcome. Whether I was working with Ron Marz, Mike Carlin and the late, great Mark Gruenwald in producing *DC vs. Marvel*, or a coterie of talented X-writers in *Messiah CompleX*, teaming up with writers whose work you respect and company you enjoy can be a fun way to approach the creative process.

Q: *Harlan Ellison (I think...ask him) once said that if a writer is not writing, he should be reading. How do you use other writers' stories for inspiration without swiping their plots or characterizations?*

A: I did ask Harlan, and he said that although he can't recall having said it specifically, he didn't rule out having said it at some point. As for using stories as inspiration, one of Harlan's favorite quotes on the subject comes from Da Vinci (or maybe Michelangelo) who said, "Where I steal an idea, there I leave my knife." To be honest, I'm not entirely sure what that means; I've come up with several interpretations and I'm not sure which one was intended. But ultimately the difference between inspiration (as you put it) and plagiarism (as I put it) is twofold.

First is intent to conceal, i.e., deliberately passing off someone's work as your own. Many years ago, back when I was working for a book publisher, a reader wrote in to inform us that we had published an entire novel that was a word-for-word rip-off from an earlier book by another writer. It was, in short, theft: Passing off someone else's work as your own. It's such a deliberate action that I don't think you'd have to ask if you're doing it. You pretty much know.

Second, when you take something that is an original (and preferably public domain) work and put your own spin on it, the new work can itself be original.

For instance: *West Side Story*. Clearly that famed musical is "inspired" by *Romeo and Juliet*, right down to every major story beat. But by setting it in modern times, steeping the hostilities in racial hatred as opposed to family feuds and adding music and dance, *West Side Story* becomes an original work while making no attempt to hide the previous work from which it derives.

From a comic book point of view, there's a short story I wrote called "The Archetype." "The Archetype" began life as an idea for a Superman story. I found myself pondering how Lois Lane ever managed to live to adulthood because of her tendency to land herself in potentially deadly situations with astounding regularity. She was never in need of rescue until Superman showed up. And I thought: What if there's a connection? What if Superman, by his very presence, causes circumstances to occur that require his services? The more I developed the story, the more I realized it wouldn't work as a Superman story because you could never do another Superman story, ever. So I basically "swiped," if you will, Superman, Lois Lane and Lex Luthor, re-created them as original characters with different names and different attributes, wrote it as a short story called "The Archetype" (the name of the Superman-equivalent hero) and sold it to *The Magazine of Fantasy & Science Fiction*. The derivation of the characters is obvious, yet it remains an original work of fiction.

Or look at *Watchmen*. All of the main characters in *Watchmen* began their fictional lives as Charlton heroes before Alan Moore made them over into the classic characters they became. Just because Doctor Manhattan started out as Captain Atom doesn't make him any less original.

Ultimately, everyone draws inspiration from the work of others. Oftentimes as writers we "write along" with other writers when we're experiencing their work. Their ideas prompt other ideas, and from those come new stories. As long as you have something new to say, the work is new.

Q: *Is there a single comic book story or arc or graphic novel which, when analyzed, is a great example of the art form? (In other words, if you were to place a single comic book on the next* Voyager *space probe, which would it be?)*

A: Most people would say *Watchmen*. Or perhaps *The Sandman* #19, "A Midsummer Night's Dream," which won the World Fantasy Award for Short Story and immediately inspired a rule change so that no comic book could ever win that award again. Personally, I'd lean toward *Amazing Fantasy* #15 since that may well be the best origin story in the history of comics. Stan Lee and Steve Ditko accomplished more in a handful of pages, and more memorably, than most other writers (not excluding myself) do in a handful of issues.

Q: *What is your opinion regarding the recent Kirkman/Bendis debate? Work for hire? Self-publishing? What are the pros and cons of each? Are there other alternatives?*

A: For those wondering what's being referred to here, Robert Kirkman—newly (as of this writing) with Image Comics—asserted that writers should cease working on company-owned characters such as Spider-Man or Superman and focus their attentions on creator-owned concepts, while Marvel and DC should be focusing their energies on producing stories that are more all-age appropriate. He felt that the comics industry is in trouble—which it is—and that the cure is steering adult comic book readers, gently but firmly, toward independent books while producing more titles that kids will be interested in reading—which it isn't.

The bottom line is that creator-owned books—even those published by major companies—sell relatively low, while teens simply aren't flocking to all-ages superhero books. Robert contended that writers can make a decent living on self-created books that sell around 25,000 copies, and that may be. But I'll betcha that retailers can't survive on that kind of volume, trade paperbacks be damned, and if the retailer base collapses, adios muchachos. Probably the industry will be saved by publishers figuring out more and more ways to milk the Internet, which doesn't have printing costs and gets

their product out to millions of people who would never set foot in a comic book store.

The ideal situation, in my opinion, is to keep your hands in as many pies as possible. Creator-owned to follow your own muse; company-owned because you enjoy the characters and the higher-profile assignment. The way to build a writing career is to keep as many options open as you can.

Q: *Which of your comics stories is your favorite? Why?*

A: There is no harsher critic of my work than me. When the final product sees print, I only see the flaws and all the seams. I am usually never satisfied, and any given story is maybe 70, 80 percent of what I think it should be. What makes a story a favorite is that it's 100 percent what I want it to be. I wouldn't change a thing. I have several that meet that criterion. *Atlantis Chronicles. Hulk: Future Imperfect. The Incredible Hulk: The End.* (I was thrilled when Marvel collected both of those into one volume.) Some issues of *Fallen Angel* (particularly the first five from IDW). *The Incredible Hulk* #467 (my last issue of my original run). Stuff like that.

Q: *Aside from the questions listed above, what other annoying questions have you been asked?*

A: Even though you didn't ask, I'll tell you my favorite unannoying (is that a word?) question. It came from a fan on the Internet who asked whether I ever feel a sense of loss when I kill off a character. And I replied, "Yes. Any number of times, I've reached a point where I've killed off a character and it had a tremendous emotional impact on me. I've even been moved to tears on a handful of occasions because I was so personally devastated by the character's death. It's only when I kill people in real life that I feel nothing at all."

Stephen Kok, Australia:
Q: *What is your point of view on this: "Most aspiring comic writers will never break into the industry. What do you think motivates them (and me) to keep trying?"*

A: It's a cliché, but as with most clichés, it's also true: Hope springs eternal. And let's face it, that determination is a requirement for all aspects of writing. The odds are formidable no matter what your talent level is, and if you don't have the determination to stick it out, you're never going to make it as a professional.

Will Jibaja, Ozone Park, NY:
Q: *Over your career you have been on titles that have had to be included in a crossover or similar events. As the writer, how do you approach it? Do you decide to take your story arc and just place it on the back burner, or do you try to tie your story into the event and sprinkle threads of the plot or your original story in it?*

A: In the old days, I had to "back burner" my storylines as I was informed that it was time for yet another crossover. There were times when crossovers got completely out of control. A storyline I launched in *Supergirl* beginning with issue #51 was intended to run for about a year. I had tie-in after themed issue after tie-in thrust upon me with such regularity—all intended to jack up sales—that the storyline inflated to nearly twenty issues. The result was that we wound up hemorrhaging readers because they complained the story was dragged out. And they were right. I don't know how things are working these days at DC, but at Marvel it's much more organic. I had a good six-month's notice when *Messiah CompleX* was on the horizon and was actually able to tailor my ongoing storylines to set up the crossover. In most other crossover events, participation is purely optional. If I think a major event is something I can tie-in with in a way that will ensure a good story, I'll definitely jump on board. If not, then, even though it means passing up on the chance to boost sales, I'll pass it up. *Secret Invasion*—the mega-storyline involving a Skrull invasion of Earth—is a good example of the former. I had introduced the concept of She-Hulk having a Skrull sidekick months before *Secret Invasion* hit my radar. When I learned about it, not only did it make sense to tie in, but it would have made no sense not to.

Q: *When laying out your story, do you plot first or use a "beat" page to keep the layout straight in your mind?*

A: If I have a clear idea of what I want to do, I'll just launch right into the story. If, on the other hand, I'm having trouble getting a handle on it, I will do a beat sheet. This basically consists of a numbered list of scenes, each one about a sentence long. It's particularly useful doing this if it's the last two issues of a limited series so I can make sure I can wrap it up within the remaining page count.

Jeremiah Allan, Ottawa, KS:
Q: *In the work-for-hire world of companies like Marvel or DC, crowded landscapes littered with thousands of super-powered heroes per square inch, how can a writer help his book seem important, especially if it stars a B-list or street-level character when there are all these cosmic events going on left and right, or even rationalize the existence of that book at all?*

I know there's some suspension of disbelief involved on the reader's part, but is there something a writer can do to emphasize the small characters and the small moments in such a way that the Sentry punching out a Galactus-level threat over New York (again) matters but doesn't overshadow stuff like the Punisher taking down a couple of street thugs?

I guess what I'm saying is this: The sheer scale of some of the surrounding super-heroics diminishes the impact of other heroes doing less heroic things. How do we make the little guys matter?

A: How "important" a book is going to be perceived is really not in the writer's control. That's in the realm of the marketing department. All you can do as a writer is produce the best story you can. And presenting the mega-events through the eyes of smaller or street-level characters can result in tales that are very accessible for the readers. Because, let's face it, whenever there's some sort of major disaster going on in the world, most of us are on the sidelines. So stories taken from that point of view, whether they be films like *Cloverfield* or comic book series such as *Marvels* by Kurt Busiek and Alex Ross, can be just as compelling, if not more so, than a big sweeping tale told from the point of view of superheroes.

Jernell Rosenthal, King of Prussia, PA
Q: *How important is revision in your work? Can you give a quick synopsis of how you develop a*

script from beginning to end, focusing on the rewrite stage? Do you write your first draft fast and loose and then clean it up, or do you spend more time laying the groundwork early on and just do a little polishing up after the first draft is written? What do you look for when revising? How do you know when you've gotten a scene or characterization right, especially when writing original characters?

A: I generally have a clear enough idea in my head of what I want to write for a script that the first draft is very close to what I want to see on the printed page in terms of the story. Generally, after writing the first draft I will go back through and read it aloud to make certain the dialogue sounds the way I want it to. You would be amazed how many shortcomings reading aloud can catch, ranging from clunky or unwieldy dialogue to flat-out misprints or wrong words. Since space is typically at a premium in word balloons, it's always wise to try and trim where you can. Actually, that's a good rule of thumb for rewrites in general. Stephen King, in his superb book *On Writing*, mentions that a second draft should be the first draft minus 10 percent, and that's never truer than in the case of comics. As for knowing when I've gotten it "right," well, I am moved to quote Da Vinci: "Art is never finished; only abandoned."

Q: *I have a tendency, I believe, to overwrite scenes. It is often said that you should enter a scene late and leave early. How do you know how much of the scene you can cut? Is there a way to distill a scene down to its basic essence during the first draft?*

A: The enter late/leave early isn't a bad rule of thumb. There's nothing duller than showing someone entering a room (through a door, that is; entering through a window or a wall is usually exciting) unless it's someone exiting a room (which is why writers always try to give characters a clever exit line). There are two purposes to pretty much any scene: Move the plot and illuminate the character. Anything that doesn't contribute to either of those should be trimmed, like fat from a steak.

Q: *There are a lot of stories being told in the comics medium, both professional and amateur, that tend*

to recycle or rehash old ideas. So much so that some creators feel that the only way to find unique stories is to take multiple disparate genres and mash them together (i.e., an Alice in Wonderland type story meets a story about depression and suicide meets some type of meta-commentary about society or relationships). While this may indeed be an interesting read, I'm wondering, is there another way to avoid clichés in plot development? Is there a way to take a familiar story or genre and make it compelling without the "Hollywood-esque" twist ending that seems like a prerequisite for storytelling since The Sixth Sense?

A: I don't accept your premise. It's not as if writers look at other properties and say, "Okay, I'm going to combine X, Y and Z, and then spin a story from it." Instead, writers come up with concepts, stories, etc., and then describe them to others (particularly those to whom they're trying to sell the stories) by saying, "It's *Xena* meets *The West Wing*." As for tweaking the familiar, that's simply a matter of looking at what's been done before and do the opposite. It's how Joss Whedon developed *Buffy the Vampire Slayer*, by twisting the old notion of the poor blonde cheerleader being the victim of monsters and instead being the one who kicks the monsters' asses.

Q: *What are some of the hallmarks of a unique character? How does one go about developing unique characterization for an original character, especially a superhero, that doesn't fall into the camp of being a Spider-Man, Wolverine, Batman, or Superman rip-off? And how does one deliver this characterization skillfully chapter by chapter without slowing down the action (i.e., fighting) that so many comic fans tend to expect? Is there a way to grow a character organically from the action, or is it the other way around?*

A: You're asking for two impossible things. The first is, basically, how to create a character with absolutely no roots in anything that's gone before. It's not really possible. Every character you cite has roots in predecessors. Furthermore, key aspects of the characters might well have been developed by someone other than the character's creators. For instance, Len Wein's original concept for Wolverine was that he was, in fact, a wolverine evolved into human form. And the characters of Batman and Superman have undergone untold permutations in their personas.

Second, at this point you're basically asking me to quantify imagination, and that's not really possible. No one knows what's really going to make a character unique or even memorable. Superman was simply the wish fulfillment of two Cleveland teenagers, who borrowed heavily from the works of Philip Wylie and Lester Dent. *Spider-Man* was a throwaway one-off story that saw print in the last issue of an unsuccessful comic book anthology series. Who knew? Not their creators, that's for sure. All you can do is create a character who is as true to yourself as you can make him. Develop a character who means something to you, and with any luck, that sincerity will cause the character to mean something to others.

I will note, though, that giving your hero an origin that involves great personal loss of some manner certainly provides readers a means of connecting. For instance, there are few things more potent to a young reader than the loss of a parent. Arguably the three most popular heroes are Superman, Batman and Spider-Man. All three are orphans, losing their parents in violent fashion. Superman lost not only his parents but also his entire race; Batman saw his folks murdered in front of him; and Peter Parker not only was an orphan, but also lost his substitute father figure courtesy of his own negligence. So obviously readers are able to become invested in characters who have suffered the kind of traumatic loss that readers know in their hearts is inevitable for themselves (although ideally it won't be when they're young and will involve less catastrophic circumstances).

In answer to your action question: Who a character is should definitely shape how he handles himself in a fight. I remember reading a so-called script by another comic book writer in which his instructions to the artist were as follows: "Pages 5 to 20—big fight. Knock yourself out." I was appalled. The writer isn't doing his job if he gives no thought to how his hero will respond in a battle situation. The Hulk will simply smash things until they stop moving. She-Hulk, on the other hand, due to both

her personality and her background as an attorney, is as likely to use rational argument and thought to defuse a situation. Spider-Man will joke his way through a fight to cover his own nervousness. Batman? Not so much with the wisecracks. Everyone should have a different fighting style, and that style informs us about his character. As for doing it skillfully, well, that comes with practice.

Q: *I find plotting to be very easy, but scene development is a much more difficult task for me. Is there a way (other than writing every day, which I do on my lunch break) for me to strengthen the skills needed to develop my scenes? How would you recommend making a scene more powerful, memorable or dramatic?*

A: The best way, honestly, is to see how other people do it. Find stories that feature scenes you find to be powerful, memorable or dramatic, and try to figure out how they did it. Was it particular twists of the characterization? Was it innovative use of the three-act structure? Was it pacing or scene selection? Seek out books by writers who describe how they went about putting their stories together. Get DVDs of films you find particularly compelling that feature audio commentary by the writers. When you're watching a movie or reading a comic, try to figure out where the writer's going. Eventually it will become second nature.

David Seidman, Los Angeles, CA:
Q: *May I make a suggestion? Please advise new writers that they shouldn't tell an editor or publisher to change ongoing characters. Don't tell DC that it should appeal to young readers by permanently turning Superman into a horny teenage stoner. Don't tell Marvel to capitalize on its success with Stephen King and Laurell K. Hamilton comics by having Spider-Man horrifically murder Aunt May. Don't tell Dark Horse and Lucasfilm to ignore* Star Wars *episodes I–III. These ideas may sound absurd, but new writers pitch ideas just as silly more often than you might expect.*

A: Consider it said. Nor does it sound absurd. I've had would-be writers come up to me and explain, with all seriousness, that they want to pitch a limited series idea to Marvel that would involve destroying the entire Marvel Universe and replacing every hero therein with newer and better models, all created (naturally) by the tyro. Explaining to editors everything that's wrong with classic characters isn't a way to ingratiate yourself. Ultimately, what you want to do, if you're trying to break in at Marvel or DC or work with any established characters, is come up with stories that will leave the characters in the same condition you found them.

Ivo Emanuel Gonçalves, Portugal:
Q: *Do you feel continuity is a tool for creating better stories or merely a reward for longtime readers?*

A: Continuity is a tool in your toolbox. Nothing more, nothing less. Utilize it when it can be of use to you, ignore it when it isn't. You shouldn't go out of your way to contradict continuity unless it's of benefit to you and doing so won't tatter the universe you're writing in too badly. For instance, I wrote a She-Hulk story in which Valkyrie showed up astride her winged horse, Aragorn, following the lead set by Jeph Loeb, who likewise depicted her in an issue of *Hulk*. Small problem: Aragorn had been killed and eaten in an issue of *The Punisher War Journal*. You know what? I didn't care. Like Jeph, I wanted Val back on her horse, and I didn't feel like giving away that image simply because another writer felt like showing how tough his bad guy was by having him dispatch Aragorn. In mythology, Thor had a chariot pulled by goats that he routinely killed and ate, and then he lay the bones down on the skins and they came back to life. If it's good enough for Norse goats, it's good enough for a winged horse being ridden by a Norse heroine. Besides, readers have been filling in continuity and plot holes since the earliest days of Marvel, when Stan Lee would award particularly clever explanations with No-Prizes.

Some fans can be absolutely obsessive about continuity, taking a writer to task because he contradicts some bit of arcane trivia from twenty years before. Basically, just try to keep your own house in order. It's your job as writer to tell the best stories you can now, not hamstring yourself because of what someone else did decades earlier.

Q: *When the bosses deem a concept to be the greatest thing ever and you know it will backfire spectacularly, but it's your next assignment anyway, what do you do?*

A: Decide if you can do it or not. Figure out if you can make it work; if you can, bring it up to the standards you've set for yourself. If you can't, pass on the assignment.

Michael Cohen, North Lauderdale, FL:
Q: *With the thousands of comic book stories out there, is there a procedure to check that your story is original (i.e., accidental plagiarism)?*

A: Plagiarism isn't accidental. Plagiarism is deliberate. That's what makes it plagiarism and unethical. I go into that in more detail on page 172.

There's absolutely no consistent way to make certain your story has no precedent. Internet searches and such can give you some idea if something matches up, in broad strokes, with concepts that you might come up with. For instance, if you decide you want to do a story involving vampire ninja pirates, enter those three words into Google and see if you have any direct hits. But you have to resign yourself to the inevitability that whatever you come up with, it's very likely going to bear a resemblance to something that someone else has done somewhere at some time. The staggering number of lawsuits in Hollywood that involve people claiming they've been ripped off by someone else attests to that. And the desire to see plagiarism where none exists can be overwhelming.

All you can do as a writer is try to protect yourself from accusations. To that end, I make it a policy never to read fan submissions because if they are at all similar to something I have in the hopper, I'd have to dump the story. It's unfortunate, but in this litigious society, it's the only option I have.

Bryan Siegbert "Ziggy" Coe, Hillsborough, NJ:
Q: *When I look for want ads online for people looking for writers to collaborate with, they always ask the interested writer to send copies of sample scripts. I am hesitant to send my original ideas out into the unknown, without knowing anything about the person receiving them, and I am wondering if it is wise to use characters that I don't own instead. For*

example, writing some short scripts about Spider-Man or Superman and the like. What else can I do for a "sample" of my work that would get me a job?

A: You're wise to be cautious. If what you're looking for is a collaborator to produce sample material that you can then send to publishers, by all means stick with using established characters. This isn't to say that artists are lurking in the high weeds, seeking to steal your ideas. Most likely they're just trying to break in, same as you. But you can never be too careful. If you wind up working with an artist on an original project, and you can afford to hire a lawyer, do so and make certain contracts are drawn up. When the Image guys first formed their company and talked about friends being in business together, I observed in *Comics Buyer's Guide* that friends and business was a dangerous mix and I sure hoped they had good lawyers. They made snippy comments in response, but a few years later various founders were suing each other, so it helps to have everything nailed down.

Q: *As I hunt for an artist online by scanning want ads, I see many artists reply to the same jobs. When it's my want ad they read and apply for, what should I ask to see from them in order to pick the best one? What kind of questions should I ask of them and what samples of their work should I ask for?*

A: You should ask to see samples of their storytelling. Too many artists think that a portfolio of splash pages is some sort of indicator of their comic book ability. It's not. You need to see storytelling samples ranging from something as simple as two people in a room talking to a major dustup in city streets. See what their strengths and weaknesses are, and how you can tailor your material to the former. That's assuming, of course, that there are enough strengths to tailor them to.

Q: *Is there any useful way to search through deviantart.com for an artist who would a) be looking for a job and not just doodling, and b) not already be a professional who is only selling their prints and thanking people for adding him to his favorites list?*

A: There's no way to avoid people who are simply trying to put together a mailing list, but certainly asking to see a list of their credits and accomplishments is a good place to start. If they're actively looking for a job, with any luck they've had jobs before, and samples of work from those jobs. Be aware that the process is going to involve a lot of trial and error.

Jason M. Bryant, Orlando, FL:
Q: *Recapping drives me nuts sometimes. Even if it's just a new character reiterating who he is and why he's there, comics often need to catch the reader up on what's going on. Since comics are only twenty-two pages, a six-issue story might spend a lot of time on people saying things like, "As I said a moment ago, I'm going to blow everything up if you don't blah blah blah."*

But sometimes the recapped information is slipped into the dialogue so naturally that it isn't even noticeable and doesn't seem to slow the story down. How do you make sure the reader is up to speed while making it sound natural and entertaining?

A: Basically by providing the reader with exactly as much information as he needs to understand what's going on. No more, no less. There are various ways you can go about it, ranging from caption narrative to such classic writer's tricks as having one character saying, "Remind me why we're sticking our necks out again?"

Q: *When writing characters, do you have to limit their vocabulary to reflect their personalities? Real people don't talk the same way all the time, but I have trouble getting variation into dialogue in a way that makes the characters feel consistent.*

A: Just because something happens in real life isn't always an acceptable excuse to put it into a work of fiction. Outrageous coincidences happen in reality that, if you put them into a story, would seem contrived. Likewise, people do things in real life that are "out of character." People say, "Peter Parker would never do that," "Clark Kent would never say that." But how often do you see news stories in which someone is accused of wrongdoing, friends and family turn out in droves to swear that the accused would never, ever do such a thing, and then a week, two weeks later there's a tearful press conference in which the accused admits to having done exactly what he was accused of?

On the other hand, word choice can be character revelatory. If you want to establish that a character from a working-class background has an advanced education, then sure, having him say "bequeathed" is a way to convey that. Likewise, having a convict say "Milady" suavely plays against the expectations of the audience. In the limited series *Madrox* I had the titular detective make a reference to "noir" while three goons held guns on him. One of the goons said sarcastically, "What's nwarr?" and one of his associates promptly delivered a perfect definition of the film movement to his edification, to both the astonishment and annoyance of the first goon.

Of course, there are some writers who seem to make no effort to distinguish characters by the way they talk, and it doesn't seem to hurt them any. Aaron Sorkin's *The West Wing* characters are pretty much interchangeable in their rapid-fire banter, erudition and wit (peppering their conversation with "yeah" or "I've got a thing," plus they all have a thorough command of Gilbert and Sullivan). And Joss Whedon produces dialogue so uniform in nature that anything resembling it is referred to as "Whedonesque." One of my favorite characters in the entirety of the Whedon-verse was Skip the demon. Massively built, monstrous in every aspect, but when he confronted the heroic Angel he said, "Hi. How ya doin'?" Skip the demon, who commuted to work and had very particular taste in movies.

That said: It's generally preferable to try and find different voices for different characters. It helps to base voices on people you know, because it's easier to figure whether the dialogue is consistent. It's also another reason to read your dialogue aloud, because that will help you catch word choice that doesn't sound right for the character.

Q: *Does every issue of a superhero comic have to have an action sequence or fight?*

A: There's no absolute rule for anything, really, other than "Thou shalt not bore the audience." You don't need a fight scene for drama. Drama only requires, at minimum, two people with goals that are in opposition with the other. If you can provide compelling conflict in a visual manner that will engage and involve the reader, no action scenes are really required. However, if you're writing a superhero comic, editors generally want you to have your hero utilizing his power, or at the very least referencing it, somewhere in every issue. Which is why sometimes you see heroes running into random bank robberies that do nothing to further the story.

Also, some comics lend themselves to non-action issues more easily. The moody Stephen King's *The Dark Tower*, plotted by Robin Furth and scripted by yours truly, has entire issues devoted to nothing but character development.

In short, no, it's not necessary.

Lee Houston Jr., Chaplin, CT:
Q: *What, if any, specialized software do you employ when writing? Personally, I just use Microsoft Word, but all the specialized programs available today might confuse the fledgling writer.*

A: I also use Microsoft Word, although darned if I know what year it is. For screenplays and teleplays, I use Final Draft.

Q: *When in need of reference material(s), what books and/or websites do you use/trust?*

A: I've gotten tremendous mileage out of a reference volume called *What's What: A Visual Glossary of the Physical World* by Reginald Bragonier and David Fisher. It hasn't been updated since 1994, but it's a marvelously detailed book that provides the actual names of all sorts of things you might want to refer to. That's really more relevant for novels than comics, but it never hurts to know what things are called. For comics, I make extensive use of Google images, often providing links for artists to specific visuals (just in case they don't happen to know what Mount Rushmore looks like). There's no single source that I trust implicitly. I might make use of Wikipedia as a starting point, for instance, but will search out additional reference sources to back up whatever I find there.

WORKS INDEX

SUBJECT INDEX

Sir Apropos of Nothing #2 cover by Michael William Kaluta © 2008 by Peter David.

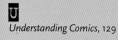

LOOK FOR THESE EXCITING TITLES!

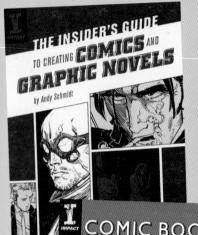

In this unprecedented, behind-the-scenes guide, former Marvel editor and current IDW senior editor Andy Schmidt and his superstar industry friends give you the inside track on creating engaging, professional-looking comic books. Written for upcoming creative stars and comic-book enthusiasts, *The Insider's Guide* covers the entire creative process from beginning to end.

ISBN-13: 978-1-60061-022-6, ISBN-10: 1-60061-022-6
Paperback, 176 PAGES, #Z1306

Comic Books 101 is the complete, definitive and super-cool guide to the universe of caped crusaders, irradiated spiders, fantastic foursomes, and the super-talents behind their creation. Chris Ryall, publisher and editor-in-chief of IDW, a San Diego-based comics publisher, and Scott Tipton, founder and editor-in-chief of comics101.com, lead you through the entire history of comic books from the very beginning up to the latest comics-based movies. Supplemented with lots of fun extras by industry greats Stan Lee, Clive Barker, Harlan Ellison and more.

ISBN-13: 978-1-60061-187-2, ISBN-10: 1-60061-187-7
Paperback, 288 pages, #Z2757

Discover the insider secrets behind eye-popping visual effects for coloring comics digitally. Follow along with expert colorist Brian Miller, founder of Hi-Fi Colour Design, as he walks you through tricks and techniques to help you flatten images, create energy glows, sparkles, warp effects and much more. Download the artwork used in the video and follow along as you learn to color the Hi-Fi way.

Introduction to Hi-Fi Digital Coloring with Brian Miller
ISBN-13: 978-1-60061-855-0, ISBN-10: 1-60061-855-3
DVD, 79 mins, Z5423

Special Effects for Digital Coloring
ISBN-13: 978-1-60061-859-8, ISBN-10: 1-60061-859-6
DVD, 52 mins, Z5427

These and other fine IMPACT books are available at your local art & craft retailer, bookstore and online supplier. Or visit our website at www.impact-books.com.